In The Beginning Was the Mother ...

To embark upon the magickal path as a Witch is to walk between the worlds of the known and the unknown. The Qabalist and the Witch meet to celebrate the mysteries of life between the worlds, within a magickal circle where the veil between the seen and unseen is thin, in a place where the Tree of Life can take root in our souls, and act as a guide and companion in our lives.

Explore the realms between the worlds in search of meaningful mystical experience through a contemporary Wiccan reformation of the Qabalah. Within these pages, Wicca and the Qabalah are melded into a healing, dynamic system for personal transformation. *Between the Worlds* is more than a translation of the Qabalah into Craft terms. This book presents the core teachings of traditional Wicca in Qabalistic terms, providing in-depth explanations of the Qabalistic significance and applications of modern Craft practices, including a complete Qabalistic Book of Shadows drawing upon the Gardnerian Tradition.

- Explore realms of human experience once thought only accessible to ceremonial magicians through modern Wiccan versions of such rituals as the Qabalistic Cross and the Middle Pillar, as well as a program of daily magickal practice for personal growth and discovery

- Use meditation to enter into a divine world filled with goddesses and gods and enhance your life by becoming aware of the patterns of reality

- Share in the energies of nature spirits through the Eucharist of the Four Elements and the Sacred Meal as you undertake the Great Work of spiritual development

- Return to the roots of the Qabalah and modern Witchcraft and discover new ways to celebrate the Sabbats and Esbats with solitary rituals attuned to the natural cycles of the moon and sun as mapped out by the Tree of Life

- Explore the Witches' Wheel and follow the Eight Paths to Spirit to achieve magickal consciousness and bring real power into your efforts to change reality

Bring the Qabalah of the Goddess into your life through *Between the Worlds'* unique program of spiritual development, and explore the Mysteries of the Craft through the Tree of Life.

ABOUT THE AUTHOR

Stuart Myers lives in the Central Florida area with his current High Priestess, Kendra Musselle, her daughter, Yasmin, and four magickal cats: Athena, Shadow, Geek, and Hop.

His experience in the Craft has spanned fourteen years, beginning with his first degree initiation into a Gardnerian coven stemming from the work of Lady Sheba (1979). A few months after receiving his third degree in August 1984, he left his parent coven and began to study the mysteries of Qabalah.

Stuart has written for a number of Pagan and New Age journals. Once a strong member of Virginia's Southern region of the WADL, he has appeared on numerous cable television programs and written a few newspaper stories about the Craft. Now, with his headline days behind him, Stuart prefers to live simply, working a full-time job and studying for his bachelor's degree at the University of Central Florida. When not working or engaged in his studies, he is writing, teaching, and working on his political/spiritual consciousness.

TO WRITE TO THE AUTHOR

If you wish to contact the author or would like more information about this book, please write to the author in care of Llewellyn Worldwide, and we will forward your request. Both the author and publisher appreciate hearing from you and learning of your enjoyment of this book. Llewellyn Worldwide cannot guarantee that every letter written to the author will be answered, but all will be forwarded. Please write to:

Stuart Myers
℅ Llewellyn Worldwide
P.O. Box 64383-K480, St. Paul, MN 55164-0383, U.S.A.

Please enclose a self-addressed stamped envelope for reply, or $1.00 to cover costs.
If outside U.S.A., enclose international postal reply coupon.

FREE CATALOG FROM LLEWELLYN WORLDWIDE

For more than 90 years, Llewellyn has brought its readers knowledge in the fields of metaphysics and human potential. Learn about the newest books in spiritual guidance, natural healing, astrology, occult philosophy, and more. Enjoy book reviews, new age articles, a calendar of events, plus current advertised products and services. To get your free copy of *Llewellyn's New Worlds of Mind and Spirit*, send your name and address to:

Llewellyn's New Worlds of Mind and Spirit
P.O. Box 64383-K480, St. Paul, MN 55164-0383, U.S.A.

Llewellyn's Modern Witchcraft Series

BETWEEN THE WORLDS

Witchcraft and the Tree of Life—
A Program of Spiritual Development

Stuart Myers

AN AUTHORS GUILD BACKINPRINT.COM EDITION

iUniverse, Inc.
New York   Bloomington

Between the Worlds: Witchcraft and the Tree of Life
A Program of Spiritual Development

AN AUTHORS GUILD BACKINPRINT.COM EDITION
Published by iUniverse, Inc.

iUniverse books may be ordered through booksellers or by contacting:

iUniverse
1663 Liberty Drive
Bloomington, IN 47403
www.iuniverse.com
1-800-Authors (1-800-288-4677)

Because of the dynamic nature of the Internet, any Web addresses or links contained in this book may have changed since publication and may no longer be valid.

ISBN: 978-1-4401-1733-6 (pbk)

Printed in the United States of America

iUniverse rev. date: 4/22/2009

ABOUT LLEWELLYN'S MODERN WITCHCRAFT SERIES

Witchcraft is a word derived from an older word, *Wicca* or *Wicce*. The older word means "to bend" or "wise." Thus, those who practiced Wicca were those who followed the path of the Wise. Those who practiced the craft of Wicca were able to bend reality to their desires: they could do magick.

Today, Witchcraft is different from what is was eons ago. Witchcraft is no longer robes and secret rites. During the Aquarian Age — the New Age — the mystical secrets of the past are being made public. The result is a set of spiritual and magickal systems with which anyone can feel comfortable. Modern Witchcraft — Wicca — may be the path for you!

Llewellyn's Modern Witchcraft Series of books will not only present the secrets of the Craft of the Wise so that anyone can use them, but will also share successful techniques that are working for Witches throughout the word. This will include philosophies and techniques that at one time were considered foreign to "the Craft," but are now being incorporated by modern Wiccans into their beliefs and procedures.

However, the core of Wicca will stay the same — that is the nature of Witchcraft. All of the books in this series will be practical and easy to use. They will all show a love of nature and a love of the Goddess as well as respect for the Masculine Force. You will find that this series of books is deeply rooted in spirituality, peacefulness, and love.

These books focus on Wicca and Wiccans today, not what was done a hundred, a thousand, or ten thousand years ago. They will help you to expand your horizons and achieve your goals. We invite you to follow this series and look toward the future of what some have called the fastest growing religion in the world, a religion that is personal, non-judgmental and non-institutional, natural and magickal — that brings forth the experience of the sacredness of ALL life. Witchcraft is called "the Old Religion" and it is found present in the oldest myths and artifacts of humanity. This series will help you see what it will develop into tomorrow.

DEDICATION

This book is dedicated to the two most important women in my life:
Virginia Henson Jenkins (08/01/25–11/10/84),
who first instilled love for the God/dess,
and Kendra Musselle, who keeps that love alive.
Blessings to you both!

TABLE OF CONTENTS

Acknowledgements ix

Introduction xi

Chapter One: Creating Sacred Space 1

Chapter Two: Working With the Elements 21

Chapter Three: Planting the Tree 51

Chapter Four: Nourishing the Tree 75

Chapter Five: Rising on the Planes 99

Chapter Six: Creating Magickal Ritual 119

Chapter Seven: Discovering the Tides of Life 149

Chapter Eight: Honoring Moon and Sun 179

Appendix One: The Sephiroth 195

Appendix Two: The Words of Power 219

Glossary 223

Bibliography 229

ACKNOWLEDGMENTS

Between the Worlds was a vision both inspired and shared by many people, but it was brought to life by Llewellyn Publications. I cannot thank my newfound family at Llewellyn enough—especially Nancy Mostad (Acquisitions and Development Manager), Carl Llewellyn Weschcke (Owner and President of Llewellyn Publications), and my editor, Jessica Thoreson. Their constant support and encouragement throughout my creative process was instrumental in the development of my work. It is a rare event in the literary world that an author finds such supportive and caring guides in a major publishing corporation; the Goddess and God blessed me with their courage, inspiration, and presence in my life! I thank them for accepting nothing less than my best work.

The contributions of Marjorie Stevens and Ann Refoe to my literary development cannot go without acknowledgment; Mrs. Stevens provided me with the original impetus to write, sharing the secret that "all true power lies in the written word." Just when I thought that I had lost that power, Ann Refoe came into my life as both an English professor and a mentor; she rekindled the creative fire that was left untended. This book began as a series of essays in her English class!

Throughout my life-long magickal odyssey, there have been few people more important in my life than the teachers/students with whom I have shared my journey. I would like to thank you all: Tammy, Denise, Nicole, Maude, and Larry (you know who you are) for helping me "ground and center" during my wild days; Tammy Corn, Sandy Clark, and Larry Pritchett, for being some of my most patient and caring critics/students; the "First Wave" of Bruce Bishop, Janine Estes, Tony Estes, Scot Kremsrieter, Stacey Schiebe, Margaret "Gibby" Scott, and Tim Wagner (we should all "time warp" again—soon!); the "Second Wave" of Scot Kremsrieter, Stacey Schiebe, Natasha McGuire, Lena de Sousa McGuire, and "Noel" (we took some great photos); my own "Sacred Grove" of Kendra Musselle, Hillary Jones, and Doug Sinning; and our three resulting sister covens of Elven Earth, Phoenix Rising, and Twisted Oak.

There have been many wonderful people with whom I have intimately shared sacred space; I cannot begin to thank you all enough: Diana Hemphill, Bob Williams, Ron and Sally Jaffe, Joy Scott, Victor Veno, Scott Lasey, Jeff Lehman, Cat Edmundson, Chris Kendall, Scott Vorkapic, Donna Mackey, Jon and Cindy Moriconi, John and Amy Ullman, Betty Jo, Suzanne LaCour, Ken "Windwalker," Judy Barrett, Carl Barrett, and Carson Humphries, all of my brothers and sisters at the Wiccan Religious Cooperative of Central Florida.

I would also like to thank the following people for their individual contributions to this work:

Kendra Musselle, for sharing her criticisms as this manuscript developed (not to mention unlimited use of her computer!). I cannot wait until her own creative project, *The Living Tarot*, is finally completed;

Bryan Zepp, for encouraging me to write when I was about to give up;

Karen Jackson of Delphi Press, for guiding me through the creative process;

Ron Jaffe, owner of Magickal Earth, Inc., for sharing his Qabalistic incense recipes with me;

Hillary Jones, owner of Dragonwood, for supporting my work with her own;

Doug Sinning, owner of Earth Tones Studios, for allowing me to use excerpts from a song that we co-wrote called "The Crone Chant";

Harper San Francisco Publishers, for allowing me to reprint Starhawk's "Faery Creation Myth" from her book *The Spiral Dance*;

Llewellyn Publications, for allowing me to quote from the writings of Israel Regardie in *A Garden of Pomegranates*.

INTRODUCTION

To practice Witchcraft, to find the elusive Tree of Life within, one must learn to create sacred space; once within the circle's boundaries, one must also learn to rend the veils between the seen and unseen, walking freely between the worlds. Much of my first year learning Qabalah and the laws of Wicca were spent within the magick circle, learning to tread the paths that lie between the mists of reality. I remember the first night that I felt I understood what it was to cast a circle; I was centering myself, growing taller with each breath. Larger than the trees, more expansive than the oceans, and moving beyond this world, I was bridging sky and earth: I was connected to sky and earth. I was a microcosm of the Macrocosm; the forces of Nature would be in my working. As I floated between the worlds, I created my first circle of power. No longer was it rote; it was magick! Qabalah teaches the structure in which one might recognize the Universe within—that is the most sacred of spaces!

—Kendra Musselle
Writer, political activist, feminist, single mother, and Witch

During my early Craft training, my first High Priestess once remarked, "Good Witches are eclectic; they'll steal anything that works!" Years passed, and we studied material from different cultures, ages, and magickal systems. Pouring through tomes of ancient mythology and magick, I became aware of an invisible thread that unraveled as history progressed: the Great Mother and Her Consort, guardians of the mysteries, spanned all times and places. Where humanity existed, they, too, existed in some form—only their aspects changed. I sensed that this elusive thread had a name; it began somewhere in our ancient past and beckoned, "Come, follow me!" Like Theseus in the labyrinth of the Minotaur, I tried to follow it to its source.

Five years passed, and the thread continued to unwind, its end nowhere in sight. After taking my third degree initiation, I emerged as an independent Witch, versed well in the mysteries of the God/dess ... or so I thought. Not long after taking my final rites, I met a man whose knowledge of the Great Mother surpassed my own. And when he told me, "No, I'm not a Witch; I'm a Qabalist," I realized that I had found the end of my magickal thread. After long conversations by moonlight,

BASIC DIVISIONS OF THE TREE OF LIFE

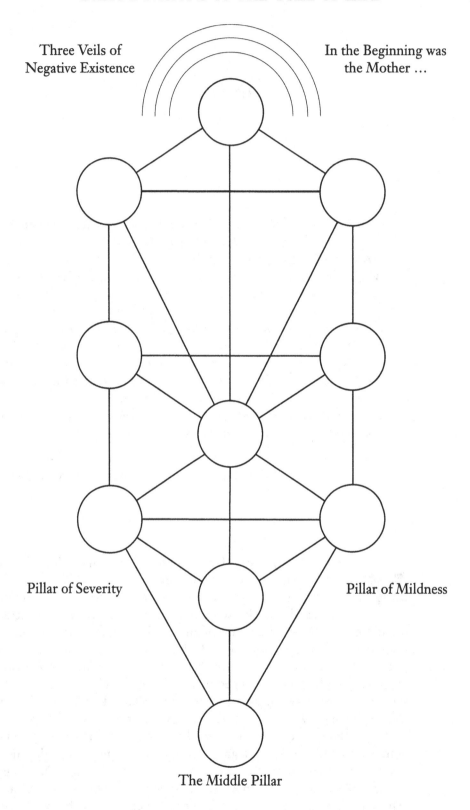

Three Veils of
Negative Existence

In the Beginning was
the Mother ...

Pillar of Severity

Pillar of Mildness

The Middle Pillar

Figure 1

nights spent in secret, lonely places evoking the raw aspects of Them, I realized that my beliefs as a Witch found completion within his system of magick. He offered to teach me the secrets held within the Tree of Life; his methods seemed to work, so I grabbed at the chance offered. Witches around me shuddered in despair and fright! I had begun my study of the Qabalah.

In earlier times, Qabalah began as a form of Hebrew mysticism known as Hechalot (ascent) or Merkabah Mysticism. Not much is known about this ancient practice, but we do know that it involved a series of techniques drawing its practitioners into higher planes of existence until they could finally gaze upon the face of Deity. Over time, as the practitioners of Hechalot learned more about the subtle realms, their practices grew into the forms we know as Qabalah.

Mythically, it is said that the early Hebrews channeled the main glyph known as the "Tree of Life" from an Archangel named Metatron. The concept of angelic forces predates both Christianity and Judaism, coming from early civilization's attempt to classify the unknown forces which permeate the physical realm. Indeed, some sought to worship the angelic forms as minor deities, alarming the early Judeo-Christian patriarchs. Within their holy texts, we find more than one verse warning against worship of these pagan concepts.

Metatron is known as the Archangel of Kether, the keeper of the highest mysteries. The name Qabalah comes from the Hebrew meaning "to receive," signifying that the whole is a system received from the higher powers. In giving us the glyph of the Tree, divinity was preparing man for a leap in consciousness, providing the tools for increasing spiritual power. Reminiscent of Prometheus bringing fire to humankind, Metatron gave us a spiritual fire to light the darkness about to descend over the followers of the God/dess; indeed, even that fire was threatened to be extinguished during the following persecutions.

Before Judaism began as an organized faith, the early Hebrews were polytheistic and Goddess-oriented, living by the tides of moon and sun. Even within the Torah, we find evidence that the leaders of the political movement behind the great exodus out of Egypt were dismayed when their people clung to the worship of the Goddesses Ashimah and Asherah and the fertility Gods Baal and Hadad. Worshippers erected wooden pillars in high places, or planted sacred trees in honor of Asherah and Baal. As these objects were revered as a symbol of the Mother Goddess of all life, followers of the new monopolist God, Jehovah, demanded that they be cut down and burned (Ex. 34:13 and Deut. 12:3).

As time passed and Judaism gained more followers, the prophets continued to demand that the pagan Hebrew sites be destroyed (Isa. 27:9; Mic. 5:14). Worshippers of the ancient Goddesses and Gods were persecuted, tortured, and murdered in the name of the new God, Jehovah. Fortunately, the Qabalah survived these fires, much as our own traditional Craft lore survived the persecution of the Catholic Church. We see the parallels between two peoples from different times, who lived and died for love of their Goddess. Their knowledge, in both instances, lives on.

Fighting to survive throughout the centuries, Qabalah was preserved within the confines of the Jewish faith, surfacing into the mainstream occasionally as the study of scholarly Jewish men. As it traveled through the ages, it began to change; its forms were adapted to relate to the theology of the times. The Goddess, however, remained a part of it, despite the objections of leaders—She became known in concepts of the Shekinah (Jewish "Holy Spirit"), and "Queen of the Sabbath," which the wife in every Jewish home represents from sunset Friday night until sunset Saturday night. But until the days of magicians such as Agrippa, Marsilio Fecino, Eliphas Levi, and Francis Barrett, Qabalah remained solely in the hands of Judaism. Indeed, transplanting the Tree of Life into ceremonial magick, which was popular in their circles, did little for its reputation; even now, Witches regard the Qabalah as a magickal remnant of a patriarchal past.

Qabalah is a magickal system that readily fits into our practice of Wicca; arguments against its use are based upon misunderstandings. At first glance, the methods may appear complex, but we find simplicity in their designs upon closer analysis. We must realize that Qabalah is a complete system in itself. A comparison that I like to use is with that of an atlas—each part of it is a map of the area to be traveled. Qabalah is a map to the soul. Each of the ten spheres of existence (sephirah, plural: sephiroth) and the twenty-two paths between them provide us with a detailed plan to follow to attain the various modes of consciousness. Describing the terrain are lists of correspondences; from the lists, which include an element, planet, and/or zodiacal sign, we may ascertain which energies are present, how to invoke them, and what to expect once we attain that level of consciousness. Witches are already familiar with the signposts and energies used; this method allows us to discover from which spiritual realms these energies originate and make more efficient use of them. Also, while working up the ladder of deity, one may use the paths and sephiroth as a means to communicate spiritual work and experience to others.

Even though it survived secretly within the Jewish faith, the mystical philosophy behind the Qabalah is based upon male and female archetypes and their union. A brief look at the structure of the Tree of Life shows that the pillars are split into three separate divisions: the pillar of severity (feminine pillar), mercy (masculine pillar), and the middle pillar (union of opposites) [See Figure 1]. But most importantly, as we look at the "Three Veils of Negative Existence" above the Tree, we notice that they are renamed "In the Beginning Was the Mother." Like the traditional Craft, Qabalah teaches the law of polarity; negative polarities always denote feminine and gestational forces.

From the start, we have a magickal system that embraces Craft philosophy!

The arguments used by Witches to avoid studying the Qabalah's magick are based upon misunderstandings; as we delve deeper into its secrets, we find that Qabalistic methods match our own. Upon first glance at the lists of books, rituals, and correspondences, the sephiroth seem complex; yet these books are the ways others have worked with the material, and the methods used may be as simple as our own. The traditional (New Forest, Gardnerian, Alexandrian) ways of making magick are based upon the Witch's Wheel and eight paths to the center; Qabalistic magick makes use of these methods, also. Both are concerned with the construction of a magickal circle, which is a place between the worlds where the veil between the seen and unseen is thin.

No matter what tradition one practices, the basic Witch powers are based upon the eight ways of making magick: meditation, trance, wine, invocations, dancing, chanting, the scourge, and the Great Rite. These methods, and combinations of them, are what we use to raise the power to complete our magick. In preparing for a spell or a ritual, we must decide what color candles, robes, and cloths to use. Some of us may use crystals, incense, and herbs in our work. We compose chants, spells, and invocations, and carefully tailor the props to match our needs. This magick uses the same techniques; once deciding the work to be done, we choose our path or sephirah and use mnemonic devices to help us tap into those energies.

Central to both systems, also, is the construction of the magick circle. Many have the misconception that a Qabalist uses the circle to keep out the "demons" he or she chooses to evoke. True, this can be one part of Ceremonial Magick, but Qabalah has little to do with these practices. Various magicians throughout the ages have absorbed its techniques into their ceremonies, as I have done. The Tree of Life teaches little of the planes known as demonic. The energies channeled by these techniques need to be contained like the energy raised by the Witch; the magick circle is much like our own in this respect. Power raised must be contained—the elements of earth, air, fire, and water are called—and then the raising of the energies needed begins. The circle, then, is the same as ours.

Both philosophies teach that the earth and the heavens are equally holy and pure. Our bodies are sacred, and all of physical existence is divine. There is an old Qabalistic saying that Malkuth (the physical plane) is in Kether (the unattainable divinity), and Kether is in Malkuth. The Tree of Life teaches us that one cannot exist without the other, and by acknowledging one without revering the other, we fall from the heights like a kite without a tether; blown about by the winds, we eventually fall and crash into the earth. Very few philosophies share this hallowing of physical existence with us.

Molding with our own system, Qabalah becomes a companion and guide to our lives as Witches; until now it has been shrouded in mystery due to its preservation by a patriarchal religion. Closer scrutiny reveals that its techniques and philosophies are much like our own—a divine world filled with myriad Gods and Goddesses that enhance our spiritual lives as humans. With so many similarities between methods and viewpoints, it is only a matter of working with the material to make it open and reveal its secrets to us. That is the purpose of this book, to make the Tree of Life flourish within us all and bring us closer to the knowledge of the Goddess and God. To all those who undertake this journey, Blessed Be!

CHAPTER ONE

CREATING SACRED SPACE

We are all one—one body, one mind, one soul—in the great circle of life!
—A Qabalistic maxim

Qabalah teaches us that there are various modes of consciousness, ranging from daily physical awareness to the misty veils of subconsciousness. To attain the ecstasy needed to work magick, we must somehow slip between the veils of physical existence and into the realms of the other worlds. Central to the practice of Wicca, also, is this belief: To become a Witch and use the old powers, the "Wise One" must part the mists between the seen and unseen, slipping between them and thus becoming closer to the energies therein. Witches must learn to still the mind to achieve awareness of the other realms and raise the needed powers.

We need a method to calm the conscious mind, make it stop its constant rattling so we may listen to the subconscious. Once stilled, we must also find a way to contain the vast amounts of power that flow from the subconscious lest the energies be lost. Casting the Witch's circle accomplishes both: in creating this vortex we speak in symbol and metaphor, ideas only the inner mind can comprehend; by its nature as a sphere, it easily contains the energies channeled. In casting the circle, we send a signal to the conscious mind telling it to shut down, allowing the deepest parts of self to shine in their glory. Sacred space is created, and within this area the seen and unseen mingle. Creating it carries us beyond the physical realm and into those of magick.

This concept of sacred space permeates all magickal traditions—consider the shaman's medicine wheel, the magician's temple, and the megalithic stone circles. However, unlike the Witch's circle, these areas are permanent spaces for magickal work. The stones used mark the boundaries of the space, which contains the energies raised. Most of us have no permanent magickal structures; we must cast the circle each time we use it. As we do so, we create a place of power that destroys mundane reality and redefines time and space. Alternate realities, existing in abundance, meet. Things we once considered to be ultimate truths become uncertain as we step between the worlds, bringing the inner truths of flexibility to life.

Once the circle is cast, the ritual begins; we are free to walk between the worlds. As Witches, as Qabalists, and as beings of light, we realize that this physical realm connects to others of more tenuous substance, and our jobs as changers-of-reality involve being able to part the veils between the seen and unseen, the known and unknown. To embark upon the magickal path, we must realize that our previous teachings about concrete reality are lies—there are other realms of existence yet uncharted. And, as we begin our study of Qabalah, we shall begin to explore the poorly charted realms of the soul and magick.

We will center our study on the glyph known as "The Tree of Life," a symbol that categorizes creation and human consciousness into energy fields consisting of ten sephiroth (states of being) and twenty-two paths (states of becoming) [See Figure 1:1]. Early mystics theorized that the Macrocosm, or universe, was a complex interplay of energies that originated from incomprehensible nothingness to tangible reality. Beginning in the physical realm and anchoring firmly to it, early magicians perfected their physical bodies as containers of the Macrocosmic energies and began to explore the more tenuous energy fields of existence. They, like Witches today, believed in the sanctity of physical existence and used it to support their exploration of the spiritual realms. To make these energies work for us, we must gather and concentrate them into a confined magickal space.

In gathering the tenuous fields of energy from other phases of existence, we realize that the circle expresses the greatest magickal truth of all: life and its possibilities are infinite and never-ending. We have a holistic view of creation; rather than the belief that the earth was created millions of years ago and will end millions of years in the future, we see it all as a continual cycle. Everything is recreated and reborn rather than destroyed or dead. All is part of a necessary whole, rather than unrelated forms massed together on one planet. Once we perceive all life as an interconnected, constantly changing whole, the possibilities for "magick" and "miracles" increase—all we touch changes for the better.

Within this circle of light, we love, adore, share, laugh, and cry together. We become interconnected; our energies mesh into a web that creates and recreates our psyches. As the sephirotic energies flow within and without, they open up new vistas of awareness that assure us, "There is no part of us that is not of the Gods." Slowly climbing and exploring the Tree branch by branch is a spiritual exercise that will intensify our experiences as Witches; a life-cycle that never ends and carries us closer to our Goddess with each celebration. Unless we perfect our magickal technique, channeling consciousness into the form and force of the magickal circle, the full impact of our magick will be lost. We begin working with our imagination, performing movements and gestures that strengthen visualizations. As this mental faculty grows in strength, forms and energies derived from beyond the Witch begin to manifest.

At first, the process may seem bizarre. Unaccustomed to magickal work, one's ego will begin to assert that it is mere drama, pure theatrics, and no more. The truth is this—circles cannot be created without a strong will, imagination, and a few theatrics to speak to the subconscious mind; a good Witch will make use of all this and more. Soon the seemingly surreal will become real, and the circle becomes a blazing emblem before us, a mandala to create and sustain the channeled magickal energies. We find ourselves in both a sacred time and a sacred place; we find ourselves within the Mother's womb.

Although confined physically within the womb, our souls are free to travel the loftiest ethereal planes in search of the God/dess, or to sink deep within the physical realm to hallow it and learn its secrets. The circle, then, is a starting point, a focus for consciousness. The only danger is in allowing our minds to wander, lost in simple revelry. A dream world cannot replace our magickal vortex, nor will it

THE PATHS AND THE SEPHIROTH ON THE TREE

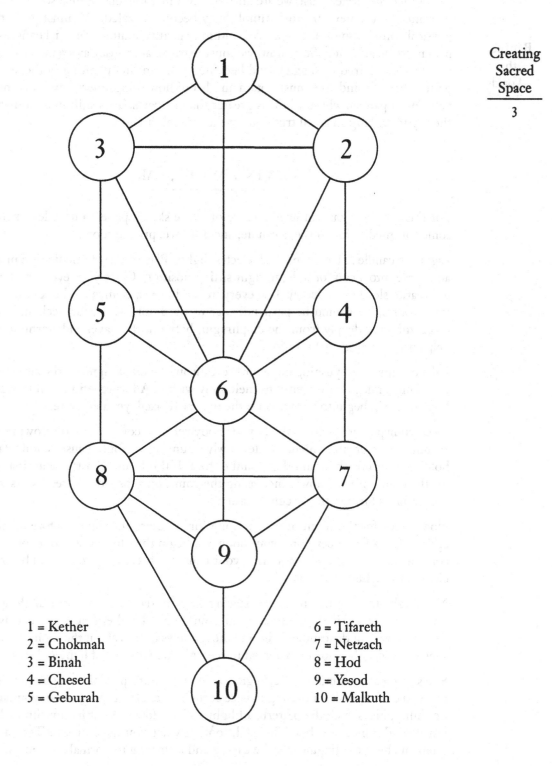

1 = Kether
2 = Chokmah
3 = Binah
4 = Chesed
5 = Geburah

6 = Tifareth
7 = Netzach
8 = Hod
9 = Yesod
10 = Malkuth

Figure 1:1

substitute for spiritual realities. We are children to the Goddess; like children, we must learn to make sense of our new surroundings.

Once the circle is cast, we are born to new inner life; our normal senses, unaccustomed to the new spiritual stimuli, may become dazzled. We must learn that physical consciousness does not work within a spiritual realm—spiritual consciousness must be achieved. Somehow, we must learn to adjust our awareness to these new levels required by magick, and become proficient in operating in the appropriate state of mind. We must obtain an idea of how things merge and mix into a pattern—a pattern whose whole is greater than its parts. This shift in awareness is the key to making spiritual truth out of theoretical thought.

BECOMING AWARE, PART I

For this exercise you will need a piece of white sketch paper, a dark lead pencil, some soft meditation music, a candle, and a secure, private room.

Light the candle and extinguish all electric lights. Play some soft meditation music, and settle into a comfortable, upright sitting position. Close your eyes, and begin to breathe slowly and deeply. Use every inhalation as a chance to check your posture; your spine should be perpendicular to the floor, with your neck and head erect. Inhaling deeply from the diaphragm, between the navel and sternum, will help correct your spinal position.

Exhale completely, pushing out your breath from the diaphragm. As the air escapes your lungs, imagine that tensions melt away with it. A few repetitions of this deep breathing will begin to put you into the proper relaxed, yet alert state.

Once your posture is aligned and your body relaxed, concentrate on slowing and evening your breath. Inhale while slowly counting to four. Pause, comfortably holding your breath for another count of four. If this is uncomfortable at first, aim for the count of two, slowly increasing the count on subsequent breaths. As your body relaxes further, this becomes easier.

Now exhale for the count of four, waiting for another four counts before inhaling again. After a few repetitions, your body will begin this rhythm without conscious commands; you will find that during your pauses in breathing, your mind becomes clear of thoughts, as it should be.

Now, light the candle and begin staring into its flame. Allow critical thinking processes to end; if thoughts arise in your mind, let them quietly float away. Become aware of the candle flame and the shadows it casts about the room. Breathe slowly and deeply, allowing yourself to see only the patterns of light and shadow.

Still staring at the candle flame, begin to sketch the interplay of the light and shadows you can see without ceasing to gaze at the flame. Don't worry about your artistic ability; just sketch the patterns of light and shadow present in your immediate visual field. Once you have finished, look at what you have drawn. Take a few moments before extinguishing the candle and returning to normal awareness.

In becoming aware of the overall patterns and not the individual pieces, we realize that all life is an interconnected whole. There is no dividing line between us and the ground we stand upon, the bird that we see soaring through the skies, or the plants growing in our gardens. Nature forms a symbiotic relationship in which everything feeds, grows, and depends upon everything else.

Imagine being truly disconnected from the environment of earth, air, water, and fire. In spirit, perhaps one could survive under such conditions. Physical form, however, must follow physical law. The Earth below us provides stability and the foundation for all other elements to exist; within Her framework an ecosystem of vast proportions has developed. Some elements may be dispensed with and cause no immediate harm; but over long periods of time no one really knows the implications of destroying a subspecies of blind shrimp found in a marine cave off the coast of Bermuda. Nature forms relationships which support and build upon each other; to take away from the pattern is risking destruction of the whole.

Our greatest limitation as humans is that we often fail to perceive the overall pattern, the big picture, of all things. Once we have truly become aware of patterns, not just individual threads, we are still limited by our inability to take in more than one part of the pattern. To illustrate this point, repeat the Becoming Aware exercise in a different part of the same room, preferably the area that was originally behind your back. Once completed, compare the two patterns. The center of the sketch where the candle was remains the same; it will be a large area of light. The remaining shadows, shades, and area of darkness will take on different forms and shapes.

They do, however, both exist; the two patterns are different parts of the same whole. If we "had eyes in the backs of our heads" we would be able to perceive the larger pattern they share. In this exercise, the candle represents our focus, our path, our point of concern, while the varying shades represent how the remainder of the environment falls into place around our focal point. Considering this, one may see how different opinions on one subject exist; different ideals, religions, governments, and political views flourish and crumble side by side in the same world. Are any right or wrong? Not necessarily, as they are all viewing their part of the whole pattern and interpreting it according to their own biases. Perhaps if our world leaders could learn to use this point of view … .

To take in and understand more of the patterns of existence we must use more than our sight; all five physical senses must blend into one another and be operative together before the sixth sense, our psychic awareness, opens up. By experiencing the present with all our physical senses, we learn to balance our experience and process material on a more intuitive level. Call it intuition, ESP, or "the sight," this inner processing of experience moves us toward the subtle realms where the big picture, or overall pattern of things, may be experienced on a broader level. The next exercise involves learning to use the five senses together to process the pattern of reality in a different way.

BECOMING AWARE, PART II

Use this exercise to become aware of the interplay of the five senses—the five separate ways one may perceive physical reality. For this exercise we need the materials from the first exercise, plus an aromatic fruit such as an orange or grapefruit.

Repeat the first exercise. Once you have slipped into the consciousness of patterns, pick up the piece of fruit in your hands. Try to feel the texture as you gaze at the orange, as opposed to rationalizing it with your mind. See the fruit and allow the awareness of its reality to transcend either the sight or the texture; feel the two modes of awareness becoming one.

Peel the fruit, listening to the subtle sounds this makes. Add this to the whole experience.

As you peel, the soft citrus aroma will permeate the area around you. Four senses are now involved in the experience: sight, sound, touch, and smell. Integrate these experiences into one.

To complete this exercise, eat the orange slowly, one piece at a time. Feel the stickiness the juices create on your fingers. Smell the aroma. See the naked flesh of the fruit. Feel the silky softness of the flesh. Finally, taste it. Internalize these sensations into one until you can arrive at a complete, here-and-now experience of the orange.

Once we perceive the big picture, once we can temporarily alchemize our experiences into one pattern, we have found the frame of mind needed to cast our circle and slip between the worlds of reality. Leaving our separatist, divide-and-conquer frame of mind behind in a trance state that embraces patterns, not individual pieces, we move into a state where we may work powerful magick.

Our magick may appear to give us the perfect freedom to do what we wish at first, but we quickly realize that by removing or changing one thread in our material designs, the others change to compensate. Throw a rock into a pool of water and ripples spread out from the point of impact, disturbing the stillness of the water. The mass of the rock itself causes a slight rise in the water level; the larger the rock, the larger the disturbance. Ripples cease, but until the added mass is removed, the water level remains the same. In removing the rock, we again disturb the stillness of the water's surface. This is the true law of karma—anything we do will influence everything in the area. There is no good or evil considered in it, only cause and effect. Sometimes even the best intentions have devastating effects. Patterns, once altered, are never truly the same again.

This defining of space and creation of a spiritual body of sorts is comparable to the choices we make before birth; those of parentage and general life circumstance. Before we create our vortex, we are limited in our working space; a room or portion of a room is used. Likewise, those of us here on earth are here because we have to be here (unlike an avatar); however, each of us chooses our parentage and general life circumstance. Choosing the magickal vehicle (body) while working within a temple (earth) is a decision left up to each of us before stepping into this world. We each come with a goal and a purpose.

Likewise, before stepping (incarnating) into the magickal circle (body), we enter with a specific goal in mind, whether it be to worship, share, or work magick. The space becomes a magickal body for us to use during our operations. While operating within the sphere, our attention turns inward to the center of the circle, an act that symbolically represents us turning inward to ourselves.

In spite of what one may have read or been taught, there are three necessary steps in casting the circle: dedication, purification, and invocation. In dedicating our circle, we begin by announcing the space as sacred, giving our subconscious a call to attention. Physical boundaries are delineated; we realize that the astral forms follow the physical designs, and thought begins the process by which we open our space. Critical and analytical functions are set aside; disbelief is suspended for a time. We also realize that the outer forms are not important. In casting the circle it is what happens within us, on the inner realms of consciousness, that creates our vortex. As we will, so mote it be!

Next comes the purification of the space. Moving in a deosil (clockwise) progression, we further enforce the circle's boundaries as we continue to cleanse it of negativity. Becoming our magickal body for a time, as the circle is cleansed, so are we. Water, incense, earth, and fire are carried about to purify the space with the four elements. We release negative thought-forms and energies from ourselves. Vibratory rates are raised, and the general area is cleansed.

Finally, having prepared and strengthened our vortex, we call the Mighty Ones into the circle. We proceed with the four elements, and finally call the God/dess. This gives us the chance to call on aspects of ourselves specific to the work that we are doing. Our operations are done with the higher parts of our beings, not just the purely human part. Magickal operations done only with the human part require more effort and often fail. Operations done under divine guidance are rapid; they become true art forms, apt to succeed. We invoke the powers and they resonate within, awakening aspects of ourselves that normally remain hidden from everyday consciousness. The circle becomes a living mandala and we are finally centered within the self.

To begin casting the circle, we must first develop the new awareness that accompanies it, a sort of twilight vision where we can see the holistic pattern and reality behind all things, not just the individual identities. For within the circle we stretch our consciousness to become one with the powers around us; the traditional separateness we feel in everyday life must be suspended for a moment so we may transcend that reality. Once we attain that awareness, we must begin to channel that new consciousness, the energy that lies within the pattern, into the form called the magick circle. In Witchcraft, we channel psychic energy with the athame.

ATHAME MEDITATION

Obtain a knife or dagger with a blunt tip and two dull edges. The three parts of the blade represent the threefold law, "What ye send forth come back to thee, so ever mind the rule of three." Because the athame is not used for cutting physical objects, the edges are dulled for safety reasons.

Some Witches paint the handle black and inscribe traditional symbols in white paint [see Diagram 1:1]; others prefer to leave the handle plain. Complete any decorations before you begin this exercise.

Begin by entering the awareness of patterns. Realize that within the patterns around us are vast storehouses of energy; as we tap into the larger patterns of Cosmos, we tap into larger stores of power.

Think of the sun, which lies millions of miles away, yet its light and heat permeate the Earth, sustaining life. Contemplate the stars that lie beyond our galaxy. This light radiates to us and we see them twinkling in the night sky. Different planets exert gravitational pulls on our planet—no matter how far out an object is in space, its energy somehow touches our own sphere. In magick, the same is true of universal energy patterns. We draw off a source; that source replenishes its stores from other patterns; all things move in an eternal circle.

By using our breathing as a channel, we can absorb and move these energies. Feel the power around your body, your aura. As you inhale, imagine that great waves of energy are drawn off the patterns around you. Hold this energy within your own pattern as you exhale.[1] To help the process, visualize the energy as white light being absorbed into the body. Do not worry about depleting the energy stores of living things in your immediate area—these, in turn, will draw off the patterns of which they are a part. Remember that all power moves cyclically.

Take the athame in your power hand. For those who are right-handed, this is the right hand; for those who are left-handed, this is the left hand. Now, as you exhale, imagine that the energy you absorbed is flowing into the athame. Energy moves with the breath, so as you breathe, the power will flow; all you have to do is guide it with the mind. Keep moving energy into the athame until it glows with a powerful, white color.

Point the blade of the athame up into the sky; on your next exhalation, will the energy to move upward through the blade in a bright shaft of light. See it as a powerful beacon that pierces the night sky as you say, "Hail Goddess and God!" Know that they shall see and hear your salute.

Spend a few moments replenishing the energies within yourself and your athame. Slowly return to normal consciousness.

Simply, as we cast the circle, we are suspending the belief in mere physical reality; there is more to the human experience than flesh and blood. We acknowledge that a spiritual reality exists within us, and as the boundaries of the circle are cast, we are extending our own magickal light so our beliefs may take form in an area that encompasses us. Here is the key to the circle's protective powers. Most of our lives are spent in denial of the divine spark within, that God/dess exists or even takes part in the affairs of humans. In casting the circle, we expand our divinity so it becomes larger than our physical selves. Shrouded by divine power, the physical becomes intoxicated by the forces of light, empowered to operate within the spiritual realms.

---

1. Athletes, who cannot afford fatigue during competition, use a special breathing technique to boost their energy levels. At the first sign that their energy is fading, they breathe in deeply through the nostrils until the abdomen is fully distended. After holding the breath for eight seconds, they exhale until the abdomen collapses inward. Three repetitions of this exercise serves to replenish their energy, allowing them to continue competition.

This breathing pattern is also used in magick; the slow inhalations allow the vital energies from the surrounding area to enter into the body; holding the breath for the count of eight allows the energies to merge with the physical body. The subsequent exhalation rids the body of the poisons which serve to deflate our energy levels. It is recommended, however, that the student continue to use the four count breathing rhythm until the lungs gain strength in this exercise, before moving on to the more demanding rhythm. And even then, increase the additional time in which the breath is retained by one second each practice, until the eight second hold is comfortably achieved. It may take awhile, but the results are well worth the effort.

Sometimes, however, what is within us is not always pure; our spiritual body can absorb toxins and poisons much as the physical body can absorb pollution, poisons, and other toxins from the environment. Suffering and diseased from improper care, our souls must be cleansed of negativity if they are to be strong enough to walk on our path. Before casting the circle, we must cleanse ourselves.

SELF-CLEANSING

Most rituals should begin with a cleansing, meaning several related techniques to rid the aura of the negativity that it picks up on a daily basis. The most common

THE MAGICKAL SYMBOLS DRAWN ON THE ATHAME

The perfect couple:
Goddess and God

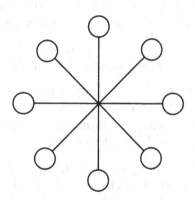

The eight ritual occasions;
the eight paths to power

The power going forth
to the astral plane

Diagram 1:1

cleansing is done with incense and water. Materials you will need for this exercise are some soft meditation music, a bowl filled with water, one red and one white candle in candle holders, some salt, some sandalwood incense, and an incense burner (use simmering potpourri in place of incense, if you prefer).

Place the materials on the altar, if you already have one, or on a special cloth on the floor used for no other purpose. Light the red candle (to your left), then the white candle (to your right). These stand for the God/dess.

Enter into the awareness of patterns. Once you are within this state, light the stick of incense and place it in the incense burner. Allow the smoke to rise freely for a few moments as you center yourself and breathe deeply.

Incense represents the mingling of fire and air. Bring the incense burner close to yourself; allow the smoke to drift up the front of your body. Feel negativity and tension being released from your aura. Imagine the energy field becoming a brilliant white as you perform this exercise.

Using your hand, draw the incense smoke to your heart area, then over your head and down your back. Waft the smoke toward your nostrils and breathe it in.

Continue this exercise throughout the room, walking around its perimeter and wafting the smoke toward the walls. Pay particular attention to the corners.

Returning to your starting point, pass any tools you will be using in your ritual (cloths, candles, containers, etc.) through the incense smoke.

Next, we shall symbolically mix the elements of water and earth (represented by the salt) to finish our cleansing of ourselves and our space.

Hold the bowl of water in your hands. Imagine the pure white light from your cleansed aura entering into the water until it, too, glows white. Say, "Blessed be thou creature of water; I cast forth all impurities that thou mayest serve me, by the powers of the gentle Goddess and powerful Horned One. So mote it be."

Putting the water down and picking up the salt, repeat the visualization and say, "Blessings be upon this creature of salt; let all impurities be cast forth, and let only good enter herein. Wherefore do I bless thee and invoke thee, that thou mayest aid me, by the powers of the gentle Goddess and powerful Horned One. Blessed Be!"

Mix the salt into the water and stir, imagining the energy swirling within. Taste it a bit, and then sprinkle a few drops on your head, imagining the energy swirling within your own energy field.

Asperse the room with water as you did with the incense, and then return to your starting point in the center and asperse all the tools you will be using in the ritual. You are now properly prepared to cast the circle.

CASTING THE CIRCLE

In an art class, the student must become familiar with the materials used for artistic expression; likewise, Witches must learn how to treat consciousness. Our awareness of things, our perceptions, makes up the artistic materials we have to create on the astral plane. True, Witchcraft is a creative expression with only one law,[2] but we must master manipulations of our materials if the resulting forms are to be true creative masterpieces of consciousness.

Once the general awareness of patterns is learned, it becomes a fairly straight-forward job to construct a circle. All that is necessary is that we slip into our altered state of consciousness, and then recreate our immediate pattern so that we are contained in a vortex of spiritual light.

Begin by envisioning that all is one; sense the play of lights, sounds, and shadows all around you. Imagine a bright ball of light expanding from within the heart area until you have a sphere of light extending roughly nine feet all about you.

Experience the inner patterns; the thoughts, cares, and concerns arising within the circle of self. This is your own individual pattern, and is as real as that existing about you before the circle was cast.

Walk to the Northern edge of your imaginary circle, traditionally the place of darkness and mystery—the home and resting place of the God/dess. Follow this line around three times clockwise. As you do, extend the athame (blade pointing to the imagined circle on the floor) and feel energy in the form of an electric blue light flowing into the boundaries of the circle and flaming up.

Return to the center of your circle. Feel the energies flowing all about you. Realize that you are contained within this sacred space.

Now that our sacred space is created, we must continue developing our magickal mandala until it is complete. Our bodies are formed from the four philosophic elements of earth, air, fire, and water; if the circle is seen as an extension of the true, inner self, it makes sense from a spiritual standpoint that we build up the elemental powers within the circle before moving on to the concepts of divinity. While it is true that the magickal elements are not material phenomena, their spiritual power does influence and vivify the physical. Their positions on the circle are: fire-South, water-West, air-East, and earth-North.

The Element of Fire

First, we must try to identify with the element of fire. Our objective here is to incorporate the element into ourselves through visualization, and once we can feel the power building within ourselves, we invoke the element to our circle. All sorts of fiery ideas come to mind: vibrant sunsets and soothing candles, raging bonfires and glowing embers. Make your concepts as aesthetically pleasing as possible, free from negative connotations. We must continue this process, expanding upon the visualizations, until they begin to spiral upon themselves; we must know what it is to be fire. As each image forms in consciousness, spend a few moments pretending that you are that concept. Feel the concept merging with your form. Once you can feel the warm and cleansing powers of fire burning within your veins, project these images into the Southern quarter.

This is the true secret of all these elemental exercises: Create an inner image of the element within the self, then visualize the image forming without the circle.

2. Within my Book of Shadows, this one law reads, "Bide the Wiccan Law ye must, in perfect love and perfect trust; eight words the Wiccan Rede fulfill—an ere ye harm none, do as ye will." Indeed, this is a law that all, not just Witches, should live by!

Soon, the powers will begin to merge. Like does attract like, and if one dwells upon the proper qualities, those same energies return from the appropriate regions. When dealing with fire, this may be a sudden onslaught of power. This experiment becomes successful when the experience becomes definite, and not leaving you wondering, "Did I really experience it?", but, "Wow! I experienced it!"

After mastering fire in the South, move on to the West with water.

The Element of Water

Elemental water must not be visualized as cold or suffocating. Begin by imagining yourself afloat in a clear, cool ocean; the water holds you gently, and you relax as the waves wash over you. Once the experience of this element is built up within, begin to visualize a vast, calm sea of clear blue water, and the sounds of the tide slowly rising on the shoreline—this visualization extends beyond the magickal circle, into infinity. Both the water within and the water without begin to connect, until you are lost in the most soothing of elements. This experience will cool the warmth created by magickal fire; first, you will feel a distinct sensation of negative debris, the charred remnants of harmful energies transformed by fire, being washed away. Then those same energies will be cleansed by the churning waves of the magickal tides flowing within and without the circle.

The Element of Air

Next, approach the Eastern quarter of the circle; within yourself, imagine that you are limitless, light, and ethereal. As these concepts begin to spiral upon themselves, feel the body dissolving, melting into the atmosphere, losing all discernable form and shape. Having been purified by fire and cleansed by water, you are now free to explore the limits of consciousness, the boundless, formless power of self. Know what it is to feel pure in spirit, and allow your expanding form the freedom to exist as one with the air, slowly churning and flowing with the ceaseless breezes and gusts of wind.

Now, imagine that without the circle, in the East, clear, blue skies stretch out toward infinity; the wind blows steadily into the circle, exhilarating and exciting the soul. Allow the energies within and without to merge, to connect into one great, relentless flow of force. Once you have known what it is to be air, turn deosil (clockwise) toward the North to experience the powers of earth.

The Element of Earth

You have been purified by fire, cleansed by water, and refreshed by air. Now come back to yourself to feel the slow, pulsing rhythms of the earth beneath your feet, the stablility of form, the force of the impermeable and immutable. It is time to experience the element of earth. Imagine yourself turning into stone, a huge, motionless boulder at the foot of a mountain. Feel what it is to resist movement, change. Lightness becomes replaced by heaviness, motion by rest—know what it means to just be still and listen to the earth.

Beyond the confines of the circle, visualize vast fields of corn and wheat melting into the horizon; perhaps, if you are more in tune with the primal aspects of nature, imagine that an ancient forest filled with pine extends along a rocky, steep

The Magickal Elements

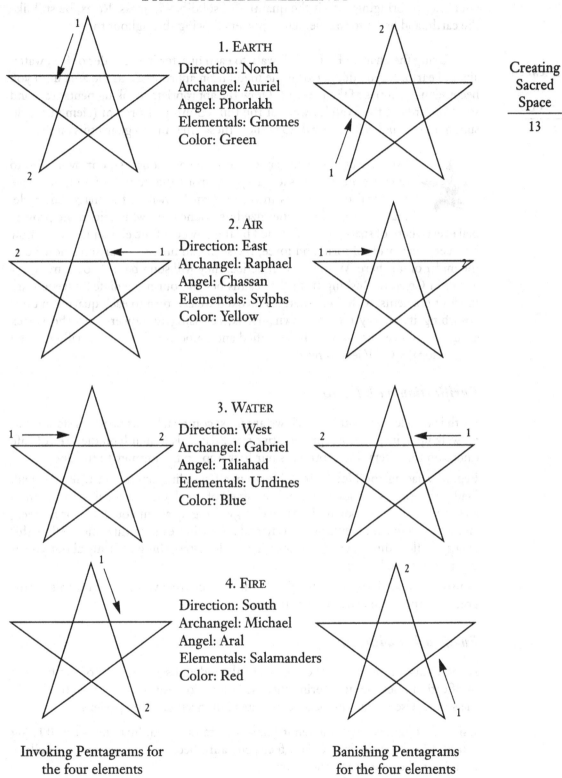

1. Earth

Direction: North
Archangel: Auriel
Angel: Phorlakh
Elementals: Gnomes
Color: Green

2. Air

Direction: East
Archangel: Raphael
Angel: Chassan
Elementals: Sylphs
Color: Yellow

3. Water

Direction: West
Archangel: Gabriel
Angel: Taliahad
Elementals: Undines
Color: Blue

4. Fire

Direction: South
Archangel: Michael
Angel: Aral
Elementals: Salamanders
Color: Red

Invoking Pentagrams for
the four elements

Banishing Pentagrams
for the four elements

Figure 1:2

mountainside. Let the energy of this earth scene permeate the circle, merging with your energy, bringing with it the qualities of solidity and mass. Relax; be still like the earth, and listen to the elemental powers flowing throughout the circle.

Using the chart in Figure 1:2, walk to each quarter in the order of fire, water, air, and earth. As you do, perform the meditation appropriate to the area until you become the qualities of the element. Draw the appropriate invoking pentagram and say, "Ye lords of the Watchtowers of the (direction), ye Lords of (element), I do summon, stir, and call you forth to witness these rites and to guard this circle."

 We have used the powers of our own consciousness, our own wills, to create a magickal, sacred space; from the center of self, we have extended our realities into the form known as the magickal circle. Having created and energized its boundaries, which lie in the proverbial everywhere of space, it was fortified by the powers of the elements; we are now between the worlds of form and force, the seen and unseen—our souls now lie in the midst of nowhere. With a little practice, they will soon be free to roam everywhere in Cosmos. Rushing from the realms beyond our immediate awareness are the four elements; with their energies invoked we can turn to each quarter in turn, absorbing its energy into our own matrix, releasing its powers into the vortex around us. Once our space is thus purified and empowered, we will finally have an area fit for the God/dess to reside.

Purification with Earth

Earth is the element within which we are most comfortable. It provides stability, as we walk upon its physical representative every day. It is Malkuth on the Tree of Life (more on this later), and represents our first step on the journey to the divine.

Begin by facing the North. Imagine yourself standing upon a vast, fertile field. Stalks of corn tower above you, and the smell of the damp and fertile earth permeates the air. Feel the cool, moist earth energy rising up about you. Its color is green, and within a few moments your body and aura vibrates with this color. Allow this energy to flow through you and into the circle, establishing it firmly about you as an impenetrable barrier.

Finish this visualization by imagining the entire circle vibrating with this earth-green energy. Turn deosil to face the East.

Purification with Air

Light a stick of incense in the East (sandalwood and sage are two of the best for purification). Set the smoldering incense before you. Allow yourself to breathe in the scent. (Use simmering potpourri instead of incense, if you prefer.)

Using your hands, direct the tendril of smoke toward you. Imagine yourself being caressed by a gentle breeze, and feel your aura becoming a gentle, pale yellow. Breathe in the energy and the color.

As your aura brightens with this yellow, allow the energy to flow through you and into the circle. Continue until the yellow color permeates the area of the circle, and air is working within to cleanse.

Finish this visualization by imagining the circle filled with gentle breezes and the color yellow. Turn deosil to the West.

Purification with Water

Have a chalice of water before you in the West. Begin by sprinkling a few drops on yourself. Imagine a waterfall pouring water all about you.

As the water cleanses you, it turns your aura a deep, blue color. Breathe in the energy and color of water. Once you are filled with it, allow the water and the blue color to spill over into the circle.

Finish this exercise by imagining the circle charged and filled with the blue color of water. Turn deosil until you face the South.

Purification with Fire

Place a red candle in the South. Feel the heat radiating from it, warming you. Imagine the fire growing in the South, and radiating a bright red color.

Breathe in as this red energy and heat fills you. Feel the fire burning away negativity, turning spiritual darkness into light. Once your aura is a bright red, allow the energies to begin mingling with the circle.

Finish this exercise by imagining the entire circle filled with the red energy. Your circle is cleansed.

Now that the circle is created and purified, we finally have a sacred space fit for the God/dess and our own higher selves to dwell. One of the beliefs central to both the Craft and Qabalah is that there is no need for an intermediate source between us and the divine beings; we partake of the two worlds ourselves and can operate as our own priests and priestesses. Stepping between the worlds puts us in a space where the worlds of mundane and spiritual reality can collide, and we can mingle the two until we effectively can be part of both.

Concepts of Goddess and God are ancient; from the earliest cave drawings until the most recent Neo-Pagan revival, there are examples of this archetype emerging from human consciousness. In invoking these archetypes, many argue that we are merely bringing hidden parts of ourselves to light; others would maintain that the God/dess in her myriad forms are all separate beings who serve to further the cause of humanity. Wiccans as a whole seem to agree that the different names of God/dess all reflect the inner reality that all is one. Perhaps it is not the actual belief that matters, rather we must experience the power and assign our own meanings to them.

As we examine the Qabalah, we find that before the Tree of Life was formed, there were three veils of negative existence (as in receptive, feminine): Ain, Ain Soph, and Ain Soph Aur (meaning void, no limit, and limitless light). These veils were considered unknowable and incomprehensible, as they were the feminine and gestational forces from which all sprang. Since the veils will never be known or touched by any in human form, I have chosen to rename them in the phrase, "In the beginning was the Mother," and leave them at that [See Figure 1:3].

Within the subtle balance of the Qabalah, we can trace this birthing of energy into Kether, the first knowable (although still unattainable) form of

God/dess. Following this manifestation that is both Goddess and God (hence the term God/dess) is the raw, directionless energy of Chokmah, the supernal archetype of God. Powerless in itself, Binah, the highest archetype of pure Goddess, must initiate the rest of creation by giving form and restriction to the boundless powers of Chokmah. Only when Binah has given form to Chokmah (as the Mother to Her divine Son/Lover, the Horned One) are the masculine powers born, no longer pure energy. By defining the indefinable, the three pillars of the Tree of Life are created. Each sephirah has a definite leaning towards male, female, or neutral energy; however, each also contains a balance of God and Goddess archetypes.

We find in the Tree of Life a central theme that is compatible with our Craft. The interplay of energies in the universe began with the Mother and ends with Her; although balance is achieved between the God/dess, She holds sway in defining what is to be. The archetypal Great Mother has the power to create life on Her own, a magickal mutation of herself—the male. Then She can integrate the masculine energy within Herself, creating the needed balance to bring all worlds into being. Through the Tree of Life, we discover what the ancients knew: all true power lies within Her; through the feminine power, man finds re-creation and "salvation." The Goddess is put back into Her rightful place as Creatrix and Great Mother, which puts our universe back into its original balance.

THE THREE VEILS

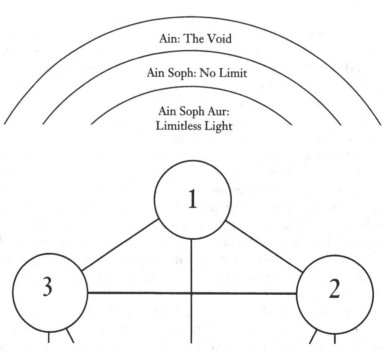

This figure is a theoretical representation of the Three Veils of Negative Existence. As negative implies feminine polarity, some Qabalists refer to these veils with the phrase "In the beginning was the Mother."

Figure 1:3

The next exercise is a simple attempt at awakening the powers of God/dess in our own consciousness and bringing these energies into the sacred space.

INVOKING GOD/DESS

Once the sacred space is cast and purified, begin by standing in the center of the circle and imagining a bright white ball of light about six inches above the crown of your head. Qabalistically, this represents the operator's Higher Self, the initial spark that enlivens and invigorates us from birth until death. This is the truly divine part of creation, and its name means "I am."

As you contemplate this spark, imagine multicolored droplets of light raining down upon your body, flashing throughout the aura. Let this light invigorate you as you breathe deeply and begin to mentally compose your invocation to the Goddess.

Visualize a pillar of black energy forming to your right. Black is the color of mystery, of silence, of the richness of the damp, fertile earth. Feel Her feminine energy flowing through you and into the circle as you say, "I invoke thee and call upon thee, Mighty Mother of us all; bringer of all fruitfulness. By seed and root, by stem and bud, by leaf and flower and fruit do I invoke thee to descend in this—our magickal circle."[3]

Again, contemplate the spark of Kether above the crown of the head. As you do, begin to mentally compose your invocation to the Horned God.

Imagine a pillar of white energy to your left. This pillar represents the Horned One as His aspect of Consort and Lover to the Goddess. Feel His masculine energy flowing through you and into the circle as you say, "Great God Cernunnos, return to earth again; come at my call and show thyself to men. Shepherd of goats upon the wild hill's way, lead thy lost flock from darkness unto day. Gone are the ways of sleep and night—men seek for these, though their eyes have lost the sight. Open the door, the mysterious door that hath no key. O mighty shepherd of goats, answer unto me!"

Once the energies of God/dess are firmly established, allow the visualization to fade, knowing that They are still with you.

By casting the circle and invoking the Goddess and Her Consort, we are engaged in an act of worship, for we acknowledge their existence within our own psyche. Craft and Qabalah teach us that the separation we feel from the worlds around us is imagined; from early childhood until death, patriarchal culture teaches us that the world is something separate and distinct from ourselves, a realm that is separate from our existence, conquerable; indeed, we must conquer it if we are to rise above the trials of life. But within the philosophies handed to us by the ancients, we are retrained to believe that the vistas of awareness and existence find their completion within ourselves: the separation we feel is imaginary. If we were to listen to what was within, reestablishing our connection with ourselves, we would find that this is true.

---

3. This invocation, and the one given for the Horned God, are derived from my copy of the Gardnerian Book of Shadows.

Now we find ourselves between the worlds; we have slipped into the aware-ness of physical patterns, and beyond into a space belonging neither within this world nor the next, but a world in which we can call upon vast vistas of awareness, new experience, and even partake in the re-creation of our world.

Our act of creating the magickal circle, which we use frequently in the Craft, has become a symphony sung to our higher selves, to the Goddess, and to the Horned God. As we leave this circle, we leave this space and its sacred energies behind. How are we to make the circle's powers and lessons a reality in our lives?

One short ritual that we perform on a monthly basis is called the sacred meal: wine and cakes. To most this is a short repast, a refreshment from the magickal work that drains much of our vitality. Needing to replenish our energies, we con-secrate our wine and cakes to the God/dess, and together share them as we replace the power we have expended.

But within this simple ritual, there is far more involved; in practice it can become a means for us to not only toast the Old Ones and replenish magickal ener-gies used, it becomes a means to bridge the apparent gap between humanity and divinity, making each of us more like the God/dess.

First, we need to take a superficial look at the chemistry behind eating. Whenever a substance is consumed, no matter what the motivation—religion, hunger, taste—in the end, the food ingested becomes a physical part of us. Diges-tion begins in the mouth, where we can absorb a small amount of the simple sugar glucose and begin to process a few starches. As it travels into the stomach, gastric juices begin to churn the material and break it chemically into smaller components. Massive absorption occurs in the small intestine, where the vital nutrients are finally sent into the body (the digestive system is considered to be outside the body; food is not in the body until it enters the bloodstream). Finally, the colon reabsorbs water and removes the waste products that cannot be absorbed.

Granted, this is a simple look at the physical processes that occur, but the point is that the substance taken into the digestive system is delivered to the body's tissues, becoming a part of the physical structure. The sacred meal, then, becomes a part of ourselves; the physical substance is broken down so it may release its stores of energy into the cellular structures. If the substance eaten is properly imbued with the divine essence of the God/dess, that also becomes a part of our physical structure.

As we perform our invocations, allowing the God/dess energies to infiltrate our consciousness, our consciousness is exalted. Temporarily, the energy also becomes a part of our matrix as the God/dess awareness infiltrates our spiritual body, but as there is no physical basis for the invocations, little of the energy remains after normal awareness returns. Our sacred meal becomes a talisman; energy from the Goddess and Her Consort is locked into the physical. While our consciousness is still in the appropriate state of mind, we make the food part of our-selves, carrying the energies it contains into our own matrix. This gives our bodies a structure to lock onto as the divine powers are released into the tissues. The for-mula is simple: take a substance symbolic of divinity, make it divine, and make it a part of yourself.

In ritual, this technique operates on two levels. The individual or individuals who have invoked the forces of the God/dess are already in tune with the energies, and as they consecrate the physical basis, create a vortex or cone of power between themselves and the ritual food. As they consume the meal, it is symbolic of the

God/dess descending into physical matter, consuming the human part and making it divine. Then, as the participants consume the ritual meal, it symbolizes the aspirants in the act of invocation, consuming the divine force and making it a part of them. Whether done in a group where this process is apparent, or alone where the Witch performs all parts alone, the ritual is symbolic of the divine descent into matter, giving true spiritual life to that which is inert.

The more often this is done, the more the Witch becomes filled with the God/dess, intoxicated by the God/dess, until every cell in the body is regenerated with the divine power. Amazingly, this one simple ritual works to transform the entire body into a vessel for the God/dess.

To begin this rite, it is important that the divine force be invoked and felt throughout the physical body as a definite energy. The rite proper follows.

THE SACRED MEAL

Within the circle, having invoked the Goddess and Her Consort, the Horned One, through two separate invocations, return awareness to the bright light of Kether above the crown of the head and strengthen the visualization of the black and white pillars of the Tree of Life.

Lift the cup of wine in salute to the powers present. Take your athame in your power hand, and lift it in salute also. Remember that you are acknowledging both the forces within and the forces without.

Lower the tip of the athame into the wine and say, "As the athame is to the male, so the cup is to the female, and thus conjoined, they are one in blessedness." Touch the tip of the athame to the bottom of the chalice, imagining that energy from both pillars travels into you, through the dagger, and into the chalice of wine. See it glow with divine power. Feel the energies of God/dess locked within it.

Now, sip the wine, feeling the liquid carrying the power into your body. Relax for a moment, giving the power a chance to merge with the physical.

Next, lift the plate of cakes in salute. Touch the tip of the athame to each one and say, "O Queen most secret, most divine, bless these cakes as you have our wine; instill within us health, wealth, joy, happiness, and love (or any other qualities you wish)." Visualize energy from the pillars beside you flowing through you and into the cakes. See them filled with the essence of the God/dess.

Eat one of the cakes, feeling the divine essence locked within it becoming a part of yourself. Finish the wine, or share it with others who may be present. The effect of this ritual is increased as the amount of the talismanic substance is increased. A few moments in meditation afterward will also increase awareness of the divine force that is becoming a part of the physical self.

Once cast, the circle becomes a reality on the inner planes of existence; before leaving the circle we must uncreate what we have created, lest it degenerate on the inner planes like a dead and decaying shell. It is not only bad magick to not uncreate this vortex, relieving the strain we have caused in the astral plane, it is also bad manners to not thank the God/dess and the myriad entities that have come to join us in working our magick. We must close what has been opened before we are free to return to normal consciousness and again walk freely within the world of form.

Closing the Circle

Return to the visualization that you used for invoking the God/dess. Imagine the visualization fading away, taking their energies with it as you say, "Gentle Goddess, powerful God, ere ye depart to your peaceful realms, I wish to thank you for attending this rite and leading me into your light. Hail and farewell!

Once completed, return to the South. See the energies that you have invoked to your circle. Draw the banishing pentagram of fire (Figure 1:2) and say, "Ye Lords of the Watchtowers of the South, ye Lords of fire, ere ye depart to your peaceful realms I wish to thank you for attending these rites and guarding this circle. And now I bid you hail and farewell, hail and farewell." Bow your head in thanks and you allow the visualization to fade, taking the energies with it. Repeat this process at every quarter: fire, water, air, and earth; use the proper element and direction in the prayer.

Now, only the circle remains. Imagine its energies slowly dissipating and flowing through you into the earth to be cleansed and recycled. Say, "I now declare this circle closed but unbroken. Merry meet, merry part, and merry meet again!"[4] Slowly return from the trance state of pattern awareness. The circle is closed.

Having cast our circle and stepped between the worlds, we are ready to begin our exploration of the realms and wonders before us. The Qabalah contains a myriad of avenues for exploration and magick; as we ascend this ladder of lights we shall increase our understanding of ourselves, our Craft, and our Goddess. Let us continue, then, and begin with the first four elements on the Tree of Life—let us explore the mysteries of earth, air, water, and fire.

---

4. Our Sabbats are normally opened to our Witch brothers and sisters from other covens, and as large gatherings, they become quite long. As we closed our circle one night, one of our friend's children fell asleep, only to be awakened by an extremely loud, joyous rendition of our "Merry meet, merry part …" closing. Her mind still clouded by sleep, she wearily asked, "Mom, who is Mary?"

Since then, we've adapted our closing to say, "… and who the heck is Mary?" It is a slight play on words, hilarious in its context, and a great way to close both the circle and the psychic centers of the mind/body complex. Guests at our Sabbat circles are taken off guard; the resulting laughter, we believe, is a welcome offering to the Goddess and God.

CHAPTER TWO

WORKING WITH THE ELEMENTS

When I became a woman, I understood intuitively the link I shared with all womyn. When I became a Witch, I realized this link extended to all beings of this world and the next. Within me was housed an entire universe. I incorporated all the elements in my being: earth, air, water, fire, and spirit. Like branches on the Tree of Life, we are all connected with this understanding. I became truly three-dimensional; my psychic self emerged, and my emphatic self became stronger.

—Kendra Musselle

To the rational, Western mind, "matter" and "energy" are two antithetic terms. The former term defines an object that has mass, occupies space, and can be perceived by one of the physical senses. The Earth, the body, and the book you are holding consist of what we collectively define as matter. Scientists define the latter term, energy, as the work matter is capable of doing in changing from its present state to its reference state. To simplify, think about the sun, or any star observable on a cloudless night: they occupy space, and thus are defined as matter. As their gases and raw materials convert from their actual state to their reference state (they change chemical composition through nuclear fusion), they produce the energy we perceive as heat and light. Lay this book on the floor for a moment. The "matter" of the book has no potential for creating energy. Now, lift the book waist high and it becomes filled with potential energy; let it drop, and as it falls it gains momentum, perhaps releasing a tiny amount of heat. The energy from its fall moves the air molecules around it. The whole action of the book's falling is described by the term "kinetic energy," the energy associated with the moving of material objects.

Until now, matter and energy have been scientifically classified as two separate states of existence in the material world; true, they can change from one form to the next, but they are separate. However, there is a new branch of physics, called quantum physics, which dispels these myths.

Examining this science briefly, we discover that a new model of matter and energy is being proposed—one that mirrors the earlier, shamanistic view of Cosmos. Early Witches and Shamans believed that the created Universe was nothing more than a vast swirling of energy; as life-forms appeared and evolved, they became temporary turbulences in the overall pattern of energy that existed in the

Universe. Carrying their theories a bit further, they believed that whenever we saw a part of that energy as being a rock, tree, mountain, or even the Earth, we were perceiving these energy forms through perceptions that I like to term our "reality agreement." As we create our own minor energy patterns within the greater pattern of energy that exists about us, we perceive the resulting energy according to belief. I believe that the energy form of a rock is a rock; my perception follows the thought. Likewise, I believe that my energy pattern of consciousness exists in a vessel of flesh and blood—and the body appears.

Let's examine how quantum physics relates to the physical body. Our material bodies contain several systems of organs that are mechanical in design. Each organ is composed of tissues—specialized groups of cells that have individual lives and a limited consciousness of duty. Within each cell are different organic molecules: hydrogen, oxygen, carbon, and nitrogen. The basic structure of these molecules is the atom [see Figure 2:1].

A superficial viewing of the atom shows us that an atomic structure is mostly vacant space. Scientific method has measured the atom as being 99.9999% empty space—which means that the "material structure" of the atom is only 0.0001% solid. Suddenly, 99.9999% of our bodies are reduced to a void, and we can only define 0.0001% of it as being what we normally term "matter." Quantum physics also gives us another problem with our traditional materialist views—the electrons, protons, and neutrons that form the basis of the atoms are constantly in motion. Moving at light speeds, they shift from appearing as actual solid objects to being nothing more than pure energy. This means that atoms are constantly fluctuating between matter and energy. Even when perceived as matter, they only occupy a minute fraction of the space in which we perceive them. As the atom is the body's

THE ATOM

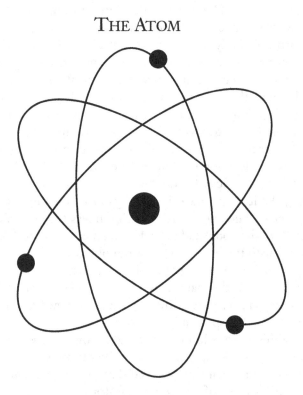

Figure 2:1

basic element, 99.9999% of our bodies are empty space. The remaining 0.0001% is the material basis. Because the components of the atom waver between being "matter" and being "energy," our bodies exist in a continual twilight that partakes of both realms. Only our perceptions keep us grounded as material beings.

Even this 0.0001% of "matter" in our bodies is of dubious existence: the protons, electrons, and neutrons are made up of smaller subatomic particles that, even with our present technology, we cannot accurately measure. These subatomic components take up a fractional amount of their overt structure, and their makeup suggests that they exist mostly as energy, not as matter.

To sum it all up: physically, we are beings of pure energy! The quantum mechanical view of nature is one that speaks of potential energy, not matter; thus, by the new science, our bodies are described in terms that match the metaphysical view of Spirit.

Returning to the Tree of Life, we also find that the Universe is examined in terms of energy—from the veils of negative existence to the realm of Malkuth, we deal with constantly evolving forms of energy. This energy flows from the sephiroth to the paths. A sephirah denotes a state of being, a mode of existence. The paths on the Tree show the states of becoming—how the energy fields of the sephiroth mix and merge to become energy. Some sephiroth have more than one path coming from different sephiroth, showing how the various powers must mix together to become the new power. Surprisingly, the physical Universe also has its own sephirah, Malkuth. To Qabalists, this world is another expression of energy, not a new form called "matter."

Not all our energy is concentrated into our spiritual/material bodies. We have, through a collective agreement called reality, bound our infinite consciousness into a finite energy pattern of body: however, something limited cannot contain the limitless; it can only symbolize its truth. Much of our energy, and consciousness, still dwells outside the body; this energy radiates outward to be perceived by others. How can this be? How can a finite concentration have an energy field that radiates beyond its material body?

First, we can point to the parts of ourselves perceived by the physical senses of others. Light energy, which becomes a part of us as it strikes our skins, is only partially absorbed. What our energy structure cannot hold, it reflects; that reflection is picked up by others as sight. In forming our thoughts into words, we absorb another form of "material energy" into ourselves—air. As we project that into the surrounding atmosphere, we send out vibrations perceived as sound by the ears. If we touch someone, the energy of our touch is picked up and perceived by the other person. Likewise, smells from our body (which are, in essence, energy by the quantum models) are smelled by others. In intimate situations, we transmit energy in the form of taste.

Research has shown that the body radiates energy in the form of heat and electromagnetic currents. Electrical impulses deep within neural tissues may be picked up on the surface of the skin. Metaphysically speaking, there is also the aura. Some speak of it as an emanation from the spiritual body contained within the physical. Perhaps a better way of analyzing it would be to perceive it as another tangible form of the vast spiritual energy that we are.

Realizing this, it is easy to conceptualize reality in terms of the ancient shamanistic view: reality, including all "material" beings in the universe, is nothing more than a series of vast, connected energy patterns. Even within the concepts of pure "matter" and "energy," the very act of sensing physical information assumes a superficial connection: right now, you are sensing these words through sight. This information travels as energy impulses to the brain; within it, energy is translated into a pattern you can understand—these words. It appears that the printed page is outside yourself—in reality, the entire image is internal. It is only a trick of the physical senses that makes this information seem external. Inwardly, we interpret the parts of the pattern we choose to sense. And it is only through our collective agreement of reality that we say the pattern is separate from ourselves.

If we think for a moment about our auras—the energy field immediately surrounding the physical body—we can also see how we are continually connected with the mundane reality about us. To a psychic, the aura is seen as an energy field that extends just past arm's length beyond the body [Figure 2:2]. As we move, our energy field moves with us, unchanging in size. So, what happens as we walk along the floor, carpet, or Earth? Does the energy field diminish so that it does not overlap the surface? No—it continually mixes with the mass and energy of the objects surrounding it. As the aura mingles with the material of Earth, it becomes a part of it; likewise, the Earth's energy field becomes a part of us.

There is nothing that I can come across that does not become, however ephemeral, an immediate part of myself. Right now, I am sitting on a chair in front of a desk; before me is a computer, an assortment of notebooks, pens, and a potted plant. Each has an energy field of its own; falling back on Craft, Qabalistic, and quantum models of thought, I realize that each thing has not only its own aura (or energy field), they are all a form of energy. My field mixes and merges with the others—right now, my reality is that the chair upon which I sit, the floor that touches my feet, the Earth below, the desk, the computer, and the plant are all a part of myself. They mix and merge into my own energy pattern.

Upon consideration, we may, by both Craft and quantum models, consider that not only is the entire Universe a part of ourselves, it also exists within us. To illustrate this point, spend some time outdoors, at night, under the light of a full moon. Relax under a tree, on a grassy hillside, or by a free-flowing stream: location does not matter; simply find someplace where you may relax alone. As you unwind, becoming aware of life around you, contemplate the stars. Realize that some of these may be planets,[1] others are stars with their own solar systems. See the patterns before you—listen to the wind rustling the leaves. Involve the five senses in experiencing the present.

Now, ponder this: you are sensing energy being sent by other energy forms—the moon, the stars, wind, insects, Earth, animals, etc. This energy moves into your aura first, then touches the part of the energy field called "the body." Accepting that we are infinite beings of energy, we realize that our perceived stimuli must first enter more subtle patterns of our energy of which we are not aware.

Upon reaching the body's energy pattern, the stimulus travels through the five senses: by our reality agreement, we perceive energy from other forms in five ways: sight, sound, taste, smell, and touch. Different frequencies enter our immediate

1. Astrologers have known for centuries that the planets, despite their seeming distance, exert their influence over us via their energy patterns. The whole system of astrological divination is based upon this belief. We can use this as evidence of our theory that "all things are a part of ourselves." Their separation is only imagined through our reality agreement. By viewing their position in the natal chart, an astrologer sees the merging of specific states of energy in a person's total energy pattern. By this method, one may ascertain the trends of any person's life.

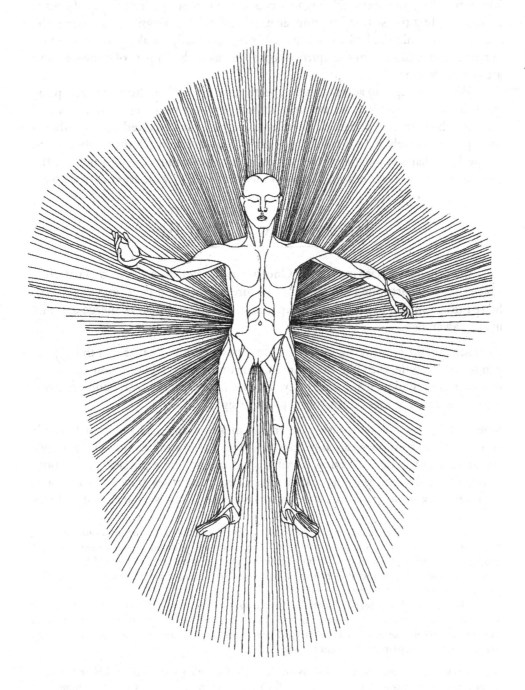

Figure 2:2

awareness by different routes.[2] In this exercise, light energy floods our awareness in the form of sight. We can also smell the aromas of grasses, flowers, and the trees about us. The Earth we sit upon is felt through touch, and so on. The actual outward image, however, lies within the brain. As long as we center our consciousness within the body, this incredible organ serves as the center of perception. All energy ends up finding translation into our terms of reality here. Physically speaking, the image exists within the brain, our physical core. Spiritually speaking, the energy we perceive also exists within our spiritual core, and as such is a part of ourselves. We are our perceptions![3]

When we begin to accept this perspective, we are well on the way to accepting the truth about ourselves: we are infinite beings who have accepted this physical form for the sake of experience. There is no part of our perceived universe that is not a part of ourselves. Our true consciousness expands to reach the furthest stars, or the bird that soars through the sky above us. Realizing this, we shall use the Becoming Aware exercise from Chapter One, with a slightly different perspective.

BECOMING AWARE, PART III

As in the original exercise in Chapter One, begin to enter the awareness of patterns. Make sure your breathing is slow, your posture is erect, and your body is relaxed. Stare into a candle's flame, letting the patterns of light and shadow merge and mix in your awareness.

Contemplate the parts of the patterns you are now sensing. Realize that the objects you see (the candle, the altar, the room in your immediate field of vision) are sending their energy to your physical body. Their energies merge with your own; you are now perceiving them through the physical sight.

Smell the aroma of the incense, hear the meditation tape, feel the floor beneath you, and sense your physical body's position in the area around you. The energies you are sensing, as our awareness is still grounded around the physical part of ourselves, come through the physical senses. Energy impulses travel to the brain: within the brain, they are translated into the images, sounds, smells, and textures

---

2. On deeper levels, we are continually aware of the energy in the environment around us. Our subconscious minds constantly monitor sensory input: if a signal demands immediate attention, it sends a "warning" to the conscious mind. Sometimes we act upon a sensory signal before conscious awareness of it. Many of us can recall having avoided sudden misfortune by reflexes that served to steer us out of danger.

Deeper awareness brings increased perception of the energy pattern about us: as we increase our perceptions, we increase our self-knowledge! This allows us to react to changes in our external energy pattern (the Universe), while still centering immediate consciousness on the smaller parts of the patterns we seem to perceive.

3. This statement holds true for all of us on all levels. One who is ignorant of his or her transcendence, feeling alone and separated from the rest of existence, fails to realize the importance of self to the Cosmos. Bound by a limited awareness of reality, one travels through life a seeming prisoner of time and space. However, as a human being assumes proper perspective of the Universe—each of us is truly the center, each of us is a distinct expression of the one divine presence that we are; life takes on new meaning—miracles increase, and personal healing takes place. The more we realize our divinity and transcendence, the more we are able to change ourselves and the world in which we live.

that we sense. Realize these sensations are the internal processing of the energies merging with our own pattern. Through our collective reality agreement, we view these objects as external. Try to sense them as internal energy structures.

Close your eyes and try to visualize the energy field around your body, the aura. See how its less tangible energy permeates the more tangible patterns of matter. The sound that travels to the ears must first merge and vibrate within the aura; the incense swirling around the physical body moves through the aura. Energy patterns that form the ground beneath us, the altar before us, and the light that shines upon us, all mix with our aura. By doing so, they become a part of our pattern.

Contemplate this until you feel connected with the energy patterns around you. Try imagining that the objects in the space around you not only mix and merge into the energy of the aura, but they are also a part of the more subtle energy that vibrates beyond the aura. Imagine a translucent, faint white energy permeating all things around yourself, growing thicker as it becomes the aura, and more opaque as it becomes the core of the "physical" energy that makes up the body.

Open your eyes, and contemplate how all perceived objects are internal. There should now be a greater connection felt.

Return to normal consciousness, carrying this sense of connection with you.

Repeat this exercise in varying locations, both outdoors and indoors. Each repetition will serve to increase your consciousness of self.

Our circle casting exercise from Chapter One now takes a new perspective: instead of expanding our consciousness and energy into the concept of a magickal circle, we are increasing the amount of self of which we are aware. Once we accept the truth of ourselves as limitless, eternal beings, once we increase our perception of self to include the energy patterns that exist about us, once we realize that the Universe, Cosmos, and God/dess all exist within us and nothing is totally without, we begin to realize the miracle that we are. Humanity is creation! We are all-knowing, all-powerful, all-transcending. As Witches, it is within our power to mold, bend, and shape the material world to our desires—for we are the creation; we are the Cosmos. The more real this perception becomes, the easier it is for us to work magick to bring needed changes.

We must also realize, however, that this is true for everyone. Any other human we meet also has this transcendence of being; regardless of race, religion, sex, sexuality, or spiritual beliefs, all humans contain within themselves the omnipotence of creation. I am a part of you, just as you are a part of myself. Our consciousness overlaps: it can be, and is, part of the same whole.

If we as a species could grasp this holistic view of self, the world's ills would be well on their way to absolution. Would a healthy, rational being destroy a part of self? Could I, knowing the implications, mutilate a part of my "physical" energy pattern? I would feel the pain and suffer. Likewise, could I harm another person or part of my "spiritual" energy pattern without feeling the resulting spiritual pain? Once this new awareness is instilled in the psyche, it becomes increasingly difficult to harm or destroy any part of nature, for it is a part of self.[4]

---

4. Examined in terms of this awareness, the old saying "We are one" takes on new meaning.

Returning to the concept of the circle, we have increased, not expanded, the amount of self of which we are aware. More of the spirit energy of self becomes compressed into its perimeter. Symbolically, the circle also represents the unknowable and unmanifest beginning to know itself and manifest self as Cosmos. Magickally, we must alter consciousness to achieve this state: in doing so, we become aware of the incredible power of spirit. As we create this new energy body, we can also perceive the energy exchange that occurs between our infinite body of spirit and the four magickal elements that combine in its creation.

As we work with these magickal elements, not only will we learn about powers existing in the Macrocosmic realm, we shall learn about the subtle energy that merges to form our spirit: this is the sum of all existence.

THE FOUR ELEMENTS AND THE CONSTITUTION OF HUMANITY

Once cast, our magick circle becomes not only a sacred space, but a spiritual body that defines a greater part of self. In expanding our mundane consciousness to the circle's boundaries, we can perceive how the four subtle elements of earth, air, water, and fire filter both within and without our energy field, which is Spirit. In earlier times, magicians and philosophers theorized that all life was made of different combinations of these elements: physical form depended on their merging into a unified whole. As scientific knowledge slowly replaced magick, the mundane models of matter and energy were proposed—the teachings of the four elements were set aside as philosophical ideas. Now, we realize that the scientific views of matter are false: there is only energy. In returning to the concepts of the four elements, we can see how this energy is created. From the greater vantage point of self offered by the circle, we can visit and use the powers of the elemental realms at will once we learn to draw upon the power they contain.

Examining the Tree of Life, we see how the elemental powers exist and merge within the human psyche. Falling back on the earlier material in this chapter, we can examine the Qabalistic statement "We are microcosms of the Macrocosm" in a new light. The term "Macrocosm" includes all energy patterns in the Universe: life-forms, planets, stars, sephiroth, and paths. Macrocosm is the all-pervasive, constantly creative energy of the Universe. "Microcosm" implies a "small universe" or limited awareness, complete in itself: it is a concentration of energy. In our physical form, Macrocosmic consciousness is compressed into the limited form of the body—the greater energy of self is part of the Universe, while that which has been limited is within the body. Because the body has become the center of our awareness, it has molded itself into a form capable of moving in the more solid energy matrix of the material world. To keep the energy systems functioning, it is said that the Tree of Life also takes form in miniature within the concentrated human energy field. It is from this theory that we shall examine the elemental makeup of the human energy field.

Qabalistically, there are four levels of being describing the creative process of the Universe; likewise, there are four levels describing the creative process of human existence. These levels range from the divine spark, our truly immortal self, to the body, which is the most tangible and transient form of creative energy. These

THE FOUR WORLDS AND THE FOUR ELEMENTS
ON THE TREE OF LIFE

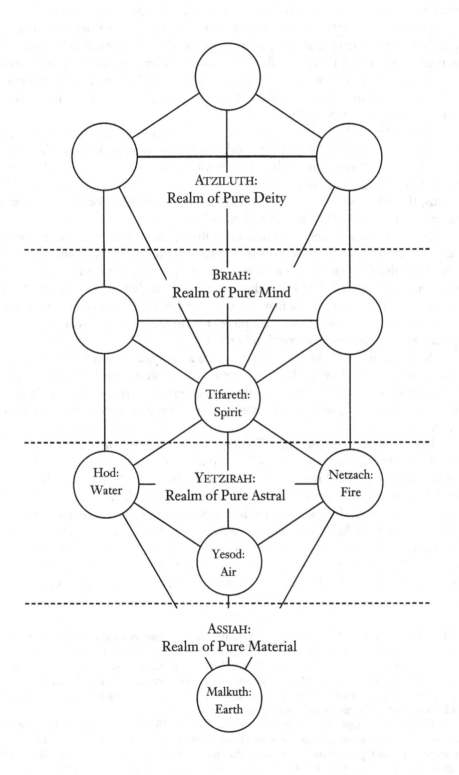

Figure 2:3

four levels of life are Atziluth (pure divinity), Briah (pure mind), Yetzirah (pure astral), and Assiah (pure material) [See Figure 2:3].

Assiah is the realm of the dense energy patterns we refer to as "matter." It is within this level that the material world exists; the energy that permeates Cosmos comes together in patterns that are cohesive only because we perceive them as such. Constantly mixing and merging with the patterns of Assiah are the sephirotic energies of the other three worlds—energies that form the parts of our energy structure called "soul," "spirit," and "mind." In our world, then, we find the center of concentration and operation of spiritual energies. The pure elemental attribution of Assiah is earth [See Figure 2:3].

Within Yetzirah, the astral realm, we find three more elements operating in their pure state: air in Yesod, water in Hod, and fire in Netzach. Each of these three elements operates within the realm of astral forms, as well as in Assiah. They form the soul, the part that vivifies the physical. Here also is the realm of emotions and dreams, the subconscious mind. When operating in the astral body we are using the level of being described by the actions of Yetzirah.

Spirit, the fifth element, is contained in Briah, the mental realm. More specifically, we find that Tifareth represents the pure action of Spirit. Some occultists claim that this fifth element is not really an element at all, but a combination of the other four. Personally, I like to view the four elements as derived from Spirit. As the God/dess created, She took the mass of energy and broke it into smaller units until She could recombine and recreate the pieces into new forms; in reworking our way up the Tree, we tend to view creation in reverse.

Atziluth, the realm of pure deity and the archetypes, is a part of the human psyche that has only recently been explored by psychology. Early pioneers of psychology, such as Jung and Freud, briefly touched upon the realm of the archetypes and their influence upon humanity's evolution. However, this is an area seldom explored.[5]

For the physical to continue, all energies from the Tree of Life, including the magickal elements, must coexist somehow within Malkuth. Likewise, as our circle is grounded in the physical realm, our elements are drawn to the physical plane. Figure 2:4 shows the cross-quarter diagram of Malkuth, with the elements in their appropriate regions. This is a key to their function in both cosmos and mankind; while the elements do have their own spheres of action, they must filter into the physical realm if our present forms are to be maintained. Thus, the early theories of life depending on the types and amounts of elements are not too far-fetched; for us to remain healthy, all levels of energy must work together to keep the psyche stable.

5. Deepak Chopra, M.D., has written several related books: *Quantum Healing, Perfect Health* and *Unconditional Life: Mastering the Forces that Shape Personal Reality*. He is a medical doctor; at one time he taught at the Boston University Medical Schools and held the position of Chief of Staff at the New England Memorial Hospital in Stoneham, Massachusetts. Currently, Dr. Chopra is writing, lecturing, and teaching about his quantum models of health and healing—theories based on both scientific and metaphysical theories.

His books and tapes are a must-have for the modern Witch; his theories, although based on Eastern teachings, are expounded upon in ways which mirror Craft and Qabalistic beliefs about reality. His tapes are published through Nightingale Conant Corporation; 7300 North Lehigh Avenue; Chicago, IL 60648. Their toll-free order/information line is 1-800-525-9000. Books may be obtained directly from the publisher: Write to Quantum Publications; P. O. Box 598; South Lancaster, MA 01523. Their toll-free number is 1-800-858-1808.

Our work with these energies will begin in Malkuth. Remember that Malkuth is the only sephirah in the realm of Assiah (physical form). A good translation of the Hebrew word "Malkuth" would be "The Kingdom"; this includes all of physical creation, and not just our own planet. All planets, solar systems, and galaxies discovered and undiscovered are included in this sephirah. With this in mind, we shall investigate how the five elements permeate our physical substance.

Referring to Figure 2:4, we can see the four divisions of Malkuth—earth, air, water, and fire. These simple divisions, when combined, produce the fifth element of Spirit (which, for now, is Malkuth). Each element also has its own Archangel, angel, magickal animal, and magickal tool. We begin our work here with the elements and the general energies present.

Earth Meditation

Remember from Chapter One that earth is the most solid and stable of the elements—it is the ground we walk upon; it supports us in our lives. We see it, touch it, and feel its strength on a daily basis. In spite of its apparent familiarity, the element of earth also represents mystery and the unseen—the womb of the Goddess.

Our ancestors, who lived by the cycles of the moon and sun, realized that those orbs never traveled in the North quadrant of the sky. The North Star, hovering high and unmoving in the night sky, became the center about which the universe revolved. Northern people pondered the mysteries of the Aurora Borealis, creating legends about its origins. The North became known as the home of the God/dess, and the final resting place for the souls of the dead.

Once the circle is cast, sit facing the North. Spend a few moments contemplating the energies of earth; feel strength and stability radiating from the North and into your body. Reach out with your power hand, drawing the invoking pentagram of earth: visualize it appearing in a vibrant, mossy-green color. A flux of stronger earth energies should enter the circle now—imagine that a great circuit of power is being opened between you and the North.

THE CROSS-QUARTER DIAGRAM OF MALKUTH

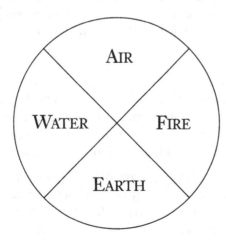

Figure 2:4

As the energies permeate the circle, peer through the pentagram with your mind and begin to see a lush forest. Trees reach toward the heavens, splitting the sunlight into thick beams that strike the mossy ground. The aroma of pine and cedar permeates the air—the dampness of the earth rises into your body. In the distance you hear footsteps, leaves crunching, an occasional branch breaking; a proud and powerful stag with massive antlers approaches. His body gleams in the sunlight, and muscles ripple beneath his fur. An image of strength, this magickal animal guards the gestative, protective, and creative powers of the North.

Feel his pervasive, protective energy all around you as he invites, "Come into my realm—share my strength and stability."

Mentally walk into the North and touch the stag, allowing yourself to feel the strength and stability radiating from him. As he lowers himself on the ground, you mount his back, and together the two of you run into the forest. As you go deeper in the forest, it grows darker; the foliage grows thicker until it all but blocks out the sunlight. The stag slows: you feel yourself growing heavier, expanding in size, until you are no longer on the stag—you are becoming the element of earth. Experience the strength, stability, and mystery of this primal darkness. Realize that you are within the magickal structure of all forms. Spend a few moments experiencing the earth.

Now imagine that the heaviness is being replaced by a more natural lightness; your consciousness is emerging from the earth and returning to you. Feel centered within your spirit body. You see yourself in the part of the forest just outside the circle: within the center of the circle, facing North, is your physical body. Before walking back and rejoining it, ask the stag for a symbol, some glyph of power to help channel the element of earth. He may describe it to you, take you on another journey to find it, or mentally transmit the image to you. Remember it, for the image is a key to the powers of earth.

The Pentacle

Obtain a disc approximately 8" in diameter and ½" thick. It may be made out of any material—wax, wood, or stone. Either paint or inscribe the earth symbol upon it; if the material lends itself to painting, the disc should be a forest green and the symbol a bright white. Other decorations may be added to suggest the element of earth, but remember that simplicity is the key to magickal tools.

Air Meditation

Within the East, we experience the element of air. This is the realm of the mind, dawn, and spring. We are contained within this element; we walk through it, touch it, breathe it, and feel its breeze upon our skin. From this realm we draw in inspiration for our work and play. It is the breath of the God/dess.

Once the circle is cast, sit facing the East. Mentally draw another invoking pentagram of air in the East. Feel the energy of the element rushing into the circle as a gentle, yet strong, breeze. Visualize bright blue skies before you, interspersed with white, fluffy clouds. Air is the most intangible of the elements. Try as we may, we cannot control it; unless we lock it into a tightly closed container, we cannot limit its movement. As a symbol of the freedom of air, its magickal animal is the eagle.

Like his element, the eagle is associated with spring, and his colors are springtime pastels and flowery shades. Sudden change is his specialty. Always in motion, the energy and gift of the eagle is transformation and activity. Freedom is his life, and when the animal touches our own lives he gives us the freedom to change whatever we wish.

Now imagine that from the distance, a creature is flying toward the circle; as it approaches, it becomes larger until you can see that it is the magickal eagle. Large and powerful, he blows great gusts of wind with every stroke of his wings. He hovers before you and invites, "Come and share my wings; ride on the waves of the wind." You climb on his back, and together you fly into the skies.

Slowly, as you soar among the clouds, you feel yourself dissolving into air, expanding until you no longer need the eagle to stay aloft. Feel your soul becoming air, moving without direction and blowing about like the wind. Once you have felt what it is like to be air, withdraw into yourself. Ask the eagle to give you a symbol representing his element. It may appear in the clouds, he may take you to it, or he may mentally transmit the symbol to you. Remember the design; this shall be your personal key to the powers of air.

The Dagger

Find a triple-edged blade, preferably smaller than the one you are using for your athame. Paint the handle a bright yellow, and once dry, paint the air symbol that the eagle gave you onto the hilt in white. Cast the circle and invoke the elements. Once you are secure within the circle, cleanse the dagger. Face the east, drawing the invoking pentagram of air with the newly cleansed dagger; visualize the influx of energy. Mentally will the powers you have invoked into the dagger, realizing that the tool is a powerful symbol that you may use to work with the powers of air.

Water Meditation

Moving deosil to the West, we find the element of water. This is the realm of the emotions, sunset, and autumn. Its nature is cool, flowing, and comforting. Earlier people believed that departed souls left this realm and entered into the summer-lands through the West. It is here where the sun sets to travel beneath the earth and into the North.

Elemental water nurtures us in times of trouble. It is blood in the rivers of our veins; it is the primal ocean.

Once the circle is cast, sit facing the West. Mentally draw the invoking pentagram of water, and feel the cool, moist energy of water flowing into the circle. Imagine a blue ocean stretching out into eternity. Slowly at first, the water begins to bubble and ripple; the ripples intensify as a dolphin breaks the surface.

She is the guardian of the elemental powers. With the dolphin's help, we learn about transformation, rejuvenation, and regeneration. Emotions are within her realm, and she can teach us how to release them harmlessly. Once we have learned this, we may touch and read the true feelings of others and help them let go of their own negative feelings. Her colors are the deep sea blues and greens found in the oceans. Her season is the fall.

Gazing into your eyes, the dolphin says, "Upon my back I shall take you to explore the mysteries of water." You mount her and together dive beneath the waves. Deeper you go, and as you do you feel yourself expanding until you have become the water. Allow the soul to flow outward, becoming the currents, waves, and water. After allowing enough time to experience the element, retreat back into yourself. Ask the dolphin to show you a symbol that you may use to invoke these powers. Again, this symbol is your personal key to the element, and it should be remembered for inscription upon the tool.

The Chalice

Obtain a chalice, seashell, or a wooden bowl which is large enough to hold about one cup of water. It may be difficult to find an appropriate object, but the effort is worth it. Paint the chalice a deep sea-blue, then paint your personal symbol in white. Other decorations may be added to suggest the element of water, but they should be kept simple as this is another of the magickal tools.

Fire Meditation

Finally, as we move into the South, we come to the element of fire. Magickal fire is not hot and destructive like its physical counterpart; rather, it is warm and cleansing. Instead of destroying, it transforms whatever it touches, burning away that which does not belong. It represents energy, will, transformation, and cleansing. Its colors are the vivid oranges, yellows, and reds found in the fiery sunset.

Once the circle is cast, sit facing the South. Mentally draw the invoking pentagram of fire in a flaming red; feel the resulting flux of warm, dry energy rushing into the circle. Visualize a vast desert of white sand extending to the horizon, with the sun hanging low and huge in the sky. From the distance approaches a single lion.

He is the guardian of the elemental energies; his fur is deep, golden, and radiates the strong energies of summer. Coming closer you see that his mane is made of fire, and silently he beseeches you onto his back.

Together, you run swiftly in the desert, the flames from the lion's mane enveloping you in fire. It is warm and soothing, not hot or painful as you allow yourself to erupt into flame. Feel its power to transform you and burn away negativity.

Before ending the meditation, ask the lion to give you a symbol for the element that he represents. Allow yourself to become aware in your body again.

The Wand

Obtain a piece of wood roughly 12" long, and at least ½" thick. Its shaft should be painted bright red, with the symbol you received on it in white. Other decorations may be added at will, but these should be kept simple, avoiding the trend to overemphasize the wand in the magickal arsenal. The fire wand is a simple tool to represent the powers of fire.

Tetragrammaton and LVX

Before continuing our elemental work, a few fundamental Qabalistic theories must be explained. Until now, the elements have been presented in the order of earth, air, water, fire, and the reverse. Most Witches will realize that this is not the traditional deosil progression; rather, this is a Qabalistic formula called Tetragrammaton, and is symbolized in the name YHVH. Most people are familiar with this lettering as the secret, unpronounceable name of the God Yahweh. A true Qabalistical secret is that this name is not a name; it hides within its letters the elements in the order of fire, water, air, and earth. The use of the two masculine and the two feminine letters denotes an energy that is genderless, an energy which we will spend much time creating.

We need to grasp the reason this order has been used, and the reason we will deviate from it for the rest of this chapter. A Qabalistic theory states that a force moves throughout the universe—a secret, magickal force eluding science to this day. Permeating all realms and dimensions, it is this energy that gives life, sustains life, and destroys life when the physical vehicle can no longer contain it. Scientists, using advanced equipment, have studied life at the cellular level and discovered the chemical components. In vain they have tried to artificially recreate cellular life; using their technology, exact duplicates of cellular structure have been created in the laboratory. But no matter how perfect the structures, they cannot make them live! That is because no one has yet invented a machine to measure, capture, or recreate this life-force. We know it as LVX (lux, Latin for light), and as we study magick, we can create vast amounts of this energy at will using our own bodies as conductors/generators.

Only a few scientists in the realm of psychology have touched upon the concept of LVX. Wilhelm Reich termed the energy "orgone." A Jungian may call this power Soul, Self, or "meaning," depending on individual interpretation. Freud called it libido, and saw its release and dispersion throughout the psyche as necessary for health on all levels. As Witches, we believe this energy can be released through ecstatic dancing, sex, chanting, and other methods. No matter what term is used, it is all LVX and may be generated at will to empower ourselves and our magick.

Without entering into a complex discussion, it will suffice to say that LVX is generated automatically when the elements are invoked and channeled in the order of fire, water, air, and earth; this provides us with the Spirit energy of which LVX is composed. Once present, this permeable and malleable light may be used to empower all our spells, chants, and invocations. The next exercise with Spirit will give us our first chance to feel LVX moving about us, and bring this energy within so we may work with it.

Spirit Meditation

Once the circle is cast, begin by walking to each element in turn, YHVH, and breathe in the central color of the element. For fire, carry the red energy in the circle. Water is blue, air is yellow, and earth is green. Sit in the center of the circle and feel all energies vibrating around you. Feel the creative energy of fire enveloping you in its swift, changing energy; follow this with the calm flow of will and water, powerful like a mighty river. Air brings an expansion of mind, permeating all space, until the final crystallization is felt within the element of earth. Slowly, a light will glow within; it will be felt as a subtle streaming of energy within the heart area. Repeat the visualization until the streaming seems to permeate your body. This is the LVX energy which you are learning to raise and control at will.

As the light and power intensifies, ask the guardians of Spirit (who will remain invisible to you) to provide you with a symbol to represent their powers. This will appear within the light, or perhaps be transmitted mentally to you. Once received, thank the powers and slowly return to normal consciousness of the circle.

The Cauldron

Cauldrons are difficult to find, and unless you have a well-stocked craft store in your area, you may have to resort to mail order. It is not necessary to find a large one on a tripod; for our work all we will need is a cauldron with an opening roughly 9" in diameter. Some of the more artistically minded may be able to create one out of clay, glazing it black and firing it in a kiln. Indeed, the more work put into a magickal tool, the more we get out of it. Inside the cauldron, draw the symbol you received in the Spirit meditation.

CONSECRATING THE MAGICKAL TOOLS

Now that the elements have been experienced individually and symbols of power obtained for each, we may begin to create the tools needed to invoke and channel these energies. There are four tools associated with the elements in the Qabalah: the pentacle for earth, the dagger for air, the chalice for water, and the wand for fire. It is important to have a tool for each element; they represent the formula of YHVH, and even when working with just one tool/element, you are working with the complete formula.

Each tool must be prepared beforehand, and then consecrated separately by the Witch. The ritual of consecration follows.

Cast the circle, invoking the four elements and the Goddess and God. It is important to remember that only one tool should be prepared at a time. Finish each consecration before beginning the next.

Once the circle is cast and the elements invoked, sit facing the North with the pentacle (or other direction with the appropriate tool). Have some consecrated water and incense sitting before you.

Now, sprinkle the tool with the water, and then pass it through the smoke of the incense. Holding it above your head with both hands, say, "Powerful Horned One, gentle Goddess, bless this magickal (name of tool) that through you, it may obtain the necessary virtue to perform all acts of love and beauty."

Lay the tool between yourself and the direction of the element, and visualize the colored energy of the element entering it. Then, sprinkle the tool with water and pass it through the smoke of the incense again. Hold it above your head and say, "Goddess and God, bless this tool prepared in your honor."

Wrap the tool in a colored cloth, preferably one in the tool's elemental color. Close the circle.

In traditional Witchcraft, the elements are followed about in the order of air, fire, water, and earth. Like the formula of Tetragrammaton, this forms this fifth element of Spirit, but instead of being geared toward creation and magick, this formula becomes centered on evolution as it follows the path of the sun. This formula is valid and useful; it has worked for Witches for centuries. So the question arises, why use Tetragrammaton?

The energy of LVX is explosive; ceremonial texts have referred to it as the holy and formless fire that flashes and darts through the hidden depths of the universe. When creating, when using the life-force to cast a spell, this specialized formula puts the specific energy we need at our fingertips. Deosil progression, the other formula with which we are familiar, puts us in touch with the parts of spirit needed for our evolution. The rest of the exercises in this chapter are attempts to facilitate this evolution and will follow the normal deosil progression; first, let us explore a practical usage of Tetragrammaton.

PRACTICAL USE OF TETRAGRAMMATON: A HERMETIC SPELL

LVX energy can have many practical uses beyond vivifying our bodies, minds, and souls. On its own, it can form the basis of our circle's energy, and hence, the cone of power. In combining the creation of LVX with the formula of Tetragrammaton, plus consecrating our circle beforehand to the creation of our magickal desire, we create an amount of life-force, a living entity that manifests on the astral plane. From our earlier training in the Craft, we realize that anything manifested deliberately on the astral eventually filters through to the physical. It is upon these principles that we will work.

Remembering this, realize that the setting of the spell begins to occur before the actual circle is cast. The climax of our formula will begin before even the formation of Yod, the element of fire. Yod is the most divine aspect of the elemental forces in the formula, and the rest are but solidifications of this energy. This means that before creating the sacred space, the object of desire must be firmly fixed in the mind, for the actual ritual brings the desire into being.

Suppose there is an unpaid bill and the money to pay it is not on hand—the desire is for enough money to pay the bill. As you center yourself and alter your awareness to enter sacred space, concentrate on the idea, repeating it in the back of your mind: "I need the money to pay this bill."

Concentrate upon this idea as the circle is cast. Once all the elements have been invoked YHVH, approach the Southern quarter and announce your intent to the powers of fire: "I need the money to pay this bill." With your fire wand, draw the invoking pentagram of fire in the air. See it made of red flames and visualize an influx of fire energy coming to empower you. The South will confer a swift, fiercely creative energy, giving your request the fire of life, the energy needed to live. Imagine that this tireless strength and energy is being imparted to your request.

Walking deosil to the West, once again announce the object of your desire. With the chalice, draw a blue invoking pentagram of water toward the quarter, and feel the power coming to energize your desires. The resulting flow of energy will be calmer than the fire, but it will be a more powerful force of will, like the force of a mighty river. Elemental water will help confer a body to your request, making it solid in the astral light.

Tread the circle deosil until you meet the powers of air in the East. Reach out with the air dagger. Again, announce your desires to the elemental forces, drawing a yellow invoking pentagram of air. As the energy permeates the circle, see it binding to your request; it will seem to expand outward and penetrate all space. The element will bestow the air of life, mind, and breath to your spell.

Finally, as you tread the circle deosil into the North, stop to draw the invoking pentagram of earth there with the pentacle. As the earth energies solidify within the circle, feel the wish crystallizing into a solid, substantial body on the astral plane. Realize that now your wish is a living entity, and soon it will take on form in the physical realm.

After working in this fashion a few times, experienced Witches will find their own artistic techniques to add; for example, pictures or effigies may be used to represent the desire. And as you tread the circle, visualize the invoked energies being added to the physical prop used. To represent the spirit formed at the end of the ritual, appropriate candles and incense may be burned as a physical aid to concentration. Dances, chants, and invocations to the God/dess may be written and choreographed to confer greater energies upon the Witch—imagination is the only limitation here.

THE ARCHANGELS OF THE ELEMENTS[6]

The chart in Figure 1:2 (see page 13) shows us that each element has its own Archangel. As we progress around the circle, we encounter each of these Archangels in turn; we must learn how to communicate with them. They are responsible for teaching us the powers of the elements, their times and seasons, and aspects of ourselves which they represent. From them, we may learn of power in all its forms, and of the ethereal realms.

These beings known as Archangels are energy forms with independent existences, much like our own. They are not physical; they have never had bodies like ours, nor will they ever manifest in the flesh for a full incarnation, although there are legends about these entities taking on physical forms for a short time. They are beings of light, formed from the energies of their respective sephirotic realms, and their sole purpose is to regulate the flow of power from the higher realms into Assiah. Although they are independent, personified by form and force, if we as Witches are to contact them and make use of their powers, we must first build up images of their form within our personal circles. As our created forms increase in strength, their force can flow from the unseen realms to inhabit these shells. Only then, when our visualization skills have increased to the level necessary to create substantial forms on the astral plane, will the Archangelic forces flow sufficiently to our circles and communicate with us. As we interact with the Archangels, we may

---

6. Archangels, angels, and other non-physical beings are beyond gender; however, it is difficult to avoid the use of he or she when writing in the third person singular. Therefore, I have chosen to refer to the Archangels and angels by the gender of their polarity: i.e., Auriel belongs to the element of earth, which is feminine, so I refer to this Archangel as "she." This does not mean that Auriel has to be envisioned as a feminine figure, for "she" is beyond gender forms.

use the potent energies at their command—control of those powers will increase with our magickal competence.

We have already learned that the magickal animals for the elements can help us discover the tools for transformation; likewise, the Archangels of the elements can give us the power to work with these tools to balance ourselves and the earth. Governing each quarter, they give us the ability to learn to control and harness the powers within ourselves, represented by each sphere. In formulating and invoking the Archangels, we work from the divine spark. True, the power transferred by the Witch is minute compared with its source; one may not accomplish anything miraculous with these energies. They must be channeled through spiritual pathways for practical results. Eventually, we will acheive a physical result, if necessary for the operation, but the deciding factor is the channeling ability of the Witch.

Before we are able to work magickally with the four Archangels, we must go around the circle and meet them.

Auriel, Archangel of the North

Directing the solidity and stability of earth is the Archangel Auriel; she is a somber entity, elderly in appearance with long, flowing salt-and-pepper hair. Her eyes are a rich, velvety black, set in a porcelain-like face. Denoting age and wisdom, she is wrinkled, but not overly so—her facial lines are few, but well set. Always robed in a vibrant forest green, she carries with her a delicate aroma of cedar and pine. Whenever Auriel manifests, the room is suffused with Mother Earth's own damp, musky scent. She changes her appearance at will: at times she comes with wings flashing the silvery-gray hues of snow, ice, and pale moonlight; when she brings news from the lands beyond the North, she travels cloaked. Her immense wings darken and slacken, forming a black cape, with scintillating, silver threads tracing the starscape of the Northern sky. Although outwardly feminine, her voice betrays her awesome strength—it rumbles with power.

Her powers are those of inner darkness. Within ourselves and the earth is a soothing, primal space—the womb, the Mother's own resting place. Deep within that darkness, however, is the light of new beginnings, new knowledge, and rebirth. Auriel knows the path through the eternal night into new life. She guides the souls of the dead who have traveled through the Western gate of death into the Eastern gate of rebirth, leaving with each the seed of new awareness. It brightens and grows under her care, and the life-force grows stronger through each incarnation.

Her magickal weapon is the shield; round and polished more meticulously than a mirror, it deflects all negativity and danger away from the unprepared soul. Auriel is the protector who leads us from hurt greater than we can handle, and in times of danger she is to be invoked to protect the unwary traveler along paths of darkness. Within her shield's polished surface, we may see our true selves, our mistakes, and our lessons. Sometimes, from behind her shield she draws out a Book of Wisdom, which we use to help us make decisions in times of turmoil. Both of her weapons, the shield and the book, offer protection and safety; Auriel is the protector of Goddess' hidden children, and it is to her that we turn when the tides of life become too harsh, seeking closure to that which is old and worn.

Raphael, Archangel of the East

Moving to the East of our magickal circle, we encounter Raphael—the Archangel of air and all its powers. To know him is to know pure youth, beauty, and exuberance. Raphael appears as an impulsive youth: not a child, yet not a man. His hair is long and flowing, billowing about his form on invisible thermal currents. His face is fresh, browned slightly by the morning sun, yet still pink like the skin of a child. Imagine the colors of a sunrise, the vibrant color palette sprayed haphazardly across the heavens as the sun breaks over the horizon, and you will know Raphael. His robe is tinted in various shades of red and yellow, and splashed with springtime hues. Always winged, he floats gracefully on the breeze he creates; at times, he conjures winds of gale force announcing his presence. When he manifests in the circle, one can smell the fresh, springtime aromas he creates.

Raphael brings spiritual consciousness to humanity, and heals the hurts we receive from our lessons in life. Auriel, the protector, kept us from encountering more than we could bear; once we have passed through the trials and tests allowed us, Raphael works to quickly heal the wounds we could, and did, withstand. He carries a sword to afford us safe space as we recover, a sword which gives us keenness of mind and the ability to make decisions about our future progress. And as we rest and absorb his healing energy, we find that around his neck hangs a vial of magickal balm on a golden chain. He uses this balm to help heal and soothe our wounds.

Raphael is the patron of travel, commerce, inventions, theatrics, and the like; it is he who should be invoked whenever beginning a venture. Through him are opened new abilities, and the power to overcome old difficulties.

Michael, Archangel of the South

Moving to the South, we come to the quarter of Michael, Archangel of fire. His image is that of masculinity; his body is strong, toned, and muscled. Like Raphael, his hair is voluminous and thick, bleached blond by the noonday sun. His skin is a rich, deep bronze with a mature tone. To know Michael is to know the pure strength of fire, the blazing afternoon sun, and the passion of summer; his robes are vibrant reds and yellows, luminescent, almost blinding in their colors. Bound around his waist is a gold girdle, and adhered to his chiseled chest is a brass breastplate inscribed with the symbol of the sun. Michael carries a long spear which he uses to destroy the forces of evil threatening the Mother's children.

Michael is said to harmonize that which arises from the misuse of natural forces. With his power to burn and transform all that is impure with fire, he destroys those aspects within our psyche that bring us into disharmony with the natural order, giving our bodies a chance to realign with the universe. His power is strong and not to be invoked frivolously, as his powers balance the more quiet and subtle powers of the North. His period is noon, his season the summer; he embodies all the qualities of these strong, potent forces.

It is said that Michael once made a promise with the Gods of this world to stand by all humans, no matter how terrible, as long as they have some amount of good left within them. This gives Michael the position of humankind's great benefactor, working to restore good on Earth as long as there are people left who are trying to achieve balance here in the physical plane. Michael is the Archangel to invoke whenever one is trying to return things to their natural order.

Gabriel, Archangel of the West

Finally, we approach Gabriel's realm in the West. She is an angel who embodies the powers of love, compassion, and tenderness; every aspect of her image is symbolic of these powers. Since her element is water, she is often pictured rising above the sea, or standing before a powerful waterfall. She comes to us with chestnut hair suspended about her face as if floating in water, amber eyes that reflect the mysterious depths of the soul, and a voice that sings with the rushing, sweet river waters. Her wings and robes are vibrant sea-blue; they all but disappear in the ocean's depths. To know unearned, unconditional love, to know the force of spiritual nourishment, to relax and be weak, one has only to call her name and let her power flow unimpeded.

Gabriel reflects the gentler issues of life—its final tides before we pass the gates of death into the unknown. Through her we find abandonment of worldly desires, fulfillment of home and hearth, and pure enjoyment of our life's accomplishments. To find sanctuary after strife, turn to the West; Gabriel will wash you with her sacred waters, calming the soul.

Like her element, Gabriel's power is soothing—the fires of unrequited love, unrestrained anger, and unreturned passion are quenched before her presence. She cries tears of both sorrow and happiness for the world—and through these tears, the hurts of a lifetime lived unwisely melt away. Physical, spiritual, and emotional death find dissolution within her arms. As life comes to a close and our magickal circle completes its cycle, we find ourselves in her loving arms with the strength to faces the mysteries ahead in the North—with Auriel.

Channeling the Archangels

For this exercise, you will need the usual ritual implements of altar candles, incense (or potpourri), and blessed water.

Begin by playing soft ritual music. Cleanse yourself with the incense and water; also, cleanse the room to be used for the ritual.

Enter the state of altered awareness and patterns, completing the circle casting exercise through the invocation of the elements.

It is important to work with the Archangels in the order of earth/Auriel, air/Raphael, fire/Michael, and water/Gabriel.

Beginning with the North/Auriel, sink into the earth visualization exercise until you have become the element. Call out the Archangel's name, and using the physical description given earlier, begin to visualize her form. Also visualize the invoking pentagram of the element in its colors. (For Auriel, this is an earthy green. For the rest of the pentagrams/attributions, refer to Figure 1:2.)

Once these have been visualized, continue to concentrate upon the Archangel's features. Don't worry if the features change slightly from the description given; my vision and your vision of Auriel will not match exactly. Do, however, be cautious that you don't allow elements from another realm to slip into your visualizations.

Once the image is firmly built, ask the Archangel if he or she will communicate with you now. Wait for a reply. If none is given, or the answer is no, simply thank the image for appearing and then close your circle. Further work with the imagery is needed before the Archangel can communicate with you.

If the Archangel will communicate with you, allow him or her to come closer. Note all appearances, mannerisms, clothing, etc. It is important to remain aware of the total experience.

Ask questions such as, "Do you have any special message for me now?" "Are you affecting any part of my life?" "Are there any lessons that I must learn from you?" and the like. Pay special attention to what the Archangel has to impart.

All magick is based on an energy exchange. Before thanking the Archangel and departing, ask if there are any special ways in which you may honor him or her now or after the circle is closed. (Sometimes the being may ask that you dance or chant within the circle to send him or her energy; at times I have had an Archangel make a request that I do something environmental dealing with the energies he or she represents.)

Thank the Archangel for his or her presence before returning to awareness of the circle. Visualize the banishing pentagram of the element to return the quarter's energy to normal. Close your sacred space, remembering to perform the task the Archangel has requested. Repeat this exercise for each Archangel.

After all the Archangels have been met and thanked, we may begin to ask their assistance in magickal tasks. If you have a need, such as an emotional healing, simply look under the descriptions given to find the one that rules the qualities of your desire. For example, this need would fall under Gabriel's domain, as she is the Archangel dealing with the emotions. Enter sacred space, and search out Gabriel in her element. Politely request her help in dealing with the situation, and then ask how you, in turn, may help her.

The Elements and the Tides of Life

In the Qabalah, we are taught that life moves in an eternal cycle—like the circle, Cosmos has no beginning, no end. For a moment, if we fall back on our reality agreement, we see life as beginning in the womb, and slowly, an individual progresses through childhood, adolescence, and then old age; the process culminates in death. This materialistic view leaves us empty: indeed, in early childhood we begin to question this process. The soul, young in linear time, intuitively feels that there has to be more. There was more; frequently, children will ask their parents, "Where was I before I was born?" Caught up in the trauma of a loved one's death, the mind not yet weighed down by reality will often look at the passing of a loved one as just that—a passing. Only when confronted with the despair of the family does a child view death as a ending, not a passage.

As Witches, we search for truth in nature: Her cycles are the cycles of life. We attempt to tune into Her rhythms—they progress, they move, and they change; within their changes we find a cycle, the rhythm of life. As time passes, She goes through light and dark, summer and winter, youth and old age. The truth is this— She moves in an eternal, mysterious cycle. Human lives, too, are bound within this cycle. If we tread our magick circle deosil, we can tune into our magickal location, our period in the cycle of Cosmos, and learn to dance the magickal dance whose rhythm permeates our lives.

We begin in the North, the "Home of the God/dess" according to the ancients, the place of mystery and darkness. The North represents paradox, a sacred time when nothing in life seems to happen, but everything for life is beginning. This is the death/rebirth time of winter when things have ceased to grow; seeds lie frozen in the earth, the trees are dormant, and the souls of the dead rest in anticipation of rebirth. Perhaps latency is the word which comes closest to describing this stage of life—as things rest, they anticipate the coming time of activity and growth. Outward activity, which has diminished, gives way to bursts of internal growth and activity. We descend into a land of darkness, quiet, and dreams.

In the North we grow old, becoming wrinkled like the earth's wizened face. It is the time when souls move from the summerlands of refreshment into the new forms of flesh; internal activity increases. We find rest and seclusion to think, to plan, and to begin to create new things. As we sleep, we align with these energies. Whenever our bodies rest and refresh themselves from hard labor, we enter the Northern tide of life. Whenever we take time to relax and reminisce about the past, gathering our thoughts and energies for future endeavors, we are under the influence of the Northern tide of life.

The Northern tide is directed by the angel Phorlakh. Under the direction of Auriel, she brings to us an understanding that there must be rest before we can emerge into the world with new forms, ideas, and plans. As an angel of power, she comes to us with frosty white hair, a wrinkled, wizened face, and a robe of brilliant white cloaked in a flowing black cape—she represents the light hidden in darkness.

As we approach the East, refreshed from our rest in the North, we find that all life is bursting with new energy. We are young, free, and renewed; with these new stores of energy at our command, we can put into action the plans we made in the North. Seeds that were frozen and dormant finally have the strength to lay down roots and send up new shoots; likewise, we burst forth from the womb of the Mother with strength and energy unmatched by the other tides of life. Under the influence of the Eastern powers, we find it easy to mold our raw energy into refined talents—our only limitation being the environment in which our own karma has placed us. But if we have laid out our plans well enough, and tap into the energies here sufficiently, even our own karma can be worked through to create new destinies for our lives.

As a woman awaits the birth of her child, she is tapping into the Eastern energies, using her own life-force to bring a child to birth. As we go to school and learn the skills to enter our chosen professions, we are using the mental, goal-achieving energies of the Eastern quadrant. Any time we dream, and choose to bring our dreams into manifestation through hard work and perseverance, we are invoking the energies of the East into our lives.

Directing these energies to us is the mighty angel Chassan. Like Raphael, he comes to us as an exuberant youth; he is, however, more child-like than his superior. Chassan appears to us with chin-length chestnut hair, light eyes and skin, and a bright yellow robe that reflects the radiance of a sunrise. He is winged and barefoot; his voice comes to us as soft and whispering, like a springtime breeze.

In the South, we explore everything without care or concern. Southern energies are those of fire and summer, a time when we are concerned with what makes us feel good. In time, under the guidance of the South, we find discrimination; we learn our true will, and what it is we came to this realm to accomplish. We discover, perhaps, that what we thought our goals were are not actually our goals; the element of fire quickly burns away that which hides our innermost talents and desires from us. We begin to to mature and watch as the work in our own lives begins to grow toward a bountiful harvest.

Often, after discovering our true wills and desires, life begins to move at a dizzying pace; all becomes a blur as the God/dess leads us deeper into our true selves. After She has made our true path known, we run, not walk, down the road that leads us to our true destiny. The South is the great AHA! experience that so many authors write about—suddenly things seem clear, and we have the needed energy and strength to establish ourselves in the world.

The mighty angel Aral directs and assists us during our fire-tide of life. Threatening to seize us with its overwhelming force and energy, Aral makes sure that we do not become overwhelmed or overworked as we fly down the path to our destinies. This angel comes to us in fiery red robes which undulate and scintillate about his body in the colors of flames: bright yellows and reds. His hair is golden like the summer sun—his voice is filled with passion and energy. Aral, like his superior, Michael, is an angel of limitless strength.

Finally, in the West, we approach the time of harvest, the autumn of our lives and plans when we prepare to collect the fruits of our labor. This is the time and the place when plants, grown from seeds once frozen in the earth, begin to give up their own seeds to the keeping of the Mother. Those who were given visions and dreams, and worked to achieve those dreams, are now responsible for giving back those dreams to the world, working to share their accumulated knowledge and experience with those around them. In the West we find the first stirrings of wisdom; people are not afraid of the unknown, nor are they afraid of those things beyond their capabilities. Total release of fear is the teaching of the Western quarter.

The West is a place of slowing down after increased activity. We are not dormant, but balancing outward and inward activity. Every time we step back to check on our creations and make sure they still follow the necessary plans, we are using the powers of the West. Whenever we contemplate the prudence of our actions or share our knowledge with others, we exercise the powers of the West.

Within the Western-tide of life, we are directed by the angel Taliahad. She appears in a robe of watery blues and greens; her hair is long, flowing, and chestnut in color. As she speaks, her voice flows like the gentle rushing of a stream; one can hear faint, bubbling sounds. As time slows for us and we weaken with age, Taliahad gives us the strength and wisdom to withstand the passage of time.

As the cycle continues, we once again find ourselves slipping through the Western gate into a sacred time, the time of the North.

Finding Your Quarter

In finding the direction that is affecting us now, we take into account more than our chronological age, we must also consider the inward, or spiritual age. In using the magickal representations of the elements, we must turn to each quarter and ask the powers which one is affecting our lives right now; then we must work with the element to learn the lessons it is trying to teach us. The following exercise will help us determine which of the four elements is working its influence upon us now.

Begin by playing some soft ritual music. Cleanse yourself with incense and water; also cleanse the room in which you will be working.

Enter the state of altered awareness of patterns, and complete the circle casting exercise through the invocation of the elements.

Walk to each quarter, beginning with the North, and feel the energy. Quietly ask the elemental powers if they are trying to teach you something at this time. It is possible that more than one quarter will be influencing you: perhaps you will find that one direction is influencing your mundane life, and another is working with you on more spiritual levels. Each direction, however, is just as important as the next—we must work to find our own personal balance.

Once an affinity is felt for a quarter, call to the Archangel of the element, asking that the angel be sent to appear. As the angels are the teachers and guides of the life-tides, they are the ones to ask what the element has to teach in our lives. It is important to establish the visualization of the angel within his or her element: i.e., Aral should be pictured standing in a vast desert, or before a roaring bonfire.

Converse with the angel, asking for advice on how you may quicken your development. Once done, make sure to ask the angel if there is anything that you may do in return; some small act of thanks to replenish the energies expended in communication. Make sure that this request is honored.

Thank the angel and close the circle.

RITUAL OF THE FOUR ELEMENTS

In Chapter One, we briefly examined the concepts behind the sacred meal of wine and cakes, and learned of the physical and metaphysical processes that took place as we ingested a talismanic substance symbolic of divinity. Once more, we shall use that formula to purify and perfect our physical bodies.

Throughout this chapter, I have emphasized that the magickal elements are the basis of the energy which forms our physical body. Earth, air, water, and fire merge to create the Spirit energy that constantly creates and recreates our beings. If these elements are the basis of our existence, if they are the basic divisions of energy that merge constantly into our energy matrix, it only stands to reason that by strengthening their patterns within ourselves, we strengthen our own energy pattern, speeding up our magickal evolution.

In Chapter One, we learned how to invoke the magickal elements to our sphere, fortifying the circle's boundaries with their power. Then, we began to use those energies to cleanse our energy pattern: the earth strengthened us, the air refreshed us, the water cleansed us, and the fire illuminated us, strengthening the power of Spirit within ourselves. Learning to alter our perception of reality, we soon concluded that the circle is more than a temporary construction on the astral plane—it is a greater awareness of self. The edges of our sacred space symbolize the boundaries of our consciousness (the edge of Cosmos): beyond the boundaries of self lie the elemental kingdoms. In purifying consciousness with these energies, we are drawing from the four foundations of our being to strengthen the self; however, as we leave the awareness of the sacred circle, we once again allow consciousness to become centered in the energy pattern of the body. As this happens, our immediate connection with the elements is lost—we lose the benefit of their purifying powers.

Somehow, we must lock these raw powers of earth, air, water, and fire into our matrix if we are to obtain long-term benefits. Once again, we turn to the concept of the sacred meal—we must take substances symbolic of the powers with which we wish to merge, change them into storehouses of that power, and then make that substance a part of ourselves. By doing this, we physically lock the elemental energies into our bodies, opening a permanent channel of energy between ourselves and the elemental realms. The ritual of the four elements is a magickal meal that shall accomplish this goal.

First, we need to personify the elemental powers in our imagination. So far, we have worked with the magickal animals, Archangels, and angels of the elements; for this area of our work, these archetypes will not suffice. The four elements are pure, raw, primal energy. The images we have worked with so far are refined archetypes—controllers and directors of the elements. By working with them, we have learned to control and mediate the energies within our psyche. Now, we need to get to the power of the elements. We will cast the circle, invoke the Watchtowers, and call upon the hierarchy of Archangels and angels to help safely channel the elements to us, but it will be the energies themselves with which we shall merge. In doing so, we shall become familiar with the elementals of the realms.

Within both the Craft and the Qabalah, we find that the four magickal elements are inhabited by spirits that do not fall into the normal classifications of Archangelic, angelic, or magickal animals: these are called elementals. There are four types: the spirits of the earth are called gnomes; those of air are called sylphs; the inhabitants of water are the undines, and the spirits of fire are called the salamanders. These are traditional names, but we can find their origins in other languages. "Gnome" is derived from the Greek word *gnoma*, which means knowledge. We can ascertain from this that the gnomes are the knowing ones of the elementals. "Sylph" comes to us from the Greek word *silphe*, which translates as butterfly. Often, these creatures are pictured with delicate butterfly wings. "Undine" comes to us from the Latin word *unda*, a wave, and these are seen as creatures of the waves. Our final classification, "Salamander," comes to us from the Greek word *salambe*, which is a fireplace. Hence, many Witches try to invoke their powers through the magick of the hearth.

These magickal spirits derive their whole existence from the realms of their creation: a gnome lives out its life through the element of earth. It is created by the elemental energies, lives out its consciousness within its realm, and eventually dissolves back into the elemental powers to be recycled and recreated. It is the same for the rest of the elementals: they are created, sustained, and dissolved within the realm of their existence. Their basic natures are easy to ascertain; in working with the elementals of the air, we meditate on the qualities of air until we intuitively understand its nature—thereby understanding the nature of the elementals from the realm.

Within their own realm, all elementals are basically the same—they are magickal robots, in a sense, with limited consciousness and duties to perform. They are a low-level, organized awareness of the elemental realm. An analogy can be drawn by looking at the human body; within ourselves, we contain many "kingdoms" which consist of the body's systems. Examine the circulatory system: the deity force of this kingdom would be the impetus for the blood to flow about the body. The deity force creates the whole of the circulatory system, which consists of the heart, arteries, veins, and the fluids therein. Overseeing the pumping of the blood through the body is the heart: this would be the Archangel of the kingdom. The heart directs the blood throughout the body in a system of tubes, arteries, and veins, which would correspond to the angelic forces of a magickal kingdom. The heart controls and directs the system's activities, while the angels carry out those orders. As blood flows throughout the circulatory system, it represents the kingdom's pool of energy—each individual part of that energy, the blood cell, represents an individual elemental of the realm.

In understanding how the bloodstream carries out its duties, it will not suffice to study the heart, arteries, or veins alone; after understanding how they work, we must move on to study the bloodstream as a whole, as well as each cell of blood. Likewise, in working with the powers of the elements, we cannot limit ourselves to the magickal animals, Archangels, or angels, even though they are carriers of the forces. We must go to the energy itself and its individual entities—the elementals.

This analogy is a simplified representation of what occurs throughout the elemental kingdoms. The deity name represents the divine creative force of the realm; the Archangel is the medium of action. The angels are the vessels in which the elemental power flows, while the elementals carry out the collective work. As such, each elemental has limited consciousness of duty, and only does what it was created to do. A red blood cell cannot carry a message from the physical brain to the muscles in the feet; likewise, an elemental of fire cannot operate or carry out its duties in the realm of water. However, they can act as channels of energy for the unified whole. The action of a single red blood cell is essential to the operation of the body, as it carries the oxygen essential for operation of the complete organism. The elemental of fire is essential to the creation of the Spirit energy that comprises our matrix, for it carries a part of the energy needed to create and sustain our energy pattern.

As such, elementals will always be what they are—but through intimate work with the Witch, they begin to gain a consciousness of their own, capable of making decisions and working magickally with the Witch. Let's look at our concept of animal familiars: entities from the animal kingdom with which the Witch works. In a sense, animals are similar to the elementals of earth, wind, fire, and water; in the wild, they are sentient beings with limited consciousness. However, as with domestic animals, when brought into human contact, they begin to develop "personalities." We separate them from their natural habitats, making them our constant companions. The bond of love is developed between the human and the animal. The wild elemental side of the entity becomes intimately bound with that of its caretaker; over a period of time, a primal intelligence begins to develop. While primarily following its natural instincts, it begins to share its owner's intelligence.

When the animal is cared for by the Witch, this personality becomes even more evident. We love the pet, care for the pet, and eventually, begin to involve it in our magickal work. As we share our divinity and our higher self with the animal, it develops an acute intelligence, partaking of our own divinity. The familiar becomes an extension of ourselves, enfolded in our immediate magickal energy matrix. As such, the animal's individuality in its kingdom becomes keen: many Witches believe that their familiars return to them after death in new forms, avoiding the remixing with the raw elemental energy that occurs in their own kingdom. Magickally, we imbue them with their individuality, and they reincarnate as the same intelligence in a new body, evolving through time with us. Reincarnation teaches us that animals may eventually achieve human status, reincarnating as a newly evolved soul.

The same can happen to the elementals with which we work. They are part of a group soul that is overseen by the Archangelic powers of their realm—as they are invoked to help us in our magickal work, the elementals become bound in our human energy pattern; they become a part of us. In joining our work, they achieve individuality from their energy pool, developing through time with us. They become our elemental familiars. And as they help us in perfecting our elemental bodies, they are allowed to glimpse the Great Work which the whole cosmos will eventually achieve—union with the Source.

As we perform the eucharist of the four elements, we invite the elementals who are present at our circle to take part in the ritual, bringing us the elemental energy which they carry. Entering our human energy pattern, they not only cleanse us with their powers, by binding their energy to the physical basis of the ritual, they assist in building our elemental bodies. Elementals, then, become magickal helpers who return to assist us in our work time and time again; in helping us become more than human, we help them to become more than just elementals. The bond which unites us with our helpers should be love; as we work together with this bond there can be no danger, only light and healing.

The Ritual

To perform the ritual of the four elements, we will need a few additional tools on our altar: a cup of wine to represent elemental water, a cake or piece of bread to represent elemental earth, a rose to represent elemental air, and a red candle to represent elemental fire. Once these items are assembled, cast the magickal circle and invoke the elements, God, and Goddess to the circle with the methods given in Chapter One.

Begin to tread the circle deosil, starting in the East and ending in the North. At every direction, stop and face outward from the circle. Imagine that the elemental energy of the direction is entering the circle and linking with its ritual symbol on the altar.

Once this is completed, stand at the South of the altar, facing North, and recite: "The gentle Goddess and the powerful God have said: 'These are the elements of our bodies—the substance of all creation! The scent of the dying rose is our breath of life; the red fire is that of our undaunted will; the cup of the wine is the blood of our hearts; the bread is the foundation of our bodies.'"

Now, walk to each direction in turn, beginning in the East, and face outward. Visualize the Archangels, angels, and elemental powers at the edge of the circle. Invoke: "Blessed be the union of the Goddess and God, for their ecstasy flows outward to the ends of the Universe, unto the elemental realms, rejoicing!"

Reach out to the edge of the circle in an act of invitation, calling now to the elemental powers assembled at the edge of your consciousness: "I invite all of you, beings of the (direction), directors of the powers of (element)—Archangels, angels, and elementals—now present at this circle, to partake with me in the meal of the four elements."

Repeat these two invocations at each quarter, moving deosil, and finish in the North.

Walk deosil to the South of the altar, and face the North. Invoke: "I invite you all to experience with me the scent of this rose, symbolic of the element of air; to feel with me the warmth of this sacred fire, which is a symbol of the element of fire; to drink with me this wine, as a symbol of elemental water; to eat with me this bread, as a symbol of the element of earth."

As you recite the invocation, perform each act in turn. Imagine that the elemental powers are flowing from the edges of the circle into the symbol; as you consume the energy by touch, smell, or taste, the energies move into you, becoming a permanent part of the energy matrix. The elemental powers—Archangels, angels, and elementals—move through your consciousness. It is important to feel the raw energy of the elementals merging into your psyche.

Consume the wine and bread. Once you have finished, say, "It is done. So mote it be!" Spend a few moments meditating on the effects of the powers and elementals which have moved through, and merged into, your matrix. Possibly you might catch glimpses of the elementals who have brought their energies to you—subsequent performances of this ritual will bring you more intimate knowledge of them.

So far, we have learned to cast the Witch's magickal circle using the methods of the Qabalah; also, we have elaborated upon those methods to investigate each quarter of the circle in turn. Now that we have anchored ourselves firmly between the worlds of the seen and unseen and mastered the methods of entering and visiting the elemental powers, we may begin to move beyond Malkuth on the Tree of Life and into the less tangible energy patterns within the sephiroth. To do this, we will need to study the Tree in depth, examining how each energy pattern fits into the whole system. Our next chapter begins our first in-depth investigation of the Tree, studying the theories of Creation, polarity, and traditional Wiccan concepts. Let us move on, then, to implant the Tree of Life in our soul, creating a living symbol of power!

CHAPTER THREE

PLANTING THE TREE

CREATION

Alone, awesome, complete within Herself, the Goddess. She whose name cannot be spoken, floated in the abyss of the outer darkness, before the beginning of all things. As She looked into the curved mirror of black space, She saw by Her own light Her radiant reflection, and fell in love with it. She drew it forth by the power that was in Her and made love to Herself, and called Her "Miria, the Wonderful."

Their ecstasy burst forth in the single song of all that is, was, or ever shall be, and with the song came motion, waves that poured outward and became all the spheres and circles of the worlds. The Goddess became filled with love, swollen with love, and She gave birth to a rain of bright spirits that filled the worlds and became all beings.

But in that great movement, Miria was swept away, and as She moved out from the Goddess, She became more masculine. First She became the Blue God, the gentle, laughing God of love. Then She became the Green One, vine-covered, rooted in the earth, the spirit of all growing things. At last She became the Horned God, the Hunter whose face is the ruddy sun and yet dark as Death. But always desire draws Him back toward the Goddess, so that He circles Her eternally, seeking to return in love.

All began in love; all seeks to return in love. Love is the law, the teacher of wisdom, and the great revealer of mysteries.[1]

We have discovered that the Universe is a vast expanse of energy—limitless, eternal, mixing and folding within itself. Within its infinite scope it contains an obvious structure: we divide our known areas of it into galaxies and solar systems. Taking those solar systems as the basic building blocks of Cosmos, we may compare them to the body's atomic structure. Each star of a system forms a nucleus, and about it orbit various planets and comets; the design is comparable to the protons, neutrons, and electrons found within an atom. Between these celestial spheres, as within the atom, lie vast fields of space. Somehow,

---

1. Starhawk. *The Spiral Dance: A Rebirth of the Ancient Religion of the Great Goddess* (San Francisco: Harper and Row, 1979), 17. Used by permission.

solar systems merge: a galactic cohesion is evident as these spheres hurtle throughout space at astronomical speeds. They move; they change; they expand; yet somehow, they all retains the same relative positions. Throughout this eternal movement and growth, new stars are formed; planets coalesce from random, swirling particles. We live and exist in a Cosmos that eternally grows, evolves, and creates itself. For every new planet formed, one is engulfed in the explosion of a supernova. Even within the grand scheme of Cosmos, Nature follows her patterns.

Likewise, we have discovered that our own bodies are made of energy: the fabric of our beings is woven from the same material that created the stars. We may "vibrate" at a different frequency; we may appear in a different form—the basic chemicals of our structures are the same. Within us are trillions of atoms whose structures mimic miniature solar systems. Those atoms combine like so many solar systems to form a galaxy; those galaxies manifest as a single cell of the human body. Millions of these cells form a tissue, which results in the creation of a single organ. Dozens of these organs align themselves, forming the human body—a compressed field of energy mimicking the design of Cosmos.

When referring to Cosmos as all creation of which we are aware (and unaware), we use the term Macrocosm.[2] We are all a part of the Macrocosm—humans, animals, plants, planets, and stars—the term is all-inclusive. Our limitless consciousness has become centered in the body's finite energy pattern. As its structure mirrors the greater pattern of Macrocosm, we refer to the body, mind, and soul complex as a microcosm[3] of the Universe. Whatever can be found within our own sphere of perception can also be found to exist within Cosmos.

If we are centered within the body's energy, and if our consciousness expands to include all creation, we must also agree that on some deeper level, we not only share universal consciousness, our true core of existence is the same. We all merge and overlap, and each individual is merely another center of action for the one force permeating Cosmos. By some mysterious process, the Goddess drew from within Her limitless being an incalculable concentration of Her own energy, continually recreating the forms until we emerged as separate and distinct, yet constantly connected, beings. Science has struggled with this process for centuries, trying to deduce a logical sequence of events that would explain the creation of the Universe. Perhaps science will never discover this answer: to explore a spiritual unknown, we must investigate the question spiritually. To find our answers, we will focus on the Tree of Life—a structure based upon the creation and renewal of all the worlds.

On its grander scheme, Qabalah speaks of creation, energy patterns, and dimensions of being. The Tree of Life gives us ten separate sephiroth, which are defined as planes of existence. Beginning with the thesis that all is a manifestation of the God/dess synergy, the ten spheres become ten different approaches to divinity. For example, I am known to friends as Stuart, while acquaintances call me Mr. Myers. Within Craft circles, I am known by a secret Witch name. In talking about me, some use the term "writer." No matter what name or title is used, I am still the same person. Only the approach to my consciousness has been different.

---

2. The term Macrocosm comes to us from two Greek words: *makros*, which means large, and *kosmos*, which means universe. Hence, Macrocosm refers to the large universe—all of creation!

3. Microcosm comes to us from two Greek words: the word *mikros*, which means small, and the word *kosmos*, which means universe. Hence, microcosm is the small universe, the human matrix of being.

So it is within the Tree of Life. Each sephirah embodies a different aspect of the same creative energy. When we speak of Malkuth, we refer to this energy as the dense patterns of material found all about us—in speaking of Kether, we refer to the least tangible energies with which we may become acquainted. Remember, though, that they are both manifestations of the same force.

If we accept the theory that we are microcosms of the Macrocosm, it follows that this theoretical structure of Cosmos also finds its counterpart within ourselves. Just as there is a universal Kether, there is also a personal Kether, and so on. And if the Tree exists within ourselves, as it does in the Universe, then it must be a living, breathing force; even the title "Tree of Life" implies a vast life-form that bridges sky and earth. Once, this philosophy was strictly an oral tradition. A pupil would learn the names of the sephiroth and paths from a master. Having memorized these, the correspondences and meditation techniques could be practiced until the Tree took life within the student's soul—he could move branch by branch with ease. The wide availability of printed material today has made the master/student relationship almost obsolete; perhaps this is not the best thing that could have happened to the Qabalah. For until the basics of this glyph are committed to memory, until the Tree has taken firm root in not just the mind, but the soul, we can never truly master its magick.

It is with these thoughts in mind that we shall begin our work, and our exploration of Creation. Like a physical tree, the Tree of Life produces seeds that are sent out upon the four winds until they land in fertile soil. Each of us contains a seed, the essence of this Tree within us, our own divine spark. As we are microcosms of the Macrocosm, each of us mirrors the processes of the Universe. If we accept that Qabalah somehow portrays the mechanics of all creation, we must also accept that Qabalah can teach us about our own existence as divine beings, and open us to the power that is our source.

This chapter is meant to be one exercise in opening to the powers of the Tree of Life. We shall create our own diagram of the Tree as we learn the meanings of each sephiroth; likewise, we shall create a magickal diagram within our energy fields, inviting the powers of the sephiroth to flow throughout our bodies.

For these exercises we will need a large piece of white poster board, markers in a variety of colors, and the familar ritual tools/equipment. Figure 3:1 shows the placement of the sephiroth on the human body to facilitate visualizations. For the exercises in this chapter, it will not be necessary to cast a formal circle; a grounding and centering exercise will be used to facilitate that. If, however, you feel full ritual is necessary, feel free to add it.

It cannot be emphasized enough that Qabalah must be tended to as if it were a physical tree. It needs to be planted in fertile soil (body/psyche), given sun and rain (our thoughts/emotions), and tender care if it is to grow from a seed to a healthy adult. One of the beliefs is that when the Tree takes root within the soul, Mezla begins to flow—a spiritual influence that descends from Kether to Malkuth, enlivening the Tree. Once we open up to this spiritual influence, things happen: we become filled with light, life, and inspiration. New knowledge wells up from within and we begin to know things intuitively. It's as if the universe itself becomes our master and teacher, and each new influx of Mezla brings a river of knowledge.

Before beginning to plant the Tree, we will learn a simple grounding and centering exercise to take the place of our more complex circle casting; this exercise is called the Qabalistic Cross.

The Qabalistic Cross, Part I

We have learned that our consciousness expands, melds, and merges with our perceptions. Only our reality agreement indulges in a feeling of separation and seclusion. Centered in the body, we experience life through the limitation of the physical senses. Through our Qabalistic rituals, we have learned to experience more of our consciousness. We have expanded our awareness. In altering consciousness, we have reached out from the body to experience the world around us as an extension of ourselves. Until now, we have worked to sense how the body fits into this pattern. Since we have centered our consciousness within it, we worked using it as our center. Hopefully, we have become accustomed to our new perceptions of reality from the physical body—now we shall begin to perceive this reality through the astral counterpart of the physical, called the Body of Light.

Moving about our daily affairs, our consciousness is centered in the physical, yet we also operate within the astral body. It is anchored within, and permeates, the physical body. At night, however, as we descend into the land of dreams, the physical body becomes still while the Body of Light is freed from its boundaries—whenever we move, talk, or think in the dream world, it is all done from our consciousness centered within the astral body. This form is made of an energy less tangible than that of the physical; hence, to the physical eye, it is imperceptible. Yet its reality is as strong and solid within its own world as that of the physical.

Our astral bodies are more responsive and malleable to our thoughts. Once centered within it, we merely will ourselves to move, and we move. Think about flying, and flight becomes possible. In the realm of dreams, which exist on the astral planes, any "material" design that we encounter can be modified by our thoughts. It is with this premise that we begin our exercise.

Although the Qabalistic Cross, and the remaining exercises in this chapter, may be done without any special ritual equipment, it should not be omitted due to laziness. We are beginning to work with levels of consciousness referred to as the subconscious: remember from Chapter One that this aspect of ourselves speaks in symbols and metaphor. Therefore, it only adds to the total experience if the Witch's altar is set up with candles, incense, and elemental tools. As a channel for psychic energy, the athame may be held in the power hand during these exercises. The whole ritual helps to impart a charge to the tools.

Once your ritual area is prepared, play some soft, soothing music as an aid to concentration. Light the candles and incense, and stand facing the East. Begin to sink into the awareness of patterns around yourself; close your eyes and relax. Begin to slow your breathing.

After becoming comfortable in your breathing and stance, begin to imagine that your body is becoming larger. As you inhale, imagine your width expanding; as you exhale, imagine your height increasing. Continue these repetitions, imagining that your astral body slips through the boundaries of the room. Watch the horizon shrink into the distance as you increase in stature. Continue this visualization until the Earth is a sphere the size of a soft ball below your feet, and your head towers above the stars. Realize that your true consciousness contains all space.

About six inches above your head, a bright white ball of light forms. This is Kether. Reach up with your athame, touch this ball with its tip, and then bring the athame down to touch your forehead. In doing this, a shaft of white light descends to touch the crown of your head. Vibrate the word "Atoh" (Ahh-tow).

Now, bring the athame down the front of your body, touching the sternum. The shaft of light should descend with the athame. Although you stop the athame at the sternum, the light should continue down to the feet, forming another sphere of light. Vibrate "Malkuth" (Mall-kooth).

The simple beginning of the Qabalistic Cross serves two functions; as we visualize our body of light expanding throughout space, we increase our consciousness and awareness of self as a divine organism, an entity that transcends time and space. We imagine ourselves growing, and our consciousness follows suit until our minds can dwell on the fact that we encompass all creation. As we establish Kether

PLANTING THE TREE

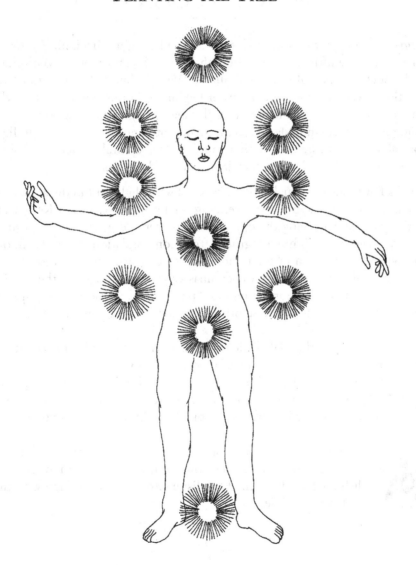

Figure 3:1

within this visualization, we emphasize that no matter how large or all-encompassing our awareness seems, there are always those parts of self that are beyond total comprehension—the eternal, immortal spark that overshadows us in our present incarnation. The light of Kether, however, is sent down into ourselves, symbolically reaching the Earth, which has taken its place at the base of our feet as Malkuth. This does not assert that the physical is subservient to the light, rather it emphasizes that it is the result of the primal forces of creation. We bring the light of higher consciousness into our physical beings, illuminating us as it progresses.

The opening of this exercise, then, has become a blessing of the physical kingdom, the Earth, and an invocation to our higher selves, the God/dess, to come and reside in the physical body. Once completed, we may move onto the second part of our exercise.

The Qabalistic Cross, Part II

Imagine that on your right shoulder, a white ball of light is beginning to form. This is the area of the fifth sephirah, Geburah, within the human aura. With the power hand, touch this ball of light and vibrate "Ve – Geburah," which translates into "and the power." Feel a surge of power beginning in this sphere, and slowly draw your right hand across your breast until a shaft of light travels across your breast, ending in your left shoulder. Here, it grows into another ball of white light, the sephirah known as Chesed. Another name for this sephirah is Gedulah. Vibrate the words "Ve – Gedulah," which translates into "and the mercy."

Spend a few moments visualizing the cross of white light within the aura. Mentally, once more trace the above steps, sending the healing energies of Kether into the Earth, and then balancing the opposites of power and mercy within your energy field. As the cross of light strengthens from contemplation, another ball of white light will begin to form in the region of the heart; we know this to be Tifareth. Allow this light to grow, until it encompasses your body. Vibrate the words "Le – Olahm. So mote it be!" translating into "for all time. So mote it be!" Spend a few moments basking in this light before returning to normal consciousness.

As we practice the Qabalistic Cross exercise, we are blessing ourselves, and the Earth, with the divine power of God/dess; likewise, we work to balance the extremes within ourselves, filling our energy fields with the purifying power of Tifareth. A few moments each day with this exercise serves to increase our consciousness of divinity within, hallowing the world in which we move.

 Our work with the Tree of Life will be in steps corresponding with the veils of negative existence down to Malkuth. It is important to establish the light from the Qabalistic Cross before working with the Tree of Life each time.

Veils of Negative Existence, or In the Beginning Was the Mother

Our universe, the complete sum of all worlds discovered and undiscovered, is conceptualized as beginning from incomprehensible nothingness. Qabalah refers to these as the three veils of negative existence: Ain, Ain Soph, and Ain Soph Aur. Negative implies receptive and feminine, hence the early pictures from Egyptian culture of the Goddess Nuit, whose body is black like the night sky, arched throughout the universe. She is the Queen of all space, the nothingness from whose breasts pours the milky substance of the stars. It is interesting to note that modern astronomers theorize the universe is curved and oval; travel far enough out into space and you eventually arrive back at your starting point. To quote from the faery tradition:

> *Alone, awesome, complete within herself. The Goddess. She whose awesome name cannot be spoken floated in the abyss of outer darkness before the beginning of all things.*

In a sense, Ain does not exist; it is no-thing. The reality of an anti-existence baffles the mind, and the closest we can come to its realization is to imagine a vacuum. This, however, is not an adequate visualization; a vacuum implies the existence of something removed from it. Obviously, that something cannot exist in the nothingness before all creation. Ain is an eternal and boundless reality on which supposition is impossible, since it transcends intellect and intuition. What is known is named: to name the ultimate is to imply limitation. Ain must be limitless!

The Veils of Negative Existence

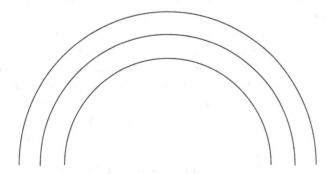

In the Beginning Was the Mother

KETHER
"The Crown"

Figure 3:2

Exercise One

Look at the three veils of negative existence shown in Figure 3:2. At the top part of your poster board in black magic marker (black implies negative/receptive), draw three dotted, curved lines. Label them, "In the Beginning Was the Mother."

Perform the Qabalistic Cross. Either standing, or lying on the floor, imagine a blackness beginning about nine inches above your head, extending into infinity. Think of the Goddess Nuit, arched out in black space, extending into infinity. Try to conceptualize anti-existence, absolute nothingness. Realize every image that comes to mind, no matter how abstract, cannot embody this concept truthfully. Allow the visualization to fade and return to awakening consciousness.

Kether

Ain quickly concentrates upon itself, becoming Ain Soph (infinity) and Ain Soph Aur (limitless light):

> *And as She gazed into the curved mirror of black space, She saw by her own radiant light her reflection and fell in love with it. She drew it forth by the power that was within Her and made love to Herself.*

For some unknown reason, the incomprehensible began to comprehend itself. Using its growing awareness of self, nothing spread into infinity, and created light energy throughout the void. In its attempt to conceive of self, Kether was created.

Kether is a difficult sphere to understand. Implying nothing concrete, it is still the creative potential upon which all draw. Some Qabalists have referred to it as the "Primum Mobile," the first swirlings of the universe. In itself it is not manifest; it is the cause of manifestation. Kether lies before force; it lies before form. The ideas of force and form have not yet been conceived.

The secret of Kether's powers lies in the magickal image—an Ancient Horned Mother in full view. This image implies two things. First, the secret to Kether's potential is found within the female archetype. The veils of negative existence have become self-aware; their reflection is opposite (nothing/something), but it is still a reflection. And what of the horns, a definite masculine symbol? Kether becomes the first sephirah of the Middle Pillar, implying balance between extremes. It receives the flow of energies reflected from Ain, definitely a negative polarity as this implies reception. But unless these powers are distilled and projected to the rest of the Tree, creation cannot occur. Thus, the receptive powers are balanced by the projective.

Yet these powers are balanced within the Mother. In Chapter One, I stated that Qabalah taught that the interplay of energies in the Universe began with the Mother and end with Her (Ain – Malkuth). Although balance is achieved between male and female archetypes, it is She who holds sway in what is to be. The interplay of energies between Ain/Kether is where we first see that principle at work. The male is alien to the original creative powers; he is seen only as a spiritual potential within a spiritual manifestation. It is not until the ideas of force and form are created that the masculine energy emerges as separate from the feminine.

To sum up, Kether was created in an act of self-love by the unknowable; the type of divine love in which physical union is but a pale shadow. The act of union between these reflections creates a swift, violent energy (a divine orgasm, if you will), simultaneously bringing the rest of the Tree into being.

Their ecstasy burst forth in a single song of all that was, is, and ever shall be, and with that song came motion, waves that poured outward and became all the spheres and circles of all the worlds. The Goddess became filled with love, swollen with love, and She gave birth to a rain of bright spirits that filled the worlds and became all things.

Swelling and overflowing with divine power, Kether filters and projects the energy into the next sephirah, Chokmah. It is here that the male emerges as a definite archetype, the primal idea of force. This is the divine son who becomes the lover, and the second Sephirah in the Tree of Life.

Exercise Two

If your poster board is white, use a gold marker to draw a circle just below the three veils; if the poster board is any other color, you will need some white paint to make the circle representing Kether. Once dry, around the top of the circle, label it "Kether," and below the circle, label it "The Crown" [Figure 3:3]. We shall label all sephiroth on our poster in this manner: Hebrew name and the English translation.

As we are labeling and drawing our sephiroth, we will be using what is called the Archangelic scale of color. Appendix One gives all attributions for the sephiroth. There are four color schemes for each sephiroth: deity, Archangelic, angelic, and planetary. The deity and angelic colors are positive scales, while the Archangelic and planetary colors are negative. The two most important are the deity and Archangelic, as they are the "power" vibrations of the sephiroth. The remaining two are used to gain entrance into the sephiroth while rising on the planes.

We shall use the Archangelic colors in our drawings and meditations. Being negative/receptive, they help draw the sephirotic energies to us as we meditate on the spheres. This serves to open us up to greater amounts of power as we progress in our meditations. Eventually, as we become proficient in our exercises, we can switch to the deity colors to project the sephirotic powers toward other goals; i.e., spell-casting, healing, etc.

KETHER

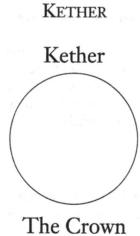

Kether

The Crown

Figure 3:3

Now, ground and center. Return to the visualization of the negative veils above you. Slowly, let the infinite blackness grow lighter; visualize it collapsing upon itself into a brilliant ball of white light about six inches above your head. This concentration of light should occur gradually, like a flashlight beam concentrating itself on a wall. This is Kether. Vibrate the word "Eheieh" (I am), and spend a few moments contemplating Kether and all it represents.

Chokmah

Kether, although it contains the potential for all existence, must divide into two concepts of force and form before it can lay down the "blueprints" for creation. If we as Witches look at the world around us and try to divide everything into two basic components, we think of polarity: Goddess and God, light and dark, positive and negative. So it is with the Tree of Life. The Great Mother who holds all potential within Herself gives birth to a "mutation," a realm of energy which is raw force (a masculine concept). Kether gives birth to Chokmah, the second sephirah on the Tree of Life. Its name means wisdom—this sphere is active.

Exactly how does this sphere come into being? The creation of this realm, as with the rest, can be explained by mathematics. The Ain, the nothingness, cannot be expressed and is written mathematically as 0. Zero is undefinable, but by some mysterious process creates a reflection of itself, Kether, which evolves zero into one. Zero by nature is undefinable; one, however, is definable. The defining of anything creates a duplicate or image of the thing defined. We create a duo of one and its reflection.

Let's carry the faery creation myth one step further. Ain sought to conceive of itself and created Kether (remember that once we name the limitless, we impress limitation upon it). Kether, in turn, by trying to see its reflection again in the mirror of space saw itself—the magickal reflection of no-thing was some-thing, and when some-thing tried to see its own reflection, it saw something back. The magickal reflection of a negative polarity becomes masculine.

> But in that great movement Miria was swept away, and as She moved out from the Goddess, She became more masculine.

Chokmah is a realm of pure spiritual force, the force that fertilizes the Mother so she may give birth to spiritual form. Here is the realm of the Great Consort in his forms as Cernunnos, Pan, Osiris, and Herne. These are not their aspects of vegetative or sexual Gods, rather these are the aspects of pure spiritual fertility of which physical sex is a pale shadow. Remember that the abstraction of physical fertility, the first primal, archetypal yearning for completion and dissolution within the female is being represented here. As a symbol of Chokmah, we find the image of the human penis.

Exercise Three

Referring to the chart in Figure 3:1, find sephirah two, Chokmah. Draw Chokmah in the Archangelic color of gray, and label it. The English translation of the Hebrew is "Wisdom."

The Tree of Life as it is pictured in our diagrams is a "snapshot" image. What is facing us to our right is actually the left; what is facing us to our left is actually our right. A photograph is an image of a person or thing in front of the photographer, as opposed to a mirror image, which refracts the light as we stand. So, the male pillar of which Chokmah is the head will be visualized on our left side, while the female pillar will be on our right.

Ground and center. Visualize Kether six inches above your head and vibrate "Eheieh." Contemplate the sephirah for a moment, then imagine a shaft of white light descending from Kether to an area above the left shoulder and parallel with the ears. From this shaft of light, a gray ball of light equal in circumference to Kether develops. This is Chokmah. Vibrate "YHVH" (Yod-Heh-Vau-Heh) and contemplate the meanings of the sphere.

Binah

Binah is the first sphere of the Goddess as we know Her. The unattainable made itself knowable, combining the dynamic aspects of Goddess and God as the receptive/projective balance based on feminine principles. That sphere, Kether, gave birth to the male principle in Chokmah, and to restore balance, Binah is born. Some Witches look at the Tree of Life and frown, for it appears that the God gives rise to the Goddess. This simply is not true! The sphere of Chokmah was birthed from Kether, a sphere that denotes balance within the female archetype. Each sephirah has three main functions: To absorb the energies from the sphere above it, to contain and balance the energies within itself, and to project these energies to the next sephirah.

Chokmah collects the energies of Kether, balances them within its own field of polarity, and sends them to Binah; this realm is created from Chokmah's yearning to be one with the Goddess again.

> But always desire draws the God back to the Goddess, so that he circles Her eternally, seeking to return in love.

This is love of self, for self is the creative energy of the Universe; it is the driving force. But pure force, represented by Chokmah, is wasted energy unless it is channeled to form. Light a match to gasoline and it blows up. Control the combustion in an engine and you create a machine capable of carrying you over great distances. Binah, a female sephirah, takes the energy of Chokmah within itself to give it form. In a sense, it is the divine engine of the universe.

Within Binah, we find the Great Mother in Her aspects of Aima (the fertile one), Mara (the Great Sea), and Ama (the dark one). To some, these may appear to be the triple Goddess of Maid, Mother, and Crone; however, those are aspects which properly belong in the sephirah known as Yesod. Binah is the first sphere given a planetary attribution, Saturn, which is the regulator of time. Within this attribution, we find keys to the triple Goddess found in Binah.

Time may be divided into three phases: the beginning, the middle, and the end. Remember that this sephirah denotes the first forms, albeit spiritual, given to creation. Aima, the Bright One, receives the energy from Chokmah and gives it form—She represents the physical beginning of all things, of time as we know it. Mara, the Great Sea, is the origin of life from which the first one-celled organisms evolved and grew into the complex forms we now know. And Ama, the dark one, represents the end of time when all that is physical evolves into something purely spiritual and rejoins the source. Here is the realm of the Great Mother as the Creatrix of Cosmos.

Exercise Four

Using Figure 3:1 as a guide, find the location of sephirah three, Binah. Draw it in the archangelic color of black, and label it. The English translation for the Hebrew is "understanding."

Next, connect the spheres of Kether, Chokmah, and Binah with three black lines, as in Figure 3:1. This completes the three Supernals in our chart.

Ground and center. Begin with the visualizations for Kether and Chokmah; once done, visualize a shaft of white light from Kether and one from Chokmah moving out and connecting in an area above the right shoulder and level with the right ear. From these two shafts of light, a black sphere equal to the rest in diameter grows. This is Binah. Vibrate "YHVH ELOHIM" (yod-heh-vau-heh ay-low-eem), contemplating the meanings of the sphere.

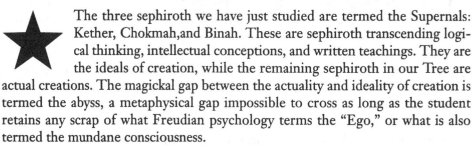 The three sephiroth we have just studied are termed the Supernals: Kether, Chokmah, and Binah. These are sephiroth transcending logical thinking, intellectual conceptions, and written teachings. They are the ideals of creation, while the remaining sephiroth in our Tree are actual creations. The magickal gap between the actuality and ideality of creation is termed the abyss, a metaphysical gap impossible to cross as long as the student retains any scrap of what Freudian psychology terms the "Ego," or what is also termed the mundane consciousness.

Mundane consciousness is the aspect with which we are most familiar; it contains our thoughts, ideas, feelings, and opinions. It is the aspect of ourselves that is continually assertive, and the part of ourselves which must be told to be silent for a time if we are to enter the altered states needed to work magick. To cross the abyss of actuality to the realm of the Supernals, all but the innermost divine self must be shed, lest it be destroyed in the darkness and seeming chaos of the abyss. I say seeming, for to the rational mind, anything that cannot be rationalized seems to be chaos. So the question arises: how may we work with the Supernals, or logically assume that they exist?

Logically, we cannot assume that the Supernals exist. This is one of the great questions that philosophers, Qabalists, Witches, and metaphysical theorists have struggled with since the dawn of time. We know that something began this universe and all the worlds it contains, seen and unseen. Basing the inner workings of the unseen realms on what we know of the physical, and then testing our hypothesis against our own growing inner awareness, we learn more of the less tangible realms. As hypothesis becomes proven magickal theory, we reach further and create more hypotheses about that which still lies beyond our grasp.

Knowing we are microcosms of the Macrocosm, mirrors of creation, we can assume that our spiritual makeup somehow suggests the spiritual makeup of Cosmos. We may not be able to travel in spirit to the Macrocosmic Kether, but by investigating our own internal/spiritual makeup, we can reach the first part of self which asserts "I am," our divine spark that begins the process of incarnation. By studying ourselves objectively, we gain a greater understanding of the world around us.

The fourth through ninth sephiroth on the Tree of Life are divided into two worlds: Briah, the World of Creation, and Yetzirah, the World of Formation. The three Supernals of the Tree represent the initial "I am," the Goddess becoming self-aware. Yearning to learn of Herself, desiring to find completion within Herself, She recreated Herself by Her own power. This sets up a domino effect: the law of inertia, stating an object (energy) in motion tends to stay in motion, sends this energy spiraling throughout Cosmos. As it expands, it changes; it recombines within itself. Moving out from the center of the Source, it changes its vibratory rate—it becomes something new. This subtle change, this evolution of power, creates the rest of Cosmos.

The Supernals represent the initial impulse of the Goddess to create, but this impulse alone is useless. The desire to create must be followed by the act of creation—ideas must pass through the abyss of formlessness and into the realm of construction. This building of forms begins in the world of Briah, and finds structure in Yetzirah before the final creation appears in Assiah. This molding of ideas is referred to as the Sephiroth Habinyon—the Potencies of Construction.

Beginning with Chesed and ending in Tifareth, we find the three basic building blocks of energy being created. The world of Briah mirrors the world of Atziluth: the abyss of formlessness repeats the initial becoming aware of the Goddess. Remember that the color scheme of Atziluth was white, gray, and black. These vibrations represent the actions of Atziluth. As these energies are reflected in Briah, we find that they become yellow, blue, and red; these are the three primary colors from which all others are created. Briah lays down the basic vibrations for all creation. The idea to create generated by the three Supernals is put into action, and becomes the first forms birthed by Binah with the force of Chokmah. We begin our study of this world with the next sephirah on the Tree of Life, which is also the first sphere of Briah—Chesed.

Chesed

As we enter the world of Creation, we encounter the sephirah Chesed, or Mercy. To restate, the unknowable feminine forces (Ain) became known, concentrating in the first sephirah of Kether. Originally containing all possibilities within Herself, the Goddess divided Her energy into two different forms, Chokmah and Binah, masculine and feminine energy, so that She could express Her existence. This primal division of self began motion, and great waves of energy washed throughout the infinite void of space. As that energy traveled away from the newly evolved forms of the God/dess, it coalesced into new forms. The ideal became actual. Between these two concepts lies the abyss, which is a gap between actualization and concentration. It is within this abyss that the intangible forces evolve into tangible concentrations: the first form manifested is Chesed. Since it all began in love, it seems logical that our first created form beyond the abyss would deal with love.

Chesed is the fourth sephirah of the Tree of Life, the first sphere in the world of Briah (creation), and the second emanation included in the masculine pillar. Although outwardly masculine, we find the feminine element of water as within this realm. This should not surprise us, for no matter what outward polarity a sephirah displays, it must contain some feminine aspect within to absorb the energies of the sephirah before it. Likewise, those sephiroth on the feminine pillar must contain an essence of the masculine if it is to project its energy into the next realm.

As Chesed emanates from Binah (understanding), it forms the perfect compliment and the next step in our faery creation myth:

First, She became the Blue God, the gentle, laughing God of love.

From this myth, we have learned that love is the force binding and controlling creation; love for self by self began the first processes that formed our world. This is not, however, love in the conventional sexual sense—that is a later concept. This is the unconditional love of acceptance that we speak of in our initiation. Perfect love and perfect trust, love that knows no boundaries, love that emerges from perfect understanding (Binah's concept) of other races, religions, creeds, and preferences. We preach it; we emote it; we rationalize it. Few but the highest souls can practice it. Emanating from Binah, Understanding, the two realms are inseparable. There cannot be love without understanding, nor can we have understanding without love.

The love of Chesed comes from a realization that we are all one; we are all God and Goddess. Emerging from this sphere, this love gives us the ability to see beyond human limitation and into the realms past Chesed. It gives us the power to see beyond the human layers, for the realm of Chesed is beyond that which we see when we look at another; it is one of the deeper levels of awareness, and one of the levels that connects us all. As we reach this sphere in our journey, we achieve the power to free ourselves from the wheel of existence, becoming one of the masters who has left this realm by the force of his or her own karma to rejoin the source of Creation.

So within its realm, we find the "Hall of Masters" or "Sphere of the Adepts." These are evolved souls who have come to understand and practice true, unconditional love. Here we find those who no longer need to incarnate, who have shed the Freudian Ego and are ready to merge with the Supernals beyond the abyss; yet they stay close to humanity, guiding us beyond the veils of physical existence.

We find a multitude of Gods within this sphere: Poseidon, Jupiter, Zeus, and Indra are placed here. Poseidon belongs to this realm, for he is the God of the seas. Water, a feminine element, rules the workings of this realm. Jupiter exists in his aspects as God of rains, storms, and thunder. Indra is here as the lord of fire and lightning. Our own aspect of the God, the Blue God, is here, for Chesed is the realm that speaks of pure, divine love.

Other attributions of Chesed are the planet Jupiter, as the beneficent planet of expansion. The angelic powers are called the Chasmalim, Brilliant Ones, and are led by Tzadkiel, Archangel of Chesed. These are the entities helpful for those who suffer from instability of any kind, whether it be physical, emotional, or spiritual. The planetary and angelic powers work together to carry and expand the love and light throughout created Cosmos.

Exercise Five

Find sephirah four, Chesed, on Figure 3:1. Draw the sphere on your diagram in the Archangelic color of blue and label it. The English translation of Chesed is "Mercy." Draw the path from Chokmah to Chesed.

Perform the Qabalistic Cross. Go through the visualizations of each of the previous sephiroth with their vibrations. Next, imagine a white shaft of light descending from Chokmah (the ball of light even with the left ear) down to the left shoulder. There, it expands into a brilliant blue ball of light. Vibrate "El" (sounds like the English letter L), and meditate on the meanings of Chesed.

Geburah

Chesed sends its energy into Geburah, which is a reflection of Binah. This sephiroth is the fifth on the Tree of Life; paired with its opposite, Chesed, the two represent the forces of expansion and contraction, and centripetal and centrifugal force. Being on the feminine pillar, that of severity, it is negative in polarity. However, most of its attributions are male and vigorous. Notice that in Chesed, most of the attributions were feminine, although that sephirah was on the masculine pillar. Throughout this book I have emphasized the necessity for equilibrium on the Tree of Life; the closer we come to form without adding matter, the more obvious this becomes.

At first glance this sphere may seem an aberration in our system, for the name Geburah translates into Might, and it is also sometimes called "Pachad," or fear. Its symbols are those of warriors and war: the planet Mars, the sword, spear, scourge, and burn find their homes in this realm. Symbolically, they speak of death, destruction, and bloodshed. Even the magickal image is dedicated to the malefic side of nature—a mighty warrior queen. In the Tree of Life, how can such an image be reconciled with the rest of the sephiroth?

Perhaps the question should be, how can the Tree of Life not contain these images? Witchcraft draws upon the patterns of nature, often called the law of polarity. Every force, every form, all manifestations of energy have an opposite in nature. We worship a Goddess and a God; we follow the patterns of light and dark throughout the natural cycle. Sheltered from the primal patterns of the Earth through our modern living, however, Witches often develop a saccharine view of Cosmos. There is love, and there is light, and there is the Great Mother who dotes upon her hidden children. This has become the underlying belief of many traditions of the modern Craft. But the truth is that the Great Mother is not a doter, She is constantly creating and in motion. Sometimes, to create, one must also destroy.

Within the realm of Geburah, we find the raw, primal powers of creation and dissolution; both are sustained through the image of strength and destruction. To a civilized soul, these powers might seem frightening. In truth, we deal with the functions of Geburah on a daily basis—these destructive forces serve to sustain our physical existence. As we consume food, we must first realize that something had to die, give its own life in order to feed our own. To reduce the environmental and ethical harm, some of us may choose to become vegetarians. This, however, still takes life, and as Witches we realize that all living forms contain some level of sentience. Digestive juices within the body must first destroy the physical structures of food before we can absorb its nutrients. Fighting to maintain homeostasis, the body's immune system is ever vigilant against intruding microbes; at the first sign of infection, an internal war is waged against the offenders. Being alive implies being at war with the forces that would intrude and destroy our own fleeting patterns.

Examining the greater cycles of nature, we also find the Geburic powers at work. Natural disasters occur on an almost daily basis: earthquakes, hurricanes, tornadoes, storms, and diseases are all part of the Earth's cleansing and creative powers. Within her vast resources, the planet contains a system of checks and balances for the ecosystem. Diseases unchecked can wipe out large numbers of humans and animals, as can the plethora of natural disasters. Natural wildfires can quickly transform aging forests and plains into fertile soil, which spawn newer and healthier habitats over a period of decades. Our most breathtaking landscapes, mountain ranges, valleys, and plains were formed by centuries of upheaval in the land masses.

It is only when humans, in their limited view of Cosmos, interfere or accelerate the Geburic functions of nature that these things become unbalanced. We over-
populate a given area, depleting natural resources, and then move into the outlying
wild places, depleting those areas at an alarming rate. In areas that have high risks
for natural disasters—coastal areas, geographic fault lines, and wildfire zones—we
live without taking proper precautions. When nature begins her cleansing process,
we suffer needlessly in our unprepared state, and then view the cycle as an unfair
catastrophe. We must remember that destruction is an important part of the natural
cycle, balancing the more joyous periods of creation. One without the other results
in an unbalanced world—by our basic beliefs as Witches, we need to view the powers of Geburah as the necessary, balancing aspect to the Great Mother of Creation.

As the world's ecosystem is thrown increasingly off balance, as humanity care-
lessly destroys vast sections of the planet, as pollution increases at an alarming rate,
the Earth must work ceaselessly to correct the imbalances. Envision the planet as a
living, evolving entity in its own right, with an organic structure mimicking our
own. For a moment, try to imagine that we are to the Earth what the helpful bac-
teria in our bodies are to us—residents in a larger, living system. As long as each
keeps its rightful place, there is harmony without and health within. But when the
microbes in our body increase at an alarming rate, when they overstep their boundaries into more delicate body systems, when their populations increase to a size
capable of poisoning the greater life that they inhabit, our bodies begin a seek-and-
destroy process. So it is with the Earth. As humanity increasingly endangers the
health and harmony of the ecosystem, nature's Geburic immune system must begin
to work harder. This means more "disasters" and more natural "destruction"
within the system. Until the Earth has restored its health and harmony, these disasters and diseases will continue to increase at alarming rates.

So Geburah, as frightening as it may seem, is yet another aspect of nature and
creation. To create new things, the old must be broken down, destroyed, to make
way for the new forms. To insure health on all levels, dangerous patterns must be
broken by the natural decay cycles. Geburah, then, is the balancing, cleansing
power of Cosmos.

Exercise Six

Locate the fifth sephirah, Geburah, on the Tree of Life [Figure 3:1] and draw it in
red on your diagram. Using black, draw the path from Binah to Geburah, and then
from Chesed to Geburah. Label the sephiroth in English ("Might") and Hebrew.

Now, perform the Qabalistic Cross. Go through the visualizations and vibrations
of the previous sephiroth until you arrive at Chesed. Imagine a line of white light
flowing from Chesed to the right shoulder; simultaneously, visualize a shaft of light
descending from Binah to the right shoulder. When they meet, they form a ball of
red light—this is Geburah. Vibrate "Elohim Gibor" (ay-low-eem gee-bor-rah) and
meditate on the sphere's meanings.

Tifareth

For Witches, this is possibly the most difficult sephirah to understand, for although
its name implies harmony and it is within the Middle Pillar of balance, its planet is
the Sun. A strong, masculine symbol in a sphere that is central to the Tree throws

a lot of us off; we are used to seeing the female essence as being the central figure, while the male is that which revolves around Her. Qabalah is not meant to be a simple study, and sometimes it takes a lot of study to get to its core. First, remember that the Tree of Life makes up the whole system—to analyze any one part properly we must understand how it relates to the rest.

First, let us return to Kether, the Crown, and the first swirlings of creation. Although Kether lies within the Middle Pillar, it too is openly feminine; it receives the initial energies of the Ain, embodies and gestates them, then gives birth to the rest of the Tree of Life. Obviously, these are functions of the female—receiving the active principle and birthing new life. The balance comes from Kether's job as a mediator; it receives energy, then projects that energy into the rest of the Tree.

In Qabalah, Tifareth is often referred to as the "Lesser Countenance," a reflection of Kether, the "Greater Countenance." Physically, reflections are opposites, as what was right becomes left, and vice versa. In magick, reflections appear as opposites also: the nothing is reflected as something, and feminine becomes masculine. Esoteric science teaches that our Sun receives its light and energy from another source; this mirrors the concept that the realm of Tifareth receives its powers from the realm of Kether.

As the sphere of the Sun, Tifareth is host to the multitudes of Sun Gods: the Egyptian Ra, Greek Apollo, and Italian Lucifer; however, most people are unaware that there are a multitude of Sun Goddesses also. Among them are Amaterasu (Japanese), Nahar (Syrian), and Yhi (Australian aboriginal). In their respective pantheons, none of these Goddesses are minor; they are the Great Mothers of their peoples. These, and the Sun Goddesses of other peoples, rightfully belong in this sphere with their male counterparts.

So, we are left with a sphere that reflects the powers of Kether, thus giving it a predominately positive (masculine) quality. Its image is that of a sacrificed God. Somewhere within these images we are to find balance and harmony. The question is—where?

My first teacher and High Priestess, Lady Cassandra, summed up the mysteries of the Goddess as the "Mysteries of the Blood."

> *There is the menstruating Maiden, who belongs to Herself; there is the gestating Mother, who belongs to the life-force within; and the bleeding Birth-Mother, who belongs to the life-force without. Serving them both as teacher and midwife is the Crone Goddess, who has beheld and experienced the mysteries since the beginning of time. The Goddess, the Creatrix of all things, bleeds from the womb to serve the life-force. And if He is to serve the life-force, if He is to be of service to Her, the God must shed his blood. He can only bleed from the heart and sacrifice Himself so that all may live.*

It is within those words that we find the balancing power of Tifareth. It mirrors Kether, and simultaneously receives the powers of the worlds of Atziluth and Briah. To serve the life-force, to impregnate the Mother on spiritual realms, to give up the spiritual essence of blood which nourishes and perpetuates the world, He must sacrifice Himself. Barren of the blood mysteries, the bleeding from the womb, He must truly bleed from the heart if life is to continue. Here is the Horned God in his aspects of God of the hunt, the sacred stag who allows himself to be killed to feed his people. We also find the vegetative Gods here—the Oak King and Holly King—however, these are their aspects as the sacrificial Consorts to the Earth Mother. And finally, every Sun God of the lesser pantheons belongs here not just because of His solar attribution, but because, in some traditions of the Craft, the Sun is said to die at Lammas, becoming another aspect of the Horned God, the Lord of Death. Also, we find the God of our Craft in His aspect as Sacred Son; the God who has just been sacrificed is reborn as the Mother's future consort. Tifareth represents the eternal cycle of death and rebirth, as seen in the Wheel of the Year, the Sabbats.

On a more personal level, Tifareth teaches us all, men and women, the greatest of all truths: if we are to serve the life-force here on Earth, that service includes making sacrifices of self, just as the Horned One sacrifices Himself for us. The world is presently in a bad state of affairs (pollution, starvation, greenhouse effect, etc.). Obviously, we can no longer blame the problems on someones else, whether that someone is our neighbor, government, or a foreign country. We must each sacrifice our time, our energies, whether they be magickal or physical, to putting things right—in harmony—the way they are supposed to be. To put ourselves in touch with this energy, the spirit of true sacrifice, Tifareth gives us two images: a divine child and a sacrificed God.

Exercise Seven

Locate Tifareth on Figure 3:1, and using the color yellow, draw it on your own diagram. Label it in Hebrew and in English (Harmony). Draw the paths in dotted black lines from Binah, Chokmah, Kether, Chesed, and Geburah to Tifareth. As Tifareth harmonizes the energies from all these spheres, take a few moments to contemplate the intersecting energies.

Next, perform the Qabalistic Cross. Starting with Kether and ending with Geburah, contemplate each sphere in turn, vibrating the name of power, and briefly contemplating its meaning. Allow the shaft of light to descend to the heart area.

For example, while contemplating Kether as balance within the female archetype, allow the shaft of light to descend to the heart area. Next, contemplate Chokmah as the supernal father while a shaft of light descends to the heart area, and so on. Once the five shafts of light have met in the heart, allow a yellow ball of light to grow from their intersection. This is Tifareth, the sphere of Harmony. Vibrate "IAO" (eee-aah-ooh) and contemplate its meanings.

Netzach

As we enter Netzach, we enter the world of Yetzirah, which we also call the world of Formation. The first three sephiroth, the Supernals, were the initial impulse to create; the unknowable and incomprehensible decided to know and conceive of itself. As it began to expand and coalesce throughout cosmos, forming the initial idea to create, it moved into Briah and began to develop the creative ideas. Archetypes and patterns were laid in what I like to refer to as the "sacred brainstorm." Now, as we move into the world of Yetzirah, we see foundations being laid upon which the physical realm is built; patterns are set into a substance referred to as the astral light. This light itself rightfully belongs to Yesod and the sphere of the moon; the sephiroth of Netzach and Hod reflect the final merging of opposites before they are imprinted into that light. Within the sphere of Netzach, we shall see the concept of the male being merged into the concept of the female.

Netzach is influenced by the planet Venus, ruling three basic things: love, victory, and the harvest. Within Netzach we find a multitude of Goddesses: Aphrodite, Venus, Psyche, and the Sacred Muse; these, however, are only Goddesses of love and inspiration. We also find the Goddess in her aspect as Lady of the harvest: Haathor, the Egyptian Goddess of the harvest whose sacred animal is the cow. Isis is here, too, presiding over the seeds scattered into the fertile earth. But, being a predominately male sephiroth, we also find the Gods of the harvest and of love: Eros, Cupid (a derivation of Eros), and the Horned One in his aspect of the warring twins, the Oak and Holly King. We saw these two earlier within Tifareth, the home of the sacrificed Gods. They belong here, too, in their aspects as God of the harvest.

> *And then She became the Green God, vine covered, rooted in the Earth, the spirit of all growing things.*

Call Him Green God, Cernunnos, Baal, or the Vegetative God, it is all the same. Like the Great Mother, the Horned Lord has many faces; each aspect has its place on the Tree of Life. But remember that the harvest speaks of more than the agricultural season. We harvest whatever we sow, whether it be on physical or spiritual planes. Here the concept is that we create, we plant, and the Horned One watches over the seeds that we sow within the Mother, tending and caring for them as they spring from Her womb, awaiting the time when they shall be harvested. In this realm He becomes the protector for growing things. When they are actually harvested, He is sacrificed with them, and it is then that He moves to his aspect as the sacrificed God in Tifareth. He is the rain which comes to refresh and replenish; he is the crop which springs from the womb. Within Netzach, we touch the energies responsible for nurturing life and growth.

Exercise Eight

Begin by locating Netzach on Figure 3:1; draw it in your diagram in the Archangelic color of emerald green. The title Netzach translates into "Victory." Label the sephiroth in both the Hebrew and the English. Two paths should be drawn on the diagram: one from Chesed into Netzach, and one from Tifareth into Netzach.

Ground and center. Starting with Kether, slowly go through all previous visualizations of the sephiroth and vibrations of the words of power. After completing those for Tifareth, pause for a moment. Will two shafts of white light to descend from both Chesed and Tifareth, intersecting at a point corresponding to the left hip. Here an emerald green ball of light forms, growing in intensity. This is Netzach. Vibrate the name "YHVH Tzabaoth" (yod-heh-vau-heh tah-zah-bay-oh-thah), and contemplate the meaning of the sphere.

Hod

Earlier, I stated that the closer we come to physical form (Assiah) without adding matter, the need for balance between polarities would become more obvious. This is openly expressed in the world of Yetzirah between Netzach and Hod. When studied together, they represent physical form (Hod) and physical force (Netzach), expansion and contraction, science and creativity. Before entering these realms, we learned how the Goddess became self-aware and self-impregnated with the life-force. Her energy spiraled and traveled in great tidal waves of force throughout Cosmos, each energy swirl becoming a new manifestation of Self. Now, as She seeks to express Her existence and draw Self out of infinite energy, She must create vehicles for expressions. This creation occurs in the realm of Hod.

Created designs must be analyzed if they are to be brought into form. Force must be given a structured channel of operation lest it be scattered uselessly. Just as a writer cannot write without the rules of grammar, as an artist cannot paint without the rules of perspective and color, the Goddess cannot birth forms in the material world without the laws of nature. Hod is the sephirah dealing with natural law, patterns, and rhythms. Both the methods of making magick and the basis of the physical senses find their roots in this realm.

As the planetary attribution is Mercury, we may interpret Hod as containing the rational power of the mind. It is the part of self, and Cosmos, that keeps the creative ideals and urges from overwhelming material designs. It offers detachment and analysis of the creative urges, giving us safe space in which we may give reign to creative impulses. The great teacher Gods and Goddesses belong to this realm in their forms as instructors of mankind in magick, myth, mysticism, and the sciences: Hermes, Thoth, Mercury, Aradia, and Athena are some examples.

To experience the powers of these realms, seek out divine inspiration—create an idea, whether it be for a sculpture, essay, poem, or painting. Spend some time searching for inspiration, the initial idea or creative spark. This is the energy of Netzach at work in the psyche. Now, begin to plan the form for your idea—what materials, forms, metaphors, and analogies will you use to bring your creation to life? Will it express the message openly, or through the use of symbols? As you plan the act of creation, you are using the energies of Hod. Once you begin to outline, sketch, or prepare the "skeleton" upon which you shall create, you are beginning to experience the power of the next sephirah, Yesod—the Foundation of Cosmos.

Exercise Nine

Locate Hod in Figure 3:1; draw this in orange on your diagram. There are three paths which must be drawn: from Geburah to Hod, from Tifareth to Hod, and from Netzach to Hod. The Hebrew name translates into glory. Label the sephiroth with both the English and the Hebrew words.

Ground and center. Perform the visualizations/vibrations for each of the sephiroth, pausing in Netzach. Visualize three shafts of light descending from Geburah, Tifareth, and Netzach into an area corresponding to the right hip; this is the realm of Hod. Vibrate the name of power, "Elohim Tzabaoth" (ay-low-eem tah-zah-bay-oh-thah), and meditate on the meanings of this sphere.

Yesod

To complete our series of three triads, we move into the realm known as Yesod, the last sephirah before form. It is formed by the union of Hod and Netzach; the creative powers of Netzach and the formative powers of Hod result in the final forms that will manifest ultimately upon the physical plane. The creative powers and mental powers imprint themselves upon a substance called the astral light, a less tangible form of matter that is passive, reflecting the images of the planes above it.

As its planetary attribution, the moon symbolizes the light of the other realms being reflected here, much as it reflects the light of the sun. This astral light is a pervasive, moving, malleable force that permeates all of Cosmos, much as the energy of the Goddess enlivens all. If we follow the patterns set up by the Tree of Life, we see that Kether is a concentration of the limitless, unknowable nothing; Tifareth is a reflection of the light of Kether, channeling the unknowable energy into manageable forms; and Yesod catches the light of Tifareth, reflecting it into the most inaccessible chasms of Cosmos.

This astral light is the power with which we work as we cast our spells and set our thought forms to do their work. It is the stuff of dreams and thoughts, for as we will, it moves; it changes; it creates. The name Yesod translates into "the foundation"—this light, although easily bent to a desire, forms the structures upon which the material designs are built. In its eternally malleable state, it renders itself open to the desires of the realms that exist beyond its sphere, reflecting them into a form that matter can build upon. In its eternally flexible state, it forms the strongest of foundations for all things.

The traditional Maid, Mother, Crone of the Craft belongs to this sphere. We find Her moving with the tides of the moon and becoming young and old as it pleases Her. Within the Earth sphere we look to Her symbol in the sky, the moon, to invoke Her powers, but in the realm of Yesod She changes form and face as it pleases Her. Thus, by traveling to this realm in mind and spirit we may invoke the aid of any form needed, at any time. We also find the Horned God here as sexual consort, the form giving his power over to the Mother as She emerges from Maidenhood. The magnetic impulses that keep the Earth tides flowing smoothly throughout their eternal cycles are found to originate here, from the union of the two in a divine lovemaking upon which physical sex is based. Whenever we work with the fertility tides of Earth, or the changing tides of the moon, or the Horned One in his aspect as Consort and fertilizer of the Goddess, we are working with the powers of Yesod.

Exercise Ten

Referring to the chart in Figure 3:1, locate Yesod and draw it on your Tree of Life. The Archangelic color for this sephiroth is violet. In translating the Hebrew into English, we find that Yesod means "the foundation." Label your diagram in both the English and the Hebrew. There are three paths that must be drawn to Yesod: one from Tifareth, one from Hod, and one from Netzach.

Ground and center. Practice the visualizations/vibrations for all the spheres, pausing after completing Hod.

Visualize three shafts of white light descending to the genitals from Tifareth, Netzach, and Hod. From their intersection a violet ball of light begins to grow; this is the sphere of Yesod. Vibrate "Shaddai el-Chai" (Shah-die el-kie) several times, contemplating the meanings of this sphere.

Malkuth

At last She became the Horned God, the Hunter whose face is the ruddy sun and yet dark as Death. But always desire draws Him back toward the Goddess, so that He circles Her eternally, seeking to return in love.

Throughout our journey, we have examined the sephiroth and the patterns of Creation, analyzing the energies as they evolved into a myriad of forms. Each realm not only synthesized the energies of the previous sephiroth into something new, but new patterns of Goddess and God emerged from Cosmos—forms that were based upon Her initial thought, "I am!" (Kether). As the great, unknowable Mother conceived of Herself, as She sought to arise from the primordial chaos that defined Her pre-existence, She set in motion forces that scattered throughout infinity. Those forces, those yearnings, those sensual emanations eventually resulted in Her final form: Malkuth.

For two-thousand-plus years, we have believed in the lie propagated by patriarchal philosophies that matter is unholy; the flesh is evil and must be reviled and tortured into submission. If we are to be pure, if we are to attain salvation and godliness, we must rise above the evils of physical existence, enjoyment, sensuality, and all other physical sensations given to us by the flesh. But by its very structure, the Qabalah teaches us that these philosophies are lies. The structure of the Tree of Life finds completion in the world of Assiah, the sphere of Malkuth—the initial creative impulses are given flesh and matter as the energy finds its way into this world. If the end result of creation is the material world, it follows that this realm is the holiest, and most blessed, of all the realms.

Its outer workings may be obvious to us, as all that we do is centered in its realm; however, on more etheric levels, Malkuth is mysterious like its counterpart, Kether. Within Malkuth, the Goddess finds Her final emanation, the Horned God. By the law of polarity set up in Her quest for self-knowledge, She arrives at Her deepest core of self, Her own masculine seed of awareness. It mutates; it personifies; it becomes Him! The great satyr Pan, the woodland hunter Herne, and the horned lord of the animals Cernunnos, all obviously male, are still the Goddess in a self-devised mask. Like Her in Kether, they retain their horns. The nurturing, supporting, and birthing qualities of the feminine become externalized as the Earth, Gaia; the personification of force becomes hardened by the elements and bronzed by the sun. Exhibiting his wild, untamed qualities, his lower torso becomes furry and his hooves cloven like the wild beasts he guards.

Our hypothesis that the Horned God is merely the externalized forces of the Goddess' projective qualities is proven by his horns: they were first worn by the Goddess in Kether, when the only power existing was Hers. Drawing off Her own existence, She alone birthed the primal forces that created Cosmos, including the God. Throughout the Tree of Life we see that His power may only be invoked and used through Hers. The horns upon the God's head imply a deeper mystery: the knowledge of the womb. If we examine the interior of a woman's body, the passages that lead to the womb, the giver of life, appear as horns. They curve and branch out into the most sacred of spaces, giving us a map to follow to the inner sanctuary of power. Emerging from within Her core, having a positive map to the interior negative and receptive spaces of Her being, this power can only emerge as masculine if it is to be of use to Her.

To become one with the Goddess again, He must follow His horns into Her womb, descending back into his place of origin. He becomes one with Her; presiding within the womb of life, He also becomes the Lord of Death. The Goddess as Mother Earth supports all life; the Goddess as Horned Lord of Shadows becomes the passage of Death. In Her final act of self-seeking, She follows Herself by way of the Horned Passage; She descends into Her own darkness and interior spaces. There, She meets what She has become, merging once more into a unified whole that gives power back to the feminine, dark, and gestative powers of night.

Like Kether, Malkuth is both positive and negative. It is the Gate of Life, and the Gate of Death. It synthesizes all forces, forms, archetypes, and powers of the Tree of Life into one unified whole. Its final message to us is simple:

> *All began in love, all seeks to return in love. Love is the law, the teacher of wisdom, and the great revealer of mysteries.*

Exercise Eleven

Locate Malkuth on the Tree of Life and draw it on your diagram. To simplify the diagram, use the color black (balancing the white of Kether). In English, Malkuth translates into "the Kingdom." Label the sephiroth in both the Hebrew and the English. There are three paths which must be drawn in our diagram: one from Yesod to Malkuth, one from Netzach to Malkuth, and one from Hod to Malkuth.

Ground and center. Follow all the visualizations/vibrations for the sephiroth on the Tree of Life. Pause at Yesod, and imagine three shafts of light descending to the area of the feet: from Yesod, Hod, and Netzach. Visualize the sphere emerging from these paths in the color black. Vibrate the name of power, "Adonai ha-Aretz" (Ah-doe-nie hah-ah-rets), and contemplate the meanings of this sphere.

Now that we have traveled in thought through the Tree of Life, opening the corresponding centers of power in our own body, we may begin a more thorough study of the sephiroth, developing and strengthening the centers of power in our own consciousness. Like the methods of the Eastern meditation techniques, there are many ways in which we may use the sephiroth we have begun to develop, experiencing more of the power and heightened consciousness of the realms. In doing this, we will increase our own awareness of the higher realms, drawing greater amounts of power into our consciousness and our circle. Let us move on, then, to developing our new awareness of the Tree, strengthening the young sapling that we have planted in our souls.

CHAPTER FOUR

NOURISHING THE TREE

When we know the world as conjoined with ourselves; when we know the black earth as the womb and the symbol of Nuit—our Lady of the Starry Heavens, our mother of delight; the beautiful, glistening moon, giving us our body as a sylphan joy to us, or to steal it softly away—for she is the emblem of continual change and Artemis the celestial huntress; when we know that great golden lion god, Ra-Hoor-Khuit bestowing on us his warmth and nourishment, or else, like a red angry lion, confronting us with gleaming open jaws, then we may realize that the universe is a living organism of which we are an integral part.

—Israel Regardie
A Garden of Pomegranates, p. 146

To know, to dare, to will, and to keep silent.

—The four powers of the sphinx

Life in any form is fragile from the start; to grow, to become a source of independent strength, fleeting youth must be nourished and protected if it is to grow to adulthood. From the beginning, we began our study of the Qabalah with the thesis that it is a valid path within the Craft. True, it was the path unknown and less traveled, but from our first step we began to see similarities to our familiar Craft practices, and new areas of development complimenting the more well-known. So, we began to develop awareness of the Tree within. Comparing it to one of the traditional myths of creation, it sprouts before our eyes as a philosophy of life, something that grows and adapts to the environment in which it finds itself. Now, having planted the Tree within our soul, we move on to strengthening the Tree within, nourishing it so the form can provide us with greater consciousness, and thus, greater magickal power.

In the Craft, developing magickal consciousness and increasing magickal power are synonymous. To build power, we must become conscious of and within its realm of origin; likewise, as we develop our awareness of the subtle realms, we begin to generate more power within our psyche. What is needed, then, are methods to reinforce what we learned in the last chapter. We planted the Tree in our psyche, now we must work until it begins to grow and flourish within.

In developing awareness of the sephiroth and working to become active within their realms, we are opening up to greater avenues of magickal power. Think of the average soul who is unaware that magick exists, or perhaps has heard of it, but denies its existence. This person would not be able to cast the simplest spell, as denial of the magickal realms implies ignorance of their existence. But one whose consciousness has awakened to the realms of possibilities realizes that magick is real, yet without the developed consciousness of the magickal realms, still cannot cast the simplest spell.

So we spend time learning altered states of awareness. Once achieved, we use those states to search out centers of power within ourselves and the created Cosmos. Power begins to flow. As it does, it opens us to greater possibilities, which increases our awareness of the states needed to find that power. The developing of magickal consciousness, and the resulting flux of power, build upon each other; it becomes a magickal spiral, a cone of power, increasing in intensity as we progress. In the Craft, then, the development of magickal powers and magickal consciousness go hand in hand.

We need methods to reinforce what we learned in the previous chapter, ways of nourishing the Tree that we have planted in our souls. Already we have opened up to the possibility that magick exists, and that the Qabalah is a valid source to empower ourselves and our Witchcraft. Realizing this system provides a practical model for attaining our Source, the God/dess, and theorizing that we mirror the Macrocosm, we have implanted a seed of awareness within ourselves, growing our own Tree of Life in the soul. Now, this life-form must be nurtured if it is to grow stronger, become a sturdy Tree withstanding the harsh realities of mundane life.

As this Tree within us grows, we grow into greater awareness of the spiritual truth unfolding daily around us. Malkuth is a spiritual plane; the Earth is sacred and divine. Our bodies, our lives, our friends, and our families are spiritual emanations, worthy of hallowing. As we help the Tree implanted in our souls flourish, we reinforce the Light, Love, and Life growing within the world. Let us continue our work, and reclaim the mysteries for ourselves.

THE QABALISTIC MODEL OF HUMANITY

Since the acts of increasing magickal knowledge and power are one and the same, it follows that self-investigation and self-knowledge are prerequisites to the pursuit of magick. As Witches, we realize that magickal power permeates the Universe, and therefore, ourselves. Some of this power is channeled through use of the physical body: dancing, chanting, singing, etc. At times, however, the power flows through deeper levels of awareness. By using trance and meditation, we tap into the subconscious, bringing more primal stores of power to the surface. We need to remember the teachings of the ancient Greeks; aspirants who wanted to contact the ancient gods would travel to the temple of Delphi. Before entering, they saw the phrase "Know thyself." Entering the holiest of temples to learn the mysteries, they found themselves within a vast, empty room. Self-knowledge was the mystery implied.

Magick brings the more creative, intuitive parts of self into actualization. Modern psychology, still an infant science, also works with these deeper levels of self. During the process of therapy, a patient accidentally comes into contact with ancient Gods, Goddesses, archetypes, and sacred mandalas buried deep within his or her psyche. As an analytical science, psychology unintentionally explores the magickal parts of self that Witches intentionally use. If we examine the concepts of magick and psychology together, we find that they are two halves of the same whole, much as mind and body are not two separate aspects, but two connected divisions of self.

Using the Tree of Life as a guide to inner experience, we may divide our consciousness into several levels. These levels correspond to the sephiroth on the Tree of Life. They are the Guph, physical body, corresponding to Malkuth; the Nephesch, the astral double, which belongs to Yesod; the Ruach, the empirical Ego, emanating from Tifareth and the spheres encircling it; the Chiah, animus, belonging to Chokmah; the Neschamah, anima, that exists in Binah; and the Yechidah, eternal, immortal self, found in the sephirah known as Kether [See Figure 4:1].

We are most familiar with the Guph. This is the physical body, which the Qabalah regards as an impermanent structure existing in the midst of constant change. The body is never the same from one moment to the next. As we go about our daily routines, at any given second there are an estimated six trillion chemical reactions occurring within the body. These reactions constantly change our internal structures, our space, and our design. Within a year's time, 98% of the body is replaced with new atoms; in two years, the atoms from the previous cycle have been totally replaced. In the brief span of seven years, not only have the atoms been replaced more than three times within the body, the complete internal structure has been cleansed—old organs are made of new particles.

From our work in Chapter Two with the quantum mechanical views of reality, we realize that the material forms of our bodies are held together by some mysterious, invisible force that permeates our design. Indeed, with trillions of chemical reactions occurring at any given second, the structure of our consciousness is changing as I write this passage and as you read this passage. Because of the multitude of internal changes that have occurred since you began reading these words, you are not exactly the same biological structure that you were a few moments ago. But you are still you. Neither one of us has undergone a change in appearance, form, or identity. Something is holding the body in its present form—what can this something be?

For a moment, let's digress and make an analogy between the human makeup and a piece of fruit. Think back to Chapter One, Becoming Aware, Part II. We used a piece of citrus fruit for the exercise, becoming aware of its overall structure. Imagine that the fruit represents the human pattern: the skin is comparable to the physical shell that we call our bodies, while the internal parts represent the internal, spiritual components of consciousness. If we peel away the skin of a citrus fruit, the fruit does not change. Its lack of a shell does not change its shape, taste, smell, or nutritive value. It is merely a piece of fruit lacking its peel. What is within the skin, however, gives form to the outer shell. It keeps the fruit's basic structure relatively unchanged throughout its life. If we were to "peel" out of our bodies we would still retain the same consciousness, minus the physical body. Operating without the physical, we would find ourselves in the part of self termed the Nephesch.

In analyzing the Nephesch, which belongs to Yesod (the foundation), we find that it is divided into two aspects: tselem and prana. Witches know the tselem as the astral body, or body of light. It is contained within the physical structure, and while in the dream state, we use the astral body's senses to act, observe, and create our nocturnal adventures. Unfortunately, many have the misunderstanding that the tselem is based upon the physical body; in truth, it is the physical body that is based upon the tselem. In Chapter Three we learned of Yesod's function as the final sephirah before form. Receiving the influences of the sephiroth before it, the powers create an imprint in the astral light, forming the foundation upon which all else is built.

THE QABALISTIC MODEL OF HUMAN CONSCIOUSNESS

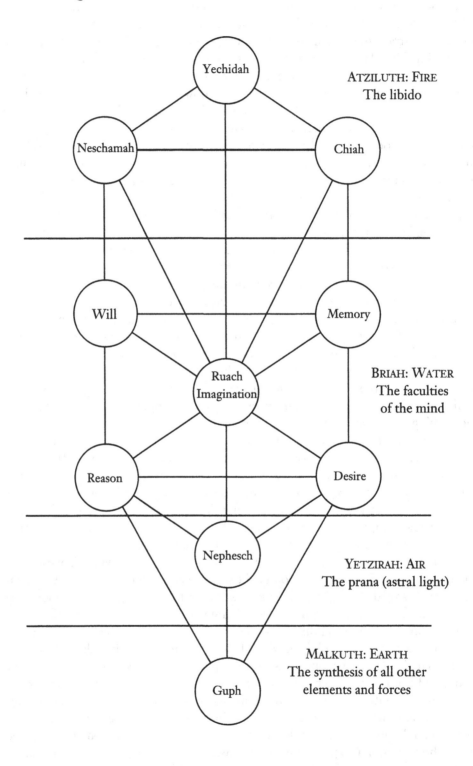

Figure 4:1

Also remember that Malkuth is the fruit of Creation—all sephirotic powers find expression and completion within this realm. Like the orange, the physical body is given form by the interior structures. Once it is peeled away from the internal systems, it quickly dissolves into its chemical components. Since the tselem is the foundation for the physical structure, the body is based upon its design—the action of the Nephesch keeps our appearance and consciousness stable throughout our lives.

Our second division of the Nephesch, the prana, is the life-force for the astral body. Just as the physical body must replenish its energy stores through the act of eating, the tselem must absorb energy from prana if it is to remain operable. Prana is a subtle, tenuous energy that permeates the astral light and energizes it; we know this energy as the five elements of earth, air, water, fire, and spirit. Prana is one division of the LVX energy, the part permeating the realm of Yetzirah. Visualize for a moment the Tree of Life, with its divisions into the four worlds of Atziluth, Briah, Yetzirah, and Assiah. Try to conceptualize the vast amounts of energy flowing throughout the Tree from Kether to Malkuth, moving through the various paths and sephiroth as it travels. This is the greater LVX energy that manifests throughout our complete system and Cosmos, enlivening all as it flows. Now, looking at Figure 4:1 again, we can see that each world has its own elemental attribution.

In Assiah, the material world, the element that corresponds to the energy system here is earth. Obviously, being the most substantial and solid of all the emanations, the energy used to sustain life in this realm would also have to be substantial. For the physical levels of life to continue, we must consume energy in its physical form—food. Within this realm, the four elements of earth, air, fire, and water are active in creating the physical forms; as we consume our meals, we are taking in these energies through a physical medium. As we move into Yetzirah, however, the finer astral parts of our systems must be sustained with a finer medium of energy—this energy is the prana. If we look back at our chart once more, we find that the elemental attribution of this sphere is air. Those of us who are familiar with Eastern techniques may recognize the Tattvas, five symbols to represent the elements. Yogis who are proficient in the use of Tattvas may observe the pranic currents as they permeate the astral counterpart of the planet by merely gazing into the air.

Each world will have its own aspect of the LVX energy that enlivens its spiritual components; it is important to remember, however, that each individual part of the light energy is necessary for the health of the complete organism. If the pranic energies of the tselem did not somehow filter into the physical body through the medium of food, the vital connection between the astral self and the physical self would deteriorate. This could result in the deterioration of health on all levels. For the sake of analysis, we are dividing individual consciousness into six levels—if all levels do not connect, overlap, and work together in the individual, health on all levels fails.

Our Nephesch also lies in a sort of twilight, a borderland between the mundane and deeper levels of awareness. This lucid state, which is necessary if one hopes to become aware of the astral body and use it to travel on the astral planes, serves as a doorway to the next level of self, the Ruach, in our Qabalistic model.

Our Ruach contains five sephiroth in its design: Chesed, Geburah, Tifareth, Netzach, and Hod. It is within this layer that we find what is often termed the intellect, the part of self that contains all perceptions, emotions, and desires. It is through the Ruach that we analyze ourselves, our environment, and the world surrounding us. We become aware of our individuality from the whole of Cosmos, and through that awareness, seek to reestablish our true place in the scheme of Cosmos.

Some writers have referred to this part of the system as the subconscious mind; this, however, is an oversimplification. Qabalah teaches us that the states of consciousness are far more complex than psychology would have us believe—each of the deeper layers of being has what one may call both a conscious and a subconscious level. Within the level known as the Guph, there are both conscious and subconscious functions: we may, on a conscious level, will our bodies to move, feel, and perceive stimulus. On a subconscious level, the body also regulates its hormonal, mechanical, and healing processes. Likewise, on a conscious level we use the Ruach whenever we study for an exam, memorize material, or try to recall important information for solving problems. On a subconscious level, it also stores every act we perform during our lifetimes; it categorizes and stores all triumphs, heartaches, traumas, and in lieu of conscious direction, it creatively solves problems we may have forgotten about. Whether we act through our wills or on instinctive levels, each aspect of self may be said to participate through conscious and subconscious volition.

The deeper we go into our spiritual makeup, the less obvious the conscious functions become. It is all but impossible for us to monitor and regulate the hormonal functions that occur within the Guph; however, through trance and meditation, we may learn how to increase or decrease their actions. When our conscious interference becomes life-threatening, as in a child holding his or her breath until a blackout occurs, the subconscious functions quickly regain control. If we were to continually monitor the functions of the mind, we would not be able to absorb and assimilate the constant barrage of perceptions and data that we process. Likewise, on deeper levels of awareness, those parts fulfill certain functions under conscious demand (such as inspiring us, delivering healing energy, perceiving psychic phenomenon), as well as operating independent of conscious awareness to keep homeostasis within the psyche.

If we dissect the Ruach into its individual sephiroth, we find that it contains the aspects of memory, will, imagination, reason, and desire. The first classification, memory, may be compared to consciousness itself. It is the part of self where the sum of all life experiences are stored from birth until death. On the Tree of Life, this is the sephirah known as Chesed. Balancing the memory is the aspect of will. Memory is a passive function, slowly absorbing the experiences undergone on a continual basis. Will is an active function, driving the organism to new experiences. Intended to be the servant—"As I do will, so mote it be!"—it can easily become the master, driving us relentlessly by the warrior powers of Geburah, its sephirotic attribution. The power of will evolves from the power of memory.

Will and memory imply dual functions in all that we do. To will a thing, we must first remember that we are not, or do not have, the thing that we will. As an example, yesterday I saw a new car. This caused me to remember, and realize, that my own car is not as nice as the one I saw. A new current of memories rose to the surface; its been five years since I bought my present car, and it was not new when I obtained it. Thoughts about the expense of upkeep to the fact that my gas mileage was not very good emerged. After remembering this information, the power of will kicked in and I began to desire a new car. I began to will the car into my possession. Through these two aspects of will and memory, I began a process that will eventually result in having a new car. But the first step was to realize that the thing I willed was not in my possession.

Our next part of Ruach, the imagination, is a much maligned faculty in human consciousness. In early childhood, the imagination is active constantly; as children, we are often told by adults, "My, what an active imagination you have!" Throughout our early childhood, however, we are often told to stop imagining things—this command by our elders is ingrained in us until the imagination becomes almost totally subconscious. For some of us, as we grow older, we still retain some scrap of consciousness of the imagination; this area of the psyche makes us more than animal, and eventually, more than human.

Although atrophied through disuse, the imagination can become the redeemer of the human soul. It is the faculty that lifts humans from animal to Deity status. Imagination is the part of us that dreams, creates, and designs; it draws upon memory and will, correlating the two into their proper balance. Imagination has brought the works of Shakespeare, the airplane, hunger-relief programs, and modern medicines. It is through the faculty of imagination that we conceive of a hunger-free, crime-free, poverty-free, and war-free world. Use the power of memory to recall how you accomplished any of your goals in this lifetime. Now, try to remember how you set these goals, how you obtained these goals, and what you did when the goals were accomplished. Was any of this possible without the imagination? No, for imagination draws off the memories in Chesed and uses the will of Geburah to perform its work. Being the spiritual harmony of Tifareth, no true evolution can be accomplished without the imagination.

Our next two aspects of the Ruach, reason and desire, Hod and Netzach, are the balancing, analytical, and emotional faculties of the psyche. They, too, are balanced within the sphere of Tifareth (imagination). For example, we will something after remembering we are not that thing. We use imagination to determine how that thing might be obtained. Then we desire it, and we become emotionally caught up in our creation. By reasoning out our desires, we keep our objective distance from our creation, keeping balance throughout the act of its creation. The process is stored in memory, which, hopefully, initiates another phase in our development.

Our Ruach is fed and sustained by the thoughts, feelings, and emotions that flood through it on a daily basis. To keep it active, to keep it functioning, we must continually use it—the faculties of will, imagination, memory, reason, and desire must be exercised to keep these aspects healthy. Since this is the link with the Supernals, our higher selves, if this region begins to atrophy and break down, we begin to lose our connection with the divine part of ourselves which is the true self.

It is through the Ruach that we are connected to the highest part of the psyche, the Supernals. Connecting Ruach with the Supernals is an area called the abyss. Here, all things exist in potential, without meaning. Below the abyss is the part of humanity that is called the "lower" self, the clothing worn for each individual incarnation. It is not the true self, rather it is a reflection of that beyond the abyss. My desires, dreams, personality, hair color, etc., are all based on choices made beyond the abyss of formlessness before birth. I am performing a role based upon artistic choices before birth. This is the false ego, the "I" of the present incarnation. Beyond the abyss, we find the true self, the part that is clothed, hidden, and protected by the lower self. The Supernals represent the real, and the ideal, existence of humanity. Here we find the transcendental ego, the unity of humanity summed up as absolute being, wisdom, and bliss.

The first division of the Supernals is the Yechidah, which is Kether on the Tree of Life. Here we have the higher self, the initial spark of incarnation that is the only real self of the individual. This is the original spark of consciousness that identifies us with every other divine spark incarnated, yet it is also the original impulse of an individualized entity. At the level of Yechidah, we all share in the same Macrocosmic flow of energy derived from the Ain. The life-blood of our individuality is the libido, LVX, which permeates Cosmos. Each spark, each personal Yechidah, is an individual concentration of this energy. We are all the same; we are all different.

The planetary attribution of the Yechidah is Neptune: this planet shares in the aspects of Nuit, Goddess of infinite space. The influence of Yechidah constantly overshadows all we do, for it is the true "I" that exists beyond life. We remember from Chapter Three that Kether is within the human energy system, but not contained in the physical matrix. This is the level of self that is lost in self-awareness and reverie; it broods upon eternal truth, floating in a chasm of cosmic energy. Alone, it can only conceive of its true, pure, and holy existence.

To become aware of self, in an effort to manifest as a created being, Yechidah must develop a magickal will, the Chiah, and a magickal understanding, the Neschamah. Chiah is the creative force of the Higher Self, and Chokmah on the Tree of Life. What could only meditate on its existence now has a will to incarnate, a will to create. But will alone can accomplish nothing. Somehow, the Yechidah must begin to understand its will to exist, its will to create. The Neschamah becomes the magickal understanding, giving the first primal forms to the force generated by the higher self. Chiah is animus; Chiah is positive and projecting. The Neschamah becomes the feminine, gestative force. It is with these two opposing principles that Yechidah becomes self-aware as a truly individual ego.

Through the evolution of the one Yechidah into the six parts of the organism, a holistic unity is created that grows, develops, and evolves as a complete organism. It begins with the spark of the God/dess asserting "I am." Through that primal acknowledgment of existence, energy spirals out into the void of Cosmos; first, it expands, and then it contracts upon itself until the intangible force of Kether becomes the tangible energy called matter. Within our model, however, we begin to see the power of evolution at work within the psyche. Remember that nature works cyclically; the energy that was sent out must be reabsorbed. Once spirit has descended into matter, it must ascend back into spirit if the cycle is to be complete, and creation be made whole. The Guph, the physical body, the unredeemed animal soul, must meet and combine with the Ruach, the deeper levels of being which often go unexplored by the average soul. Imagination, reason, memory, and will must be balanced with the eternally changing, self-asserting power of the physical self.

Once the two aspects of self become one force committed to self-awareness, a magickal unification takes place. The unrelenting physical desires become hallowed to the forces of love and light that permeate Cosmos; an inner marriage takes place in which the deeper self is understood by the mundane self. This is the magickal healing so many new-age texts try to facilitate. Two forces that were once in opposition achieve understanding and knowledge of the realm of Binah, where the Chiah resides. Perfect understanding of Cosmos and self gives us knowledge of our true wills—our purpose in life. Once the will is understood, we may finally bask in the light of the Higher Self and the Goddess, becoming perfect instruments to perform Her will in the world.

As we develop our magickal consciousness and power with the following exercises, we will be consciously activating the deeper levels of self, experiencing and analyzing each in its proper realm. Through continual use and exercise, we will strengthen our connections with the subtle realms of existence, becoming more aware of what was once resigned to subconscious workings. Establishing solid connections with the roots of our existence, we become strong; we heal and prepare ourselves to be true spiritual warriors in an age that needs spiritual strength. Our light will grow and our love will show; through it all, we will become more of what we were meant to be—spiritual emanations of the Goddess.

THE MIDDLE PILLAR

The Middle Pillar is perhaps the most ignored, yet most important, of any magickal technique we may learn. In it are the keys to success in the art of magick; it is an excellent exercise for aligning the Witch with the internal, sephirotic powers that absorb and channel energies from the universal centers of power. This is the force we need to make our spells and rituals work; many texts written on the practice of Witchcraft have implied that the success of a ritual depends on a dance being done a certain way, or the use of candles, incense, and words spoken in a forceful manner. Even worse, some texts have argued that the entire success of a ritual supposes the invocation of some great and mighty deity from the heavens, a degenerate return to the days of sacrifice and propitiation of the gods. The truth is that all magickal power comes from within, and if the above methods work at all, it is in spite of themselves and due to the natural talent of the operator. However, even the most talented Witch could benefit from an exercise developing the ability to channel magickal power.

By working with this technique, we are again attempting to invoke the highest, most unattainable part of self, working to bring this light into conscious awareness. We exalt, purify, and empower our bodies to be instruments of the God/dess' light, love, and life. As its name implies, the Middle Pillar exercise is based upon the Middle Pillar of the Tree of Life: Kether, Daath (the abyss), Tifareth, Yesod, and Malkuth. The diagram given in Figure 4:2 shows the anatomical locations of these sephiroth; we have already developed them with our work in Chapter Three. As we invoke the energies of the Middle Pillar into ourselves, we are working to find balance between extremes (remember the balancing of power and mercy in the Qabalistic Cross), and to exalt our own consciousness into Kether.

But why use the Middle Pillar? Once again we are led back to the tenet that Malkuth and Kether are interconnected—each is as holy and divine as is the other. Kether represents our highest link with the unknown, while Malkuth represents the sum of all existence. As we climb the Tree of Life, we work until we are perched in the uppermost branches, established in the realm of Kether. There are three paths that we can climb; the first, the pillar of severity, alone can take us no further than the sephirah of Binah, the sphere of the Great Mother. Climbing up the pillar of mercy leaves us stranded in the realm of Chokmah, the archetypal Father. But if we ascend by way of the Middle Pillar, we find ourselves in the highest realm possible, the realm of Kether.

In Chapter Two we spoke briefly about the powers of Tetragrammaton and the LVX energies generated in our technique of casting the magickal circle. The Middle Pillar also uses the formula of Tetragrammaton to create the LVX energies, but instead of the lesser form used in the creating sacred space exercise, we are using the greater formula as it relates to the Middle Pillar. Remember that the spiritual world, Kether, is contained in the world of Atziluth, the highest creative urge. In our formula, this become the first letter of Tetragrammaton, the Yod, representing the element of fire. Traveling through Daath and into Tifareth, we enter the world of Briah, the archangelic powers, and encounter the element of water, the second letter from our formula. Yesod lies in the realm of Yetzirah, the formative powers, and is the element of air. Finally, Malkuth becomes the final element, earth, and represents the solidification of all the spiritual realms.

THE MIDDLE PILLAR IN THE ENERGY FIELD

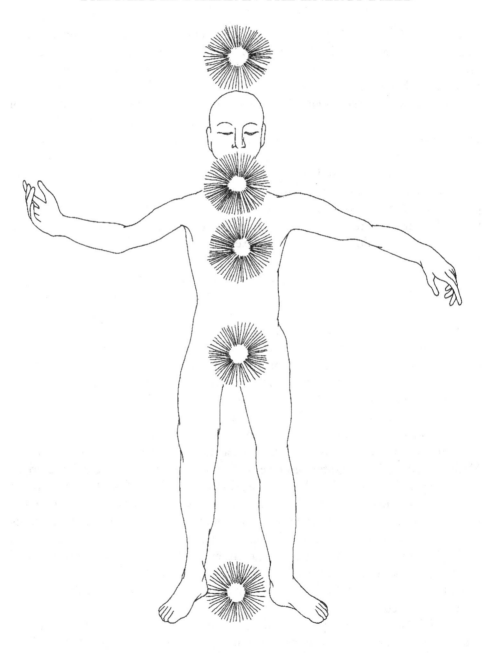

Figure 4:2

As a further note, it should be emphasized that when used in this fashion, the four letters of Tetragrammaton represent the elemental man, unregenerate, who lives daily in the body, drinking, eating, talking, and going about his daily chores with little thought or care about spiritual concerns. But as we work with the greater formula of Tetragrammaton, something wonderful begins to happen. The LVX, or spirit energy, is not only generated, it begins to take shape within the Witch's body. This descent of spirit into matter changes the formula into another, Pentagrammaton, representing the spiritual man vivified by the spiritual powers of Cosmos. In Hebrew, spirit is represented by the Hebrew letter Shin, and when inserted into the four letters of YHVH they become YHShVH, pronounced "Yeheshua" or "Yahovashah." It is from these names that the Christians got the corruption "Jesus," implying that he was not the savior of man, but a man who had attained spiritual consciousness.

During the course of our practices, the Witch shall regenerate and purify consciousness, becoming a living vehicle for the light of the divine. There is a familiar Craft symbol, the pentagram, which we have already used several times throughout this book: it symbolizes the powers of Pentagrammaton. In Figure 4:3 we are shown this symbol with its elemental attributions; we already know of its power to invoke and banish the elemental powers at will. In its upright position, the four elements of fire, water, air, and earth are overshadowed by the regenerating power of Spirit; some traditions of the Craft also use it in its inverted position as a symbol of the second degree. When the top point is pointing downward, it shows one in whom the light of God/dess has descended, yet it is not balanced and working to control the lesser elements of existence.

THE ELEMENTAL ATTRIBUTIONS OF THE PENTAGRAM

In the upright position, the Pentagram represents the forces of Spirit presiding over the power of the four elements. In the inverted position, it represents the four elements unbalanced, but still forming the Spirit energy.

Figure 4:3

Before beginning to work the Middle Pillar, we must spend a few moments studying the theoretical addition of the shadowy center called Daath. If you remember from the exercises in Chapter Three, we worked with ten sephiroth, not eleven, and only briefly mentioned the area between the Supernals and the rest of the Tree of Life, calling this area the "abyss." It was a region of seeming chaos to the personality, a place transcending logic and reason. Perhaps Daath can best be described as a magickal filter for the Tree of Life. It was created after creation; it is a shadowy center that acts as a sephiroth, yet does not really fit into the Qabalistic system. As we invoke the light into our spheres, Daath is there, working as a filter for that light, not allowing more to enter than our fledgling psyche can withstand. As we work our way up the Tree, it stands there as a guardian, not allowing us to become blinded by a brilliance our souls are not ready to withstand. One almost could call it a safety feature in the system, added after humanity first became aware of its divine origins and attempted to see the light. Daath develops as we learn to control our mental/emotional makeup. It is a symbolic link, self-devised and induced, between the highest realms of the God/dess and the conscious self of which we are most aware.

With this in mind, we will begin to establish the Middle Pillar in the body.[1]

EXERCISE ONE

Begin by performing the Qabalistic Cross, establishing the cross of white light in the aura and then enveloping yourself in the protective, balancing power of Tifareth. Remain facing East, and return your attention to the sphere of white light that was approximately six inches above the crown of your head.

Spend a few moments contemplating this sphere, Kether, meditating on its significance as your own higher self. Its archangelic color is pure, bright white; concentrate to visualize it as the most brilliant white possible. Slowly, vibrate the word "Eheieh" as you did in the Chapter Three exercises; repeat this vibration three times, imagining that the sound emanates not from your mouth, but from the sphere of light above your head.

Now that Kether has been opened and energized, imagine a white shaft of light traveling down into the top of your head, ending within the larynx. Here is Daath, the magickal filter and mediator of the light as it travels between the Supernals and the rest of the Tree of Life. As the shaft of white light strikes this area, it grows and becomes a lavender-blue ball of light. The name Daath translates into "the link;" think about this concept as you vibrate the name "YHVH Elohim" (yod-heh-vau-heh eh-loh-eem). Repeat the vibration three times.

Next, imagine the shaft of white light continuing down your spine to the heart area. Here, allow it to expand into a ball of bright yellow light. This is Tifareth, the great harmonizer. Vibrate the name "IAO" three times, allowing the sphere to grow in power and intensity.

---

1. In addition to the material presented in this chapter, I would like to recommend another book published by Llewellyn Publications: *The Middle Pillar*, written by Israel Regardie, is the most informative and insightful text written about this exercise. All writers, myself included, draw upon his teachings on this subject. If the volume is not readily available in bookstores, it may be ordered directly from Llewellyn Publications.

Once again, visualize a shaft of white light emanating from Tifareth, traveling down the spine until it reaches the area of the genitals. Expand the light into a violet ball of light and vibrate the name "Shaddai El-Chai" three times, imagining that the whole of the vibration is centered within the light.

Finally, send another shaft of light into Malkuth. Allow it to expand into a ball of black light and vibrate "Adonai Ha-Aretz" three times. Visualize the sphere becoming solid and powerful.

Spend a few moments contemplating the sephiroth in the psyche, allowing them to balance you. Finish the exercise with the Qabalistic Cross.

Now that we have followed the above pattern, establishing the Middle Pillar within the aura, we may move onto the next step in the process, which is circulating the vast amounts of energy raised, evenly distributing it throughout the psyche. As we open our sephiroth step by step, we are opening channels to power; it cannot be emphasized enough that these spheres of action that we open in ourselves correspond to, and draw power from, the greater sources in the Macrocosm. As we progress in our exercises, more energy is raised that must be circulated evenly throughout the body's systems, lest any one part become overloaded and unbalanced. We know that the energy in our own fields can be moved; we have already done this as we sent the overflow of energy from one sephirah into the next. What is needed, then, is a method to distribute it evenly throughout the body.

Energy follows the breath and thought processes, so we shall work with this in mind to facilitate the flow of energy throughout the body. There are three ways of moving the power generated from this exercise so it flows smoothly: side to side, front to back, and in a spiral. Realize that after the energies are balanced throughout the body, the excess will safely be distributed into the area surrounding us. What we are aiming for here is to make sure no one part of the body/mind/soul complex is overwhelmed in comparison to the rest. All parts of the body must be exposed to an evenly distributed amount of these psychic energies.

In a sense, the body of light has its own circulatory system, mirroring that of the physical. Conceptualize each sephirah within the body as a center of activity much like our own heart. Energy comes in from the universe, is pumped through the paths (like magickal arteries), and then must be collected and moved back to the centers of action by mental activity, just as the blood in our veins is moved by muscular activity. If the energy grows stagnant, like the venous blood in our bodies, and is not subject to movement, all sorts of problems can occur. We become prey to a host of mental/psychic disturbances, eventually resulting in physical breakdowns. We have all experienced what we call low-energy days, times when we just don't feel like getting out of bed. Usually these are short-lived, as the subconscious functions quickly work to restore the energy balance. But sometimes, the movement of the energies is so blocked that it takes conscious effort to get the system working again. Without this effort, the physical, which depends on the workings of the more subtle energies, begins to break down.

In practicing the Middle Pillar and the following circulation of energy, we increase our vitality, and hence, our health. The deeper levels of self become refreshed and invigorated by the influx of stronger, fresher energies; the resulting daily circulation of them makes sure that each part of our spiritual make-up is contacting this flow. As the astral body becomes stronger, so does the physical, and it shows over time as we continue our practices. At first we simply feel more energetic. As time passes, we begin to look better, feel younger, and find great stores of energy at our disposal.

To circulate this energy properly, we first need to repeat the above exercises (the Qabalistic Cross and the Middle Pillar). Follow the steps slowly and deliberately, feeling the resulting flow of energies permeating your matrix. Pause for a few moments, feeling the energy flooding throughout your psyche. Eventually, you will begin to sense the energy-blocked areas; perhaps these will correspond to actual physical complaints. Quite often, the area blocked corresponds symbolically to the physical problem; for instance, one who is having difficulty overcoming a cold may find that the blockage of energy is not centered in the respiratory system, rather, it is centered around Geburah and the right shoulder. White blood cells, which create the antibodies we need to fight infections, perform a Geburic function: attack and destroy. Obviously, if this center is being blocked from its influx of energy, or if the energies generated there cannot reach the rest of the energy centers, it will stagnate within the system. As we circulate the energy throughout our auras, we will need to specifically concentrate on pushing the power through any blocked areas, releasing the imprisoned energies to the rest of the body.

Exercise Two

Perform the Qabalistic Cross and open the sephiroth along the Middle Pillar. Spend a few moments sensing the energy flow throughout the body; feel it reaching out to the farthest limits of your aura. Try to sense if there are any blockages in its flow; this will be felt as a heaviness in your body or auric energy system, or perhaps seen as an area of blackness where the power flows in, but does not flow out. Unless you have been involved with some sort of self-cleansing regimen (working to relieve stress, tension, etc.), you may find that there are several blocked areas. Not to worry, this exercise will begin to relieve that.

Within the Tree of Life, there are two sephiroth which receive and send all the energies generated by the Tree: Kether and Malkuth. They are the two major hearts for the sephirotic system. Kether takes the powers from the unknown and sends them to the rest of the Tree, while Malkuth receives the influences of all the sephiroth and works to send them back to Kether. We shall begin by contemplating Kether.

Imagine that Kether begins to fill with power—light energy is generated from the unknown until the sephirah is ready to burst with light. Begin to will the energy to move; at first, it may seem difficult to put it in motion. Try making it flow with your breath. As you breathe in, feel Kether taking in its energy from the Cosmos. As you exhale, send the energy down the front of your body with your breath, until it enters Malkuth. Now, inhale once more, and feel Malkuth receiving the energy that filters into it from the rest of the Tree of Life, adding the energies sent from Kether into it. Now exhale, and imagine that the energy is traveling from Malkuth through the back of your body and into Kether, where it joins with the energy still entering the sephirah there. Repeat the breathing and visualizations at least ten times.

Allow your mind to contemplate Kether once more. Will the sephirah to gather energy again, but instead of sending it down the front and up the back sides of your body, allow it to flow down the left side and up the right. Remember, we are not just aiming to move our energies over the body, but throughout the body's internal systems and the external aura as well. Perform this exercise ten times.

Now that we have immersed the body complex in these circulations of energy, pause for a moment. Mentally look over your energy pattern, feeling if there are any places where the light is still blocked. Remember that deep, rhythmic breathing and visualization are keys to making the light flow; if there are still blockages, repeat the above exercises with the intention of removing the stagnant patterns from the aura.

As you progress in these exercises, you may notice that the rest of the sephiroth within your Tree begin to open into conscious awareness automatically; that is how it should be. As the energies flowing between Malkuth and Kether are consciously circulated throughout the body systems, they will automatically energize the other spheres of existence. No one part of the Tree can exist without the other, they all work together as a whole, even if we do not consciously open them.

Now that we have the energies from the sephiroth circulating freely, we may perform the final part of the circulation exercise. We will wrap ourselves in this light that we have generated, enveloping ourselves in a magickal cocoon that will both comfort and protect. Perhaps some of us have used simpler shielding exercises, drawing energy from the world around us, visualizing it as a protective white light that keeps harmful energies at bay. This exercise is an elaboration of that technique, using the power that we have generated from the Tree of Life to form a protective cocoon. As we solidify the energy around us, we empower our auras with the maximum amount of light that it can hold at this time; the rest simply radiates outward. Perhaps you have seen people who you have described as radiating or glowing. One reason for this is that these people naturally exude large amounts of psychic energy, and their auras simply cannot contain the amount of light and love that they generate. The excess flies off their system, and those of us who need the extra boost are drawn to their power. This is one of the signs of a natural healer.

Now that the Middle Pillar is established with energy circulating freely throughout the system, begin to contemplate the sphere of Malkuth. Watch as it receives the flowing energy that comes to it through the Tree of Life. Allow it to gather power for a moment, then will the light to emerge from it in the form of a white band. Wrap the physical body with this band tightly, starting with the feet, and ending with Kether above the head. Repeat this three times until the body is seen as glowing and radiating from within a blanket of white light, interspersed with the colors of the sephiroth within. Allow any excess energy that you cannot hold within this filter of light to radiate from within, illuminating your aura and the area surrounding you. Finish this exercise with the Qabalistic Cross.

MAGNETIZING THE AURA

While we have been working to establish the Tree of Life in our aura, we have been using a scale of color called the Archangelic scale; that is, we have used the colors of the sephiroth which are receptive to the powers we have been trying to harness and explore. Remember that in Witchcraft we work on the principle of polarity; we have both positive and negative, opposites seeking to attract each other and form a balance. We conceptualize this as Goddess and God merging into what I have termed throughout this book as God/dess. This principle is seen creatively on the physical plane as the joining of opposites, masculine and feminine. In magick, and on the higher planes of existence, the law of polarity also holds true—opposites attract. Thus, by using the receptive colors in the Archangelic scale, we have been attracting the powers of the sephiroth to us; we became receptive and negative so the projective and positive powers of the spheres may reach us.

There is another scale of color that we may use, the Deity scale, which is positive and projective. We have worked only with the Archangelic scale of color until now because we have been trying to open the sephiroth within our psyche; now we are going to put those sephiroth to use in magickal ways, and for some of our magick it will be necessary for us to use the projecting scale of color.

As we learn how to magnetize the aura, projecting or receiving sephirotic powers at will, we will once again learn a technique opening us to greater avenues of power. Instead of working with one sephirah in a specific anatomical region, we will concentrate on the energy coming through that one sephirah, until our whole energy system is vibrating with its power. We will, in a sense, consecrate all of consciousness to dwell on the principles that the area represents.

Doing these exercises will develop our control of the aura, our knowledge of the individual energy patterns of the sephiroth, and give us our first taste of pure Qabalistic Witchcraft. Like I mentioned at the beginning of this chapter, magickal consciousness and power are synonymous in the Craft, and we will be putting our awareness of the sephiroth to practical use here.

EXERCISE THREE

It is best to work with this exercise over the next ten days, beginning with Malkuth, and moving sequentially until we reach the sphere of Kether on the Tree. Review the Archangelic and Deity colors for the sephiroth as given in Appendix One. These two colors should be committed to memory before beginning the exercise.

Once you have this information memorized, perform the Qabalistic Cross and Middle Pillar exercise. Give each part of the body of light exercise one circulation, allowing the other sephiroth to open up in the aura. Now, focus on the sephirah chosen, Malkuth. As the energies of the Tree filter through Malkuth, concentrate on the white becoming tinged with black, citrine, olive, and russet, the Archangelic colors of Malkuth. Allow this energy to circulate throughout the aura; each circulation through and around the area of Malkuth makes these colors deeper still, until the whole aura vibrates with the Archangelic colors. Feel the energies of Malkuth permeating all of your consciousness, not just your physical feet. Feel how this changes your overall consciousness.

Now, as the energy continues to circulate throughout your aura, allow the colors to be caught once more in the sephirotic area of Malkuth. This sephirah acts as its own filter, until the energies circulating return to their normal white. The Deity color of Malkuth is yellow; this is also the positive, projecting color. Still concentrating on the area of Malkuth, will the sephirotic color to change to yellow. Once the visualization is firmly established, return to circulating the white energy throughout the aura, allowing it to pick up the color yellow. As the entire energy system changes to this vibration, feel the difference it makes in your consciousness of Malkuth. The overall level remains the same; however, instead of receiving the sephirotic energies into yourself, you are now radiating them from within, projecting them outward. Allow the sephirah of Malkuth to once more filter the energies out of your aura, will them back to the Archangelic colors, and end with the Qabalistic Cross.

Over the next nine days, repeat the exercise for the remaining nine sephiroth, in the order of Yesod, Hod, Netzach, Tifareth, Geburah, Chesed, Binah, Chokmah, and Kether.

For this type of magickal work, there are seven spheres we may use: Yesod, Hod, Netzach, Tifareth, Chesed, Geburah, and Binah. Malkuth will be omitted because it becomes the plane of manifestation for all practical work. Likewise, Chokmah and Kether are not used in this type of magick, as their forces lie before magickal form. We will work only with the sephiroth giving rise to the ideas and principles of manifestation. Below, guidelines are given for the magickal uses of the sephirotic energies.

Yesod: The Sphere of the Moon

Projective qualities: Travel, domestic life, medicine, agriculture (nourishing life), luck (for others), feminine aspect and problems (others), waters, emotions (others), publicity, illusions, personality (how others see you), sense reactions, preventing war, voyages, cooking, the sea, natural medicines and herbs (to bless and empower).

Receptive qualities: Agriculture (planting), vision, luck (for self), feminine aspects and problems (self), birth, time, theft, changes, illusions, personality (inward), knowledge of astral travel, reconciliation, food, milk, and dairy products, the family, clairvoyance, natural medicines and herbs (receiving knowledge of).

Hod: The Sphere of Mercury

Projective qualities: Influencing others, theatrical success, authors, short trips, bargain-hunting, schools, teaching, communication, business matters, contracts.

Receptive qualities: Success in tests, divination of future, writing, medicine, predictions, self-improvement, celibacy, the mind, learning, conjurations (knowledge of), predictions, eloquence, speed, improvement of mind, power, poetry, inspiration, healing of nervous disorders.

Netzach: The Sphere of Venus

Projective qualities: Beauty (how others see you), friendship, luxury, jewels, partnerships, spiritual harmony (with another), offspring, younger people.

Receptive qualities: Natural harmony, beauty (from within), obtaining love, insuring pleasure, art, music, parties, aphrodisiacs, scents, perfumes, compassion, extravagance.

Tifareth: The Sphere of the Sun

Projective qualities: Health, harmony, and luck; preventing war, influencing superiors, employees, executives, officials, obtaining confidence.

Receptive qualities: Obtaining friendship, health, harmony, and luck; finding money, patronage, peace, and missing property; regaining youth, illumination, immediacy, promotions, labor, and divine power. Increasing vitality.

Geburah: The Sphere of Mars

Projective qualities: Overthrow of enemies, wounds, war, acts of destruction and oppression.

Receptive qualities: Courage, surgery, physical strength, defense, endurance, energy, construction, vitality, and magnetism.

Chesed: The Sphere of Jupiter

Projective qualities: Creating wealth, abundance, growth, leadership, career success, expansion.

Receptive qualities: Speculation, gambling, acquiring wealth, abundance, bankers, divination of the past, obtaining friendship, health, honors, luck, law, money. Obtaining honors, religion, trade, treasure, dreams, and legal matters.

Binah: The Sphere of Saturn

Projective qualities: Reincarnation, destruction of diseases and pests, terminations and death. Acquiring consciousness on the astral plane. Projecting all qualities of time, space, and eternity. Buildings, the elderly, funerals, plans, and debts. Slowing terminal disease in another. Sending destruction or death.

Receptive qualities: Plans, acquiring real estate, inheritances, antiques, studying for exams, receiving esoteric knowledge. Slowing terminal disease within. Bringing destruction or death. Duties, responsibilities, finding familiars, learning, meditation, life, doctrines, repayments of debts, conversing with those who died a natural death.

Notice that the above lists have been divided into two parts: the positive qualities and the negative qualities. This is for convenience in deciding which scale of color, the Deity or Archangelic, you will need to use. The exercise for using these correspondences follows.

EXERCISE FOUR

Determine the object of the ritual, the sephirah to use, and the scale of color needed before the actual ritual is begun.

Perform the Qabalistic Cross and the Middle Pillar exercise. Circulate the energies throughout the aura, allowing the other sephiroth to open. Begin concentrating on the one which corresponds to the work you wish to do. Slowly, imagine it changing to the color scale in which it needs to be; if that color is the Archangelic, just relax and continue to strengthen the visualization and your awareness of the sphere. As the white energy generated by this exercise begins to flow through and wash over the sephirah, imagine it becoming colored by the energy. Continue the visualization until your entire aura is filled with this light.

If you are trying to obtain something from another source, use the Archangelic color. Visualize your need as off in the distance, and the color of your aura creating an irresistible pull toward the object. The stronger the visualization, the stronger the emotion, the stronger the magnetism of your aura. Imagine the thing you want being pulled by the Archangelic colors within your sphere.

If you use the Deity scale of color, then you will need to imagine the thing or quality within yourself. As the color in your aura becomes stronger, imagine that it is being pushed out of you and into the place it needs to be. Remember, the stronger the visualization, the stronger and quicker the magick works.

Once the visualization is finished, allow the sephirah you worked with to act as a filter, clearing the colored energy out of your aura. Return it to the Archangelic scale if the polarity was reversed, and finish with the Qabalistic Cross.

VIBRATIONS

Until now, we have spoken of vibrations as methods of intoning the various names of power so they resonate in a singing, chanting manner throughout the Witch's body, aura, and the surrounding space. This is only one use of a magickal vibration; in conjunction with the Middle Pillar exercise, there is a method of using the vibratory technique so that the vibration travels throughout space, finding its destination within the Macrocosmic sephiroth, and reverberating back to the Witch, bringing Macrocosmic energy with it.

We may compare this technique to the text given in the Gardnerian Book of Shadows, the section on the calls:

> *Of old there were many chants and songs used, especially in the dances. Many of these have been forgotten by us here; but we know they used cries of IAU, HAU, which seems much like the cry of the ancients: EVO or EAVOE. Much depends on the pronunciation if this be so. In my youth when I heard the cry IAU it seemed to be AEIOU, or rather HAAEE IOOUU or AA EE IOOOOUU. This may be the way to prolong it to make it fit for a call; but it suggests that these be initials of an invocation, as AGLA used to be. And the whole Hebrew alphabet is said to be such and for this reason is recited as a most*

powerful charm. At least this is certain, these cries during the dances do have a powerful effect, as I myself have seen.[2]

It is interesting to note that within this text, we find the call EVO and IAU. As we can see from our work with the Tree of Life within, the power vibration for the sephirah of Tifareth, IAO, ends up sounding like IAU, and possibly EVO, if the vowels are not properly intoned. Traditionally, we are taught that these two calls are vibrations that evoke the Goddess' sacrificial Consort. Tifareth is the sphere in which the concept of the sacrificial God is found. Also, the writer's reference to the Hebrew alphabet may signify that the Qabalistic use of vibrations was known, if not practiced, by the Witches of an earlier era.

Like the traditional calls used in the mainstream Craft, the vibrational formula we are about to employ will evoke a greater amount of specific energies into our consciousness. We can use this technique to evoke greater consciousness of the sephiroth; after mastering this, we may use the formula to invoke the God/dess in myriad forms, creating a more intimate bond between our energy complex and theirs.

As with the calls, the theory behind the vibrational formula is simple: send a deliberate call/vibration out into Cosmos, and the energy you are trying to call will respond. This assumes two things: first, the specific energy you are trying to reach exists; second, you know the name by which it must be called.

The medium of exchange by which the call travels is our own trained consciousness. Within ourselves, we open up to the microcosmic part of self corresponding to the area of Macrocosm we wish to contact. Then, by magnetizing our aura, we create a conduit between the lesser and greater areas by which the vibration travels.

EXERCISE FIVE

For this exercise, we will begin in Malkuth, working our way up the Tree into Kether. This exercise will be outlined for Malkuth; as you work the remaining nine sephiroth, merely substitute the proper colors, names, and vibratory rates. It is important that, before beginning, you turn to Appendix One to memorize a few facts: the positive and negative colors of the sephirah (Archangelic and Deity colors), the vibratory name you will be using (the name of power in this exercise), and the proper English spelling of that name. Complete memorization of this material assures us that the whole of our consciousness will be centered upon the task at hand.

Once the necessary information has been memorized, begin by entering into the awareness of patterns about you. Perform the Qabalistic Cross, and open the Middle Pillar within the aura. When we work with the sephiroth in the Middle Pillar (Kether, Tifareth, Yesod, and Malkuth), it is not necessary to open up the rest of the Tree of Life. If, however, we find ourselves working with any of the spheres contained within either the Pillar of Mercy or Severity, open up all ten sephiroth briefly. For exercises such as these, always include the Daath, which shields us from receiving more of the light than our spiritual bodies can withstand.

---

2. From my version of the Gardnerian Book of Shadows.

Next, begin to center on the Archangelic colors of Malkuth. Perform the circulation of energy from Kether to Malkuth, parts one and two, allowing the white light to take on the swirling colors of pale yellow, yellow-brown, black flecked with gold, and olive. Continue until the entire aura is suffused with this color. We are magnetizing the aura with the Archangelic colors because we desire to receive greater amounts of the sephirotic energy from the Macrocosmic Malkuth.

We are going to further tax the powers of visualization by imagining that the colors of the sephiroth on the Middle Pillar are beginning to shine so brightly that they show through the colors of Malkuth swirling within the aura. Even the sephiroth proper of Malkuth within the aura glows brighter than the colors swirling about you. This may take a serious, concentrated effort, but this visualization must be maintained. Continue to breathe slowly and deeply; the colors will begin to intensify.

In the air before you, imagine that the divine name of "Adonai Ha-Aretz" is flashing in the Deity color of Malkuth: pure yellow. Take your time to establish this visualization firmly. Exhale the entire contents of your lungs, and as you inhale slowly and deeply, breathe in the colored name. Allow it to enter through your nostrils, descending into Tifareth by way of the Middle Pillar. Return your awareness to Kether, willing the sephirah to send a shaft of white light into Tifareth and the Deity name of Malkuth. Without opening your mouth, hum the name so that it vibrates throughout your chest area. Inhale deeply, sending the name into Yesod, allowing the shaft of light from Kether to descend upon it. Hum the syllables. Once again, inhale deeply, pushing the name by way of the Middle Pillar into Malkuth, and will another shaft of light to descend upon it from Kether. Once again, hum the name, imagining that the vibration takes place within Malkuth. We have consecrated the magickal name three times with the light of Kether, blessing and purifying the name by the power of the four creative worlds.

Inhale deeply again, holding your breath for just a moment as you visualize the empowered name rushing from the area of Malkuth and into Yesod, then Tifareth; as it ascends through the Daath, vibrate the word forcefully and loudly; no longer humming, send it out in an audible, loud vibration, "aah-dooh-nie hah-aah-reh-tah-zah," and visualize the name hurtling out into space until you can no longer see it. Then, after a moment of silence and absence of breathing, imagine that the name comes rushing back to you in a brilliant ball of yellow light. As the Deity color of Malkuth is drawn to you, breath in forcefully, allowing it to shoot into your core. The aura flashes in both the receptive and projective colors of the sephirah, and for a moment you are lost and blinded by the powers evoked within.

Once equilibrium has been regained, it is important to restore the Archangelic color of Malkuth back into the proper anatomical position. Filter all light through the sephirah until your aura turns back to its proper white color. Finish this exercise with the Qabalistic Cross.

The first several attempts at this exercise will bring minimal results; it is complex, and will take a few trials before all the steps can be smoothly assimilated. Once the technique is memorized and you have gone through a few practice runs, results will follow. The secret is in using slow, prolonged breathing as you inhale and exhale the words, as well as long, drawn-out vibrations. Success will bring a temporary "blackout" in consciousness; you will be lost in a world of color and sound as the vibration returns from the Macrocosm, bringing an onslaught of power that will take a few moments to be properly assimilated by your psyche. Eventually, after your consciousness has become accustomed to the increasing forces, the next sephirah may be evoked in the same manner.

ASSUMPTION OF ASTRAL FORMS

There is another technique that we may use to generate greater amounts of power with the Middle Pillar: the assumption of astral forms. Most of us are already familiar with this; we use it in conjunction with another well-known Craft ritual, the Drawing Down of the moon and sun. Those who are experienced in this invocation usually employ a method of enflaming the mind so the God/dess is met halfway—they imagine that, as the invocation is being employed by their working partner, the form of the God/dess is enveloping their own, so that an overlapping in consciousness occurs. By putting on the "magickal clothing" of the form invoked, and employing a second party to also invoke the God/dess, a conduit between the two is set up, so that the Witch's human self is overtaken by the divine form. This is the assumption of an astral form.

For our work at this time, we will once again be using the pure sephirotic energies in this exercise. We will attempt to assume the astral forms of the magickal images of the sephiroth; detailed drawings of all ten can be found in Appendix One of this book. We are beginning our work with the magickal images, for they represent a purity of consciousness—as we establish our vibrational rates within the newly formed sephiroth, we overlap our consciousness with a form that embodies the purest consciousness of the realm. Later, as we gain proficiency in accessing these states of consciousness, we may substitute the name of a God or Goddess attributed to any one sphere, say, Persephone in Malkuth, and employ Her magickal image and the vibration of Her name within the realm of Malkuth to learn more about Her in that sphere, as well as wield the powers She has for empowering our spells.

For now, until proficiency is gained, we shall stick with the pure consciousness of the sephirah. Each God or Goddess contained within any one sephirah only contains one specific aspect of the realm's consciousness. For example, Yesod is the realm of the moon, the foundation for the world of Yetzirah and the astral counterpart of the physical realm. In attaining awareness of this sephirah, we are learning of all its functions on the astral plane. Diana is a moon Goddess who is also attributed to the sphere of Yesod; by choosing her image and name over others of the realm she belongs to on the Tree of Life, we learn about her powers and aspects only. In this case we learn of her function as part of the Triple Goddess, and how the powers of the Maiden that belong only to Diana fit in with the scheme of the whole. Notice that through her, we learn little of the greater Maiden, Mother, and Crone who exist as archetypes, nor do we learn anything about the place of Yesod in the scheme of created Cosmos. So, we tackle the greater awareness before learning to deal with the smaller aspects and divisions.

Also, by achieving the overall awareness of the pattern of any one sephirah, we find that our later exercises to obtain intimate knowledge about a divine, Archangelic, or angelic form is comparatively easy. We are accomplishing the toughest work first, so that our subsequent work appears almost effortless.

EXERCISE SIX

As in our last exercise, we will outline the steps for assuming the magickal image of Malkuth. When approaching the sephiroth beyond this, simply insert the appropriate colors, names, and images into the exercises.

The best way to begin is to study the magickal image of Malkuth given in Appendix One. Gaze at it, trying to see it as a complete picture. Then, begin to study each part, until even the lines forming the eyes are committed to memory. Know the image so completely that if you were to close your eyes, you could conjure up a solid vision of it before you.

Now, perform the Qabalistic Cross and the opening to the Middle Pillar exercise. Circulate the light generated about you; once it is flowing evenly, begin to concentrate on your awareness of Malkuth in the Middle Pillar. As in the technique of vibrating the divine names, if you are employing any sephirah on the Middle Pillar, there is no need to establish the rest of the Tree of Life. If, however, you are working with anything on either the masculine or feminine pillars, spend a few moments opening all the sephiroth.

As the energy moves through and about Malkuth, visualize the Archangelic colors diffusing into the aura until you are flashing in olive, pale yellow, yellow-brown, and black. Keep filtering the colors into your energy system until they are solid and bright. This establishes your body's vibration in the energy of Malkuth.

Next, begin to visualize the magickal image for the sephirah. Imagine it standing before you, but sharing the energies that you are emitting. Allow your mind to slowly conjure up every detail until it is solid before you, as real as anything else you might encounter if you were to open your eyes. If you have spent sufficient time contemplating the image, this should pose few problems, as the exercises in this book will have honed and tuned your powers of visualization. The important thing to remember is to take your time, skimping on none of the details.

Once the image stands solidly before you, inhale deeply and imagine that it is floating closer to you by the currents set up with your breath. Allow it to touch you, merge with you, until you can feel the form enveloping your own. Slowly, adjust your physical body without opening your eyes, so that your posture matches the image's. This will shift your consciousness subtly; as you imagine the form over your own, slowly becoming one with your pattern, you will feel your own consciousness beginning to merge with that of the magickal image. Once begun, the process moves of its own accord; allow yourself to experience the union.

As the visualization becomes complete, perform the vibratory technique for the Deity name of Malkuth, "Adonai Ha-Aretz." As the name is vibrated both within and without, you will achieve a greater connection with the form; you may even begin to hear Her own thoughts within your pattern. The resulting influx of energy from the Macrocosm will be greater than before; you will now have established a stronger strain within the light, magnetizing the aura to such a degree with the image that it will pull a flood of power to you.

Once this is completed, imagine that the image is pulling away from you, establishing itself once more as a separate force. As before, the process will continue once it is begun; allow the visualization of the image to fade. Filter your energy through Malkuth until it is once more a solid, white color; balance and cleanse yourself with the Qabalistic Cross.

As we progress with the exercises in this chapter, slowly increasing our consciousness of the magickal realms on the Tree of Life, we will find that increasing amounts of power are being opened to us. Remember that increasing magickal consciousness and magickal power are synonymous within the Craft. Still more lies ahead; building on the techniques that we have just learned, the next chapter will give us methods of traveling both mentally and astrally into the realms of which we have been increasing conscious awareness within our body/soul complex. Our work here has taken our young sapling of a Tree into adolescence; let us continue to nurture the life we have birthed into full adulthood.

CHAPTER FIVE

RISING ON THE PLANES

✦ *April 29, 1989.[1] The night was alive, filled with the sounds of insects, lonely animals baying in the distance, and an angry river swelling and churning below. A breeze wafted about us, and with it came the musty scent of damp earth and pine—all around, I could feel the throbbing of life; the ever-growing, yearning forces of Earth awakening to a titanic pulse of power. Intoxicating. Scintillating. Teasing the physical senses with promises of pleasure to yet unveil.*

Amidst the growing life-tide, Krystal and I stood together on a cliff overlooking Mott's Run, a winding, frothing length of the Rappahannock River. A breeze softly soughed through our cloaks, filmy and translucent; they billowed out into the night, playing with the tendrils of incense smoke that dissipated throughout our magick circle. Our only light was that of a full moon that loomed low among towering trees; for a long time, we stood and gazed at Her face. Krystal was telling me about her visions of Yesod: a tantalizing, voluptuous Maiden taunting the Young Stag across the hillside. Delicate yet dangerous, she whispered promises of sensual delights, of dissolution within the source. The Bealtaine love-chase, awaiting consummation.

Again and again, peering into Yesod from the safety of her temple, Krystal had seen the same images played out before her. To experience the chase, to learn its secrets on the night before Bealtaine Eve, she would venture into Yesod; she would become part of their world. Firsthand, she would see the magickal love-chase played out before her. She would be a witness, a participant, not merely a distant voyeur.

To recreate the scene, making our outer temple as close to the symbols she had seen in her vision, we chose to work along this hillside. To the West was the river; to the North, a forest; the East turned into a sloping, curving field, the direction of our breeze. Facing the moon, absorbing its soft, magnetic glow into her own energy, Krystal would use the planet of Yesod to light her way into the sephirah.

I watched her sit on the rough, slate surface of the cliff; her eyelids fluttered shut, the face relaxed and became expressionless. Soon, her voice rose into the night sky. Strong and sensuous was her chant, "Yay-soo-dah." The vibration swelled within the circle, its power spiraling out into the surrounding darkness. Sinking along the hillside, its force echoed and melted into the sound of the churning river below. Each chant filled our circle with power; the force throbbed around us, poured through us, slowly becoming a pale violet. As the energies merged

---

1. From my magickal diary.

into the patterns of Yesod, her voice rose higher: it became a vortex, a cone of power, a piercing dagger that ripped and sliced through reality. Ecstasy!

Then, there was silence. No chanting, no vibrations, no more life in the night outside our circle. The world … stood still. Or perhaps we were cut off from the world by the strength of Krystal's vibrations. Entranced, I could see a faint outline imposing itself upon the circle's boundary; for a moment, I was within an ancient Greek temple. Krystal's refuge. It flashed, then faded. Her body tightened; the energy in our sacred space began to collapse upon her; it coalesced around her body, sinking into her body, disappearing into her form. The tidal wave of energy returned, swirling back into Krystal, its source, washing her spirit beyond our space between the worlds.

I was alone, sitting in the circle with Krystal's physical form. Her mind, however, was gone; she had ventured into Yesod.

Whenever we turn in for the night, falling into a deep, restful sleep, we all but lose awareness of the physical body. The mind withdraws upon itself, turning inward, and we begin to operate on more subtle levels of being. Descending into the land of dreams, a vast and powerful world of symbols and metaphors is opened to us. We play with newfound friends; we fight with unknown enemies—sometimes our awareness emerges into worlds with unfamiliar shapes and scenery. Approaching a dream object, we can perceive it with our senses of sight, taste, smell, sound, and touch. Sometimes, the more subtle senses open; we begin to perceive our dream-scapes through the faculties of psychic awareness. Past, present, and future merge: time loses meaning. Space begins to warp. Our bodies become malleable, molding their shape and size to our will. In the dream-state, we become creators and creations of our own consciousness.

While the body lies silent, unmoving in its unconscious state, the mind retains its consciousness. Free of its physical boundaries, it emerges in a new body, a new form, and flies to regions inaccessible to us in our physical forms. A mind once fettered by flesh is allowed, for a time, freedom in the tselem—we drift away into the land of dreams. In this world, we explore chasms of consciousness inaccessible to the physical body; higher realms in which the lower self may not travel.

Roughly one-third of our incarnation is spent in this state: that averages out to twenty-five years of astral adventures. Yet, ask Witches if they can leave their bodies at will, and the answer is usually no. Since we perform this feat every time we dream, everyone can answer that, yes, projection at will is possible—simply enter the dream state. Using astral projection for practical purposes, however, is another problem altogether. Once in the dream-state, we function on subconscious levels, playing out scenes decided upon by its design. When we awaken, we bring new knowledge about ourselves into conscious awareness; this exploration is good for us inwardly. But if we are to employ our natural skills for practical purposes, like any other ability, we must learn to control them when control is needed.

Obviously, the dream-state is not good for our magickal work: we cannot ensure, even with advanced training, that we can gain and keep control of our astral adventures. During times of danger, stress, or exhaustion, the subconscious mind quickly regains control of its operations—anything that seeks to unbalance the mind's homeostasis becomes a danger to subconscious functions. Even if we use our dreams as an entrance to the more tenuous realms of existence, our experiences still occur while in the dream-state. Somehow, we need to gain entrance to these worlds from our conscious state by using a specific technique.

This technique, conscious projection, is often referred to as rising on the planes: a skill that many of the great magickal masters have written about, yet few of us have attempted. When confronted with the possibility that we can leave the physical and explore realms which the body cannot, students begin to tremble with fear and doubt. They rationalize that it is an advanced technique, not easily mastered. Well, it is an advanced technique; yet projection is easily mastered. Our first attempts will result in imaginary adventures—this is how it should be. We teach ourselves what is to be encountered in the realms beyond our own world. Then, as we become secure in exploring the sephiroth as they exist in our own body/mind complex, we slowly make the transition over to mental travel. The mind begins to explore that which exists outside its own awareness; the sixth sense opens up and we can see into realms beyond our own. The mind has learned to take its first, fleeting steps. As the mind becomes stronger, exercising mental muscles that it did not know existed, we become free in spirit—free to explore the other worlds.

Some spheres will be easier than others; it takes an advanced soul to progress beyond Yesod in the astral body, and few but the most adept will ever truly travel beyond Tifareth. No matter what level we operate on within a sphere—imaginary, mental, or astral—all will serve to open us up to the magick of the region, and put vast amounts of power at our fingertips as we invoke what we cannot visit.

As we rise on the planes, we will stop at various points to establish what are called magickal temples; regions created by the Witch within the sephirotic worlds to act as focal points for the powers there. These will be exercises of the mind and soul as weight training is for the body. Visualizations will be simple at first, but will grow in intensity until we can conjure up visions of complex temples. At first, it will seem as though our visualizations are make-believe—our mental eyes have atrophied due to lack of use, and unless our training has included intense conscious visualizations, those muscles will not be strong. Not to worry, for as we progress in our work we will soon find fascinating images rising before us. The first solid visualizations we receive will be startling at first, and they will shock us back into the make-believe mode. But as we practice, we will become more secure in these exercises.

Appendix One includes the attributions for the ten sephiroth, Kether through Malkuth; these are the signposts we will use to create and test the visions received in our work. Also, in the beginning, we will use these correspondences to build up the temples in which we shall work. In working with these correspondences, it is important that we do not assume any connection between them beyond their being attributed to a particular sephiroth. Many students have studied these correspondences and assumed that on the magickal planes, one equals the other. The moon is a planet found in Yesod, and we also find the attributions of the dagger, air, and ginseng. This means that these things all teach us about some aspect of Yesod, and together can be used in ritual to create the state of mind needed to enter the realm. As we journey within the sphere, we may also encounter these things somewhere in the landscape. But this in no way implies that the moon, dagger, and ginseng are all different forms of the same thing. Nor does this imply that if a spell calls for ginseng, we may use the dagger instead. Each is separate and distinct, and has its own special use within the sphere.

It cannot be emphasized enough that the correspondences must be committed to memory. While in the trance state appropriate to Yesod, we cannot revert back to Malkuth to check our books, verifying that an herb we encounter is really found within this sphere. Nor can we ask our coworker within the circle to do this for us. Before setting out along the path, we must know the basics of what we can expect. If we encounter anything unusual, we test it against what we already know, and accept it as part of a valid vision if it passes our test. Then, after returning to normal consciousness, we check our lists to see if this information is included in our notes. If not, we continue to work with the vision to see if we have truly discovered something new, or if the older information has been assimilated in a new fashion. This memorization of the material frees our minds to wander in the higher realms.

As we begin, we will work from within our sacred space—the magick circle. However, at this point in our training we have a few options available to us. We may either use the complete ritual given for casting the circle in Chapter One, or we may use a simpler exercise based on the Golden Dawn's Lesser Banishing Ritual of the Pentagram. We already know that the pentagram is a sacred symbol used to control the five elements of earth, air, water, fire, and Spirit, but when used in the following ritual it serves to create the magickal circle and invoke the Archangels of the four elements to its perimeter, guarding us during the time we spend exploring the invisible realms. The form given below is based on the original given in Israel Regardie's volume titled *The Complete System of the Golden Dawn.*

Perform the Qabalistic Cross.

Still facing the East, draw in a slow, deep breath. Begin to imagine a large pentagram before you, burning in a deep, electric blue. If you feel the need, you may draw the pentagram using the athame; the form drawn should be that of the banishing pentagram of earth.

As you exhale, vibrate the word of power, "YHVH" (Yod-heh-vau-heh). Imagine the sound traveling out into Cosmos. See the pentagram blaze brighter, illuminating the Eastern area of your circle in a bright, blue light.

Turn deosil to face the South. Imagine or draw the banishing pentagram there (again using the earth banishing pentagram), and vibrate the word "Adonai" (Aah-doe-nigh). See the pentagram blaze brighter, illuminating the southern area of your circle.

Turn deosil to the West. Repeat the gesture of the pentagram to this quarter, vibrating "Eheieh" (Ay-huh-yae).

Turn deosil to the North. Repeat the gesture of the pentagram to this quarter, and vibrate "Agla" (Ah-gah-lah).

Turn Deosil once more to face the East. Imagine the Archangel Raphael before you. From behind him comes the sunrise and a swift, rushing wind. Behind you, visualize Gabriel standing within a great waterfall, sending a cool mist into the circle. In the South, see Michael in all his bright, fiery splendor. And from the North see Auriel standing in a vast field of corn. Chant, "Before me, Raphael; behind me, Gabriel; on my right hand, Michael; on my left hand, Auriel." Vibrate the name of each Archangel, allowing their forms to become more stable in your imagination.

Once more, visualize the pentagrams in the four quarters; the Archangels should be standing just behind them. See the energies of their realms pouring into the circle from the center of the pentagrams. Chant, "For about me flame the pentagrams, and within me shines the light, love, and life of the God/dess."

Repeat the Qabalistic Cross. The circle is cast.

When opening the circle with the Lesser Banishing Ritual of the Pentagram, make sure to close with it also. Each ritual should have a definite beginning, the opening of the circle; a middle, the ritual itself; and an end, the closing of the circle. To make the ceremony complete, leaving no loose energies floating around, it should be opened and closed in the same manner. Just as using the Lesser Banishing Ritual of the Pentagram ritual will open the circle, it will also close it.

A practice that will be helpful with these exercises is the creation of a magickal diary, a personal journal used for recording the results of all magickal experiments and journeys. The material in this chapter will put us in contact with the inhabitants of the other sephirotic realms—we will journey in mind and spirit to planes of existence that contain new vistas for exploration. We can intellectually study Yesod through Kether by reading the writings of others who have explored these realms; however, as we progress deeper into the Tree of Life, we will explore parts of the sephiroth that are psychologically important to us as individuals. Within an incarnation, each individual student of the magickal arts has certain dispositions and tendencies that develop over time as we work with the higher planes of consciousness. As I explore Yesod, I may obtain detailed visions of the Maiden, Mother, and Crone, along with the areas of Yesod in which they hold power. Someone who is working on inner levels to establish a stronger connection with the male archetypes might wander through the area inhabited by various Horned God figures—the aspect of Him the one who fertilizes the Mother.

Both parts of Yesod are equally important; both visions would be valid. During our initial explorations, we tend to visit parts of the realm that symbolize internal, subconscious workings. By keeping a magickal diary, two students may compare notes on the visions of the sephirah visited, and together share and learn more about the overall working of the sphere. Also, as we begin to individualize our practices, our diary will show certain trends. Some of us may have better results working during the night, while others obtain more detailed visions during daylight hours. Individual cycles vary with the cycles of the moon and sun. Keeping a magickal diary helps us learn more about personal cycles that will increase our magickal effectiveness.

Beyond this, the diary serves as a reference work, and years after these initial investigations are but a clouded memory, we may turn to its pages and review the consciousness-altering work that we have done. In Figure 5:1, I have included a diagram of the format my own journal takes, along with explanations for each entry. This format is only a suggestion; over time you will come up with your own style for recording information.

Now that we are about to begin rising on the planes, there is one question that remains: How are we to approach what may be the most difficult rituals we have done thus far? In spite of their seeming impossibility (mental/astral projection on command), we must remember that soul travel is a subconscious function that occurs naturally every time we dream. Our subconscious minds prefer to

THE MAGICKAL JOURNAL

Date: _____ Lunar Phase: _____

Time: _____ Time Ended: _____

Rituals Performed: *This is a record of the rituals you will be attempting at this time.*
Include an accurate record of the people involved, the parts of ritual performed by each per-
son, and the steps that you go through in order. Keeping this information ensures that a suc-
cessful ritual may be studied and repeated at a later time. _____

_____

_____

_____

Performance Evaluation: *Here, give the ritual's overall success a rating: poor, average,*
good, or excellent. Explain what could have been done better, and how you will improve sub-
sequent rituals. _____

_____

_____

_____

_____

Record: *Give the complete results of the ritual. Make sure that you include all thoughts,*
feelings, and intuitive insights received during the time spent in ritual. This is the most
important part of the journal entry; as memory is weakened over time, we may return to
this record and remember previous work. _____

_____

_____

_____

Figure 5:1

work in a playful fashion, unbound by conscious restrictions and worries. As I stated earlier in this chapter, we need to create a childlike approach to these exercises, relaxing our conscious restrictions and reality agreement. Previous mental conditioning has taught us that the body/mind/soul complex is a complete unit, melded together into a whole throughout our lifetimes. Realize that although these elements function as one, they also function separately for the health and vitality of the whole. Approach these exercises with the attitude of sacred play; slowly, the subconscious functions will participate in these exercises, freeing us to explore the more subtle realms of existence.

With this in mind, let us begin to explore the sephiroth on the Tree of Life!

ENTERING MALKUTH

Malkuth is the easiest sephirah for us to experience; it is here, in the world of material forms, where our consciousness is normally centered. We walk, talk, work, and play within its boundaries every day, yet few of us experience its inner workings. Rising on the planes may seem a contradiction when traveling throughout Malkuth, for rising implies an ascension into another realm. Malkuth is a multi-level reality, and many secrets are hidden in its more etheric energy pattern: this energy unites the patterns imprinted in Yesod with the material forms found in Malkuth. By rising within this realm, we enter the more subtle patterns found in the world of manifestation, experiencing parts of this world still hidden from our physical senses.

To begin, we need to memorize eight pieces of information about this realm: the vibratory names and colors. Turning to Appendix One of this book, the information is found under the four scales of color (Malkuth): planetary, angelic, Archangelic, and Deity. Likewise, there is a section under each sephiroth for the vibrations that accompany the colors. Using colors and sounds, we can exalt the mind/body complex until our entire matrix vibrates with the energies of Malkuth.

As we use these vibrations of sound and color, it is important to remember that they are forms of energy. We not only conjure up the images of the colors and surround ourselves with sound, we invoke the energies of Malkuth through their use. In this way, we surround ourselves with the energy of Malkuth, allowing it to permeate our bodies, minds, and souls. As an illustration, imagine a tuning fork being struck—the vibrations of sound permeate the air in its vicinity, causing the air to vibrate to its pitch. Likewise, the sound of the vibration "Adonai ha-Aretz" causes the energy around us to vibrate to Malkuth's frequency; in return, those vibrations permeate our consciousness. The whole of our energy pattern becomes attuned to the patterns of Malkuth.

By using the vibrations of color and sound, allowing those energies to permeate the magickal circle and our matrix, we begin to vibrate to the conjured frequency. Concentrating the whole mind on the visualization allows the mind to move into an altered state in which Malkuth may be perceived. Surrounding the body with the visualization creates subtle changes in its pattern; the proper sound frequency reinforces this. Atomically, sound changes the pattern in which molecules move. Following this subtle change in the pattern of the body and mind, we effortlessly slip into the awareness of Malkuth.

In Chapter One, we learned that unless energies are properly confined within a magick circle, they continue to radiate and disperse into Cosmos—their immediate effect is lost, as they do not concentrate in the area around us. Our vibrations raise power that must be contained. If the circle is not properly prepared and consecrated before beginning our magickal work, our meditations will be weakened. We may achieve the altered state of consciousness needed to enter Malkuth, or any of the higher realms, but we will not remain in that realm. The power raised through the vibrations continually changes our consciousness, maintaining the mental/spiritual state needed to remain in altered awareness. If that power dissipates, our bodies and minds reassert their natural vibratory rates, and we plummet from the heights back into our normal state of awareness. The secret to rising on the planes, then, is to invoke the vibratory rate of the sephirah desired through intense meditation, concentration, and chanting; then we must contain the power of those vibrations in the area immediately around ourselves.

Therefore, no detail must be omitted from creating sacred space; we must spare no effort to ensure that our immediate circle of consciousness is secure from the mundane world about us. Once we are safe within its boundaries, once the powers of the elements are invoked to be the guardians of the sphere, once the God/dess is called to heighten and sensitize our awareness, we merely begin to use the proper vibratory rates to ensure that our energy dwells in the sephirah desired.

Rising on the Planes, Part I

Create sacred space. As with any ritual, remember to set up your altar and the complete set of magickal tools; they gain strength from these operations.

Secure within the circle, once more perform the Qabalistic Cross to purify your mind and further enforce the boundaries of the circle. Relax into a comfortable sitting position, remembering to keep your spine straight and your chin parallel to the floor. Any clothing should be loosened, as free breathing enhances energy flow.

Begin by visualizing the planetary color of Malkuth flowing about you, black with yellow rays throughout it. Breathe this color in, letting it permeate your body. Feel it growing and spreading to every tissue and pore within, the light growing and emanating from you and into the circle without. As the planetary colors become darker and stronger, make sure you can still visualize the boundary of the circle containing the energies you are invoking. Once this energy is seen in the imagination and felt to be permeating the body, vibrate the name of the sephirah, "Malkuth."

Feel the sound resonating within your chest and spreading throughout your body. Let the sound spiral within your circle, rebounding off its perimeter and coming back to you full-force. Feel your body beginning to move and vibrate with the sound; feel your consciousness freed from the baser material of Malkuth, moving into the more etheric realms. Malkuth is the tenth sephirah—this and all other vibrations should be repeated a total of ten times.

Continue your visualizations with the angelic colors of Malkuth: pale yellow, yellow-brown, olive, and black flecked with gold. Once again, make sure that the colors are not only visualized as present within the circle, but present within the systems of the body. Allow them to vibrate within and without, until you are submersed in color.

Begin to vibrate the angelic name of power, "Kerubim." Once again, feel the sound resonating within your chest and spreading outward to your extremities; also, be aware that the power invoked by your voice is reflected back to you by the circle's perimeter. Repeat this vibration ten times.

Begin to visualize the Archangelic colors: pale yellow, yellow-brown, olive, and black. Once the colors have permeated your energy field and circle, vibrate the Archangelic name "Sandalphon" ten times.

Begin to visualize the Deity color, which is pure yellow, and allow it to permeate your body's systems. Vibrate the name "Adonai ha-Aretz" a total of ten times.

To firmly establish yourself in the sphere of Malkuth, return to the Archangelic color, vibrating the name "Sandalphon" ten more times. The Archangelic color is the negative/receptive color, and being within its energy helps us to attract the sephirotic powers to us. As the circle becomes filled with the Archangelic vibrations of Malkuth, visualize that the magnetic, receptive colors automatically draw more of the sephirotic energies into the circle. Your consciousness is permeated by the vibrations of sound and color. Remain for a few moments in the Archangelic colors of Malkuth, trying to remember everything you have learned about this sphere thus far.

To return safely to everyday consciousness, reverse the pattern of entrance. Rise to the Deity color of Malkuth, vibrating the name "Adonai ha-Aretz" ten times. Then, descend to the Archangelic color, repeating the vibrations. Finish by going through both the angelic and planetary colors and vibrations. Slowly open your eyes as your consciousness returns to normal.

Finish this exercise by closing the circle, using the same methods that you used to open it. As the circle is declared closed, but unbroken, visualize any remaining vibrational energy spiraling out into Cosmos, rejoining its point of origin.

As you become proficient with this manner of entrance into Malkuth, you may practice an alternate route given in Chapter Four with the Tree of Life exercises. Begin to establish the Tree of Life within the aura, beginning with Kether and ending with Malkuth. The Archangelic colors for all the spheres are already present, we just need to concentrate on the sephirah of Malkuth, channeling the energies into the circle about us. Using the exercise given in the section on magnetizing the aura, allow the Archangelic colors of the sephiroth to permeate the aura, then extend to fill the circle. Just channel the energies throughout the vortex as you did in the previous exercise. This method will not exalt the consciousness as in the previous exercise; however, once the first method is mastered, this second technique will be a short-cut for the already trained consciousness.

CREATING THE MAGICKAL TEMPLE

Now that we have attuned ourselves to the frequencies of Malkuth, we must still find some way to enter into the sphere, investigating our surroundings and landscape. Obviously, while we are surrounded by the colors, we cannot see what our minds are tuned into; likewise, since the colors are sustaining us in the energy field of Malkuth, if we cease our visualization of them there is the danger that we will plummet back into the awareness of our bodies. Somehow, we must create another field of energy that will serve as a midway point between our circle and the realm we wish to investigate. What we need is a magickal temple, a special form built in the world of Malkuth to anchor consciousness within its realm.

Remember that the circle, once created, allows our entire matrix of energy to exist between the worlds of the seen and unseen. In our previous exercise, we began rising on the planes by shifting out of ordinary consciousness; we moved our body/mind complex from the mundane world into a realm that exists between the seen and unseen—the circle. Using specialized vibrations, we shifted our awareness into the etheric energy fields of Malkuth. Still centered within the body, we invoked the energies to permeate and share sacred space with us. Two worlds, mundane reality and Malkuth, met in a neutral, in-between space. Before the rising in consciousness, our circle merely existed between the seen realm and the unseen. Manipulating our awareness into a higher state, we shifted the circle to lie between mundane reality and Malkuth.

As long as our vortex is permeated by Malkuth's energy, we shall remain in partial contact with the realm. If, however, we cease channeling these energies, our circle shifts and loses touch with the realm. Somehow, we must anchor the circle in Malkuth's etheric field, just as it is firmly anchored in the mundane world. Our imagined boundaries within our place of working serve as an anchor to the physical; the imagined temple of Malkuth will also serve as an anchor to that sephirah. Even though awareness of that realm consists solely of the energy permeating sacred space, if we mold that energy into a magickal temple, it will shift and exist on the plane of Malkuth. Then, by concentrating on its form, we can effortlessly slip into that realm, just as the body effortlessly sits within the circle.

By the power of pure consciousness, a Witch can venture into realms the physical body may never visit. Our Guph is forever bound into mundane reality; the five physical senses limit us to the reality of matter as solid and impermeable. By allowing the consciousness to wander free of physical restraints, we can peer not only into areas of the physical realm that once denied us access, we may form an "astral body," or a body of light made up of the sephirah's substance. While in Malkuth, we will eventually find ourselves operating in a form that exactly matches the physical, made of the heavy, etheric vibrations of Malkuth. In this form, we cannot permeate any of the higher realms.

Progressing into Yesod, our minds will operate in the pure tselem, as this is the realm that gives our shadowy counterparts their material. But beyond Yesod lies the Ruach—pure mind. Each realm has its own energy upon which we will draw to create our bodies of light. Our minds cannot even cross beyond the Ruach, for pure consciousness and existence are beyond the abyss. Actual travel into the realms of Binah, Chokmah, and Kether is a skill that will be denied most of us, although the mind may glimpse fleeting images through the abyss. These images speak in symbols, for the Supernals transcend the mind and its logical, reasoning processes in all ways.

In traveling into these sacred realms, the physical anchors and reality agreements we have become accustomed to will begin to fade; we can fly at lightening speeds, exhibit super strength, and mentally read the thoughts of other beings. Space has no meaning, as great distances can be traversed with a single thought. Time begins to warp around us, for on the higher planes of existence, time begins to have little or no meaning. At first, these powers may make us uncomfortable, telling us that all our experiences are pure imagination. But as we become accustomed to the laws of the new lands we visit, we will grow more self-assured and comfortable with these changes.

Before any of these things can be experienced, we need to succeed in traveling to the sephiroth; to do that, we must create our magickal temple of Malkuth. In creating our temples, we must take into account the correspondences given for the sephirah in which we will work. Nothing must be placed arbitrarily into these temples; everything must have purpose and meaning. It simply will not do to place an image of a god of war in a temple of Malkuth, even if that god is one's patron. Inharmonious elements must be dispensed with if we are to ensure pure states of consciousness while within these realms.

Figure 5:2 gives an example of a temple that could be used within Malkuth. Let me express that this is not my magickal temple; indeed, it is unwise to show others from outside your own coven, or even those in your coven who are not involved in your work, these creations of personal consciousness. What occurs within these temples is a personal affair, involving work within your deeper awareness. It would be perilous for others to gain entrance to the depths of your own psyche.

There are times when a coven can and should come together within a magickal temple on the inner planes of existence; for work such as this the temple should be created by a group, allowing no one from outside the group to see the actual image. The image only exists on the astral plane once the circle is cast, and the Witch(es) who will be working within the temple have activated its image on the inner planes. This is a valuable safeguard to the temples, for once dissolved on the astral, they are like locked doors, allowing access to no one without a key. The key is the knowledge of the temple coupled with the actual creation of the magickal circle giving the temple's creators access to the spiritual realms. Also, one of the marvels of working within the magickal temples is that the people within it need not be together within the same circle, nor, if they are experienced in such things, do they need to be together at the same time. Five Witches in five separate geographic locations, at five different times of the day, can still all come together within the same temple as a unified group. This is one of the powers learned through practice with the Tree and the magickal temples.

In creating these magickal temples, we begin with the correspondences given in Appendix One. From this list of attributions, we work to build a diagram of the temple we wish to create. Let's look at how I developed the simple design in Figure 5:2. First of all, since Malkuth is the tenth emanation on the Tree of Life, I began with a decagram, a simple ten-sided figure. In each corner, I placed a column to help support the imaginary roof which I will build above the supports. The use of the number ten has given me the basic structure of my temple; likewise, the number of the sephirotic emanation can be used for most of the temples we build.

As a focal point for my work, I decided to build an altar in the temple. The precious stone used in this sphere is the rock crystal, so the altar itself is conceived as a ten-sided figure, waist-high, built of solid rock crystal. The element of this realm is earth, so a large pentacle, much like Auriel's shield, is in the center of the altar. However, because all four elements permeate this realm, I have chosen to color the floor in the elemental colors of Malkuth: red for fire, blue for water, yellow for air, and green for earth. Other decorations which I may choose to add could be lily and ivy plants interspersed among ten statues of various Gods and Goddesses around the perimeter of the temple. Also, there is an open arch in the

Figure 5:2

southern part of my temple, leading to the "outside" world within the sphere of Malkuth. This is not an entrance/exit to and from physical consciousness, but a doorway into the magickal, etheric realm of the sephiroth so we may view the hidden workings of this sphere.

The next exercise, then, is to develop a blueprint of the magickal temple. Some of the basics will be the same as the items in Figure 5:2; for instance, the use of the number ten to create the building and the use of the precious stones. However, feel free to create using the correspondences. Some people may choose to use the planetary colors to build up the design on the floor, then revert to the angelic color to create the colored walls, the Archangelic color for the ceiling, and design the altar out of the willow tree's wood and stain it yellow, the Deity color. Others may choose to change the design of the inner temple itself, using ten large candle-holders in place of the pillars, or do away with the pillars altogether. What is important is that everything has a purpose; nothing is to be placed within the temple without good reason.

Once the design is completed, it should be permanently recorded in the magickal journal and shown to no one, save those directly involved in your magickal work. Magickal exploration is a personal affair, involving deep psychological processes unique to each student. Even well-meaning, unintentional interference from another student may hinder the healing, developmental processes involved.

Now that the temple is created on paper, we need only to proceed into the sephirotic energies and work to establish this structure on the other side of our circle, giving us our anchor within Malkuth.

Begin by casting the circle.

Using the Rising on the Planes technique already given, rise into the Deity colors of Malkuth. Fall back into the Archangelic, allowing the energies to anchor you in this state of consciousness.

Once you are firmly established in Malkuth, gaze into the colors swirling about you. Contemplate the basic design of your temple—the ten-sided figure in whatever manner you have chosen to conceptualize it. Mentally will the sides to form. This may take a concentrated effort, for you are using the raw energy you have evoked to create a structure within the etheric energy patterns. Center yourself on the task at hand and proceed, knowing that your visualizations will begin to take form.

As the sides begin to take form, turn in your imagination, gazing at each wall. Command the energy to take on solid shape before you. Walk to each side, touching it with your hands, feeling its substance. Try to use as many of the five senses as you are able in creating its reality.

You may notice that as the walls take form, the Archangelic energies around you will begin to fade; this is how it should be. Vibrate the Archangelic name ten more times to channel more of the energies into your temple. Once the energies are present, use them to create the symbols and images you have incorporated into the structure's design: columns, altar, floor designs, weapons, statues, etc. Then turn to the area that you have designated as your doorway to the outside realm of Malkuth, and create that also.

Whenever the energies become depleted, simply renew them with the vibratory technique. They will continue to flow into your area.

Using the energy, create any remaining details of the temple. Remember to experience each part of your area with as many of the five senses as you are able.

Now, consecrate the temple. Using your imagination, conjure up the water, salt, and incense. Invoke an astral counterpart to your physical athame. Follow the steps for casting the circle; only instead of the circle, visualize the energies flowing into the side of the temple.

Spend a few moments relaxing within your creation. Chant the Archangelic name a few times to replenish depleted energies. Name your temple; this is the key word to calling it into existence whenever you rise to this plane. Close it by pronouncing the name backward and visualizing the walls dissolving into the Archangelic colors; descend, using the reverse of the vibratory formula, back into your physical body.

At first, calling the temple into existence will take a concentrated effort. During our first few visits, we will not only have to rise into the energy matrix of Malkuth and say the temple's name to open it, we will also have to proceed through complex visualizations to give the area its reality. The whole process is slow, and it may take a dozen or more repetitions before our powers of concentration and visualization are strong enough to conjure up the form of the temple. Perseverance is the key to success. As the temple is both a protection and a sanctuary grounding us in the vibrations of Malkuth, it is important to ensure that the form becomes a strong reality on the etheric planes.

Once our temple is created and strengthened, we have firmly established our consciousness within the sephirah and may move freely within it. Before a visit to the realm outside our temple, however, we must spend some time learning what to expect beyond the temple walls. To do this, we will first call upon the magickal image of the sphere, given in Appendix One, and work with the image to learn some of the secrets of Malkuth.

Begin by creating sacred space. Work your way up the vibratory scales of Malkuth; drop and rest in the Archangelic colors and call the temple into being.

Now, begin to visualize the image of Malkuth in the Eastern part of the temple. See it slowly developing, as if in a mist. Keep working to create the magickal image until it is as solid as the temple itself.

Next, walk around the image, viewing it from all sides. Try to create a solid, three-dimensional shape within the temple.

Now that the image is firmly established, try communicating with it. Talk to it, sing to it, send mental messages; the image itself may choose to either communicate verbally or mentally. Try to listen to what it has to teach you.

The next part of this exercise is to be attempted only after proficiency is gained in visualizing and communicating with the magickal image. Facing the image, pose yourself in the same manner. Try to mimic the posture of the image. This may facilitate greater communication. Visualize your body taking on its form and shape; remold your own image to match that of the image. Once done, imagine that you are merging with the image of Malkuth. Become the magickal image; try to think her thoughts, see with her eyes. Once you are satisfied that you have merged with her, walk out of the figure, assuming your own form.[1]

Although you are still within the temple of Malkuth, you may use the magickal image to show you parts of the realm's exterior landscape. Reverently, ask the form to show you what you will see within her realm; behind her image, the outer landscape will appear. It is important to remember what you are shown so that you can record it in your magickal diary.

Thank the magickal image for any guidance and advice given. Bid her hail and farewell, allowing the visualization to fade into nothingness. Become fully aware of the magickal temple once more before pronouncing its name backward and descending back to the physical body. Record your experiences: thoughts, feelings, and images.

Now that we have learned from the image of Malkuth, we shall invoke the Archangel of this realm, Sandalphon.[2] In any realm that we enter, the Archangels are responsible for the safety of the magickal explorer. Through them, we may obtain guides to the realms beyond the confines of the temple; these guides will keep us from wandering into areas that we may not be ready to perceive (darker areas of the psyche). The technique is similar to that of using the magickal image. Merely invoke Sandalphon (or the Archangel of the sephirah you are in), and request that a guide be provided.

Create sacred space, and enter Malkuth. Open your temple with the secret name.

Begin to chant Sandalphon's name, asking him to appear before you. Visualize his form taking shape in the North.

Communicate with Sandalphon; tell him what you have learned from the magickal image of Malkuth, and ask if he can elaborate. Messages from Sandalphon can be received in a variety of ways, so make sure you are listening to him.

Sandalphon may show you a variety of images and landscapes you should explore; remember to record this information in your magickal diary. Next, request that Sandalphon provide you with a guide, your own magickal companion to the world beyond the magickal temple.

If you are ready to venture into the sephirah, Sandalphon will provide a guide. It may appear as a solid, angelic form, or as an energy being with no discernible form. It is important to ask Sandalphon if this is your guide. Once an affirmative reply is received, ask Sandalphon for the name of your guide. Finally, ask the energy being present if he or she will respond to this name. If not, ask what title or name it would like to use.

---

1. In assuming an astral form while operating in the mental/astral bodies, we actually become the image invoked. Obviously, the physical body cannot change its overt structure; this is due to the reality agreement that we abide by while in physical form. On the astral planes, however, the astral bodies are malleable to thought. Imagine that you are the magickal image of any sephiroth, and you become that image.

As we proceed in our exercises, these new powers will emerge and strengthen in ways unfathomed by the Witch. Practice, experiment—you will excel!

2. Descriptions of the Archangels of the sephiroth are given in Appendix One.

Thank the guide for offering its assistance, and thank Sandalphon for providing you with the guide. Bid them both farewell before closing the temple and descending back into the magickal circle.

Rising on the Planes, Part II

We have entered a sacred space, centered between the worlds. Using this magickal circle as an anchor between opposite realities, we have met the powers of a higher plane, Malkuth, halfway by invoking the energies of the sephiroth into the sphere. Our bodies, protected by the sanctuary of the circle, can relax safely while the mind and soul slowly enter the higher planes of existence through the medium of a magickal temple, created from the energies we have invoked. Without strain, we have slowly developed our powers of visualization and entered a higher realm. Although not aware of it, we have left the body's energy matrix behind, training the soul to soar into realms it once thought impossible to reach. The next step in our practices, then, is to leave the magickal temple we have created and explore the wonders of Malkuth that await us.

Already, we have used both the magickal image of Malkuth and the Archangel, Sandalphon, to mentally peer into the parts of Malkuth that we will encounter in our present stage of spiritual evolution. But what the mind can see, the mind can visit, and we can learn to interact with the landscape and the inhabitants of the realm we are about to enter. First, however, we need to familiarize ourselves with the territory that we will be entering.

This is where our magickal journal begins to assist us. If we have kept accurate records, we can turn back to our earlier visions and reread the entries made, reviewing the landscape and territory that we will visit with our guides. Consider these entries as an itinerary presented by a tour guide; they are the most important parts of the areas that we will be visiting, and as such it is important to concentrate on these areas. Later, as we become familiar with what is already planned for us, we may begin to wander on our own, becoming familiar with the sights that lay beyond our planned itinerary.

Also, we need to study the information given in Appendix One about the sephirah of Malkuth. These correspondences serve as landmarks, things that identify our state of consciousness. Whenever we seem to be lost, roaming in an unknown part of the sephirah, we can begin to vibrate the various names of power and look for these symbols in the landscape of Malkuth to verify that, yes, we are within the sephirah.

Just as in entering the energy pattern of Malkuth, there are certain steps that, in the beginning, we should follow exactly. Later, as we gain proficiency in these exercises, we may begin to alter our methods of working to suit our needs. In the beginning, however, you will have the best results if you follow the pattern below.

Create your sacred space, and rise through the vibrations of sound and color until you are safely established in the energy patterns of Malkuth. Pause for a moment, gathering strength, and then call your magickal temple into being. Take a few moments to ensure that you are firmly within its energy matrix; turn slowly within its perimeter and make sure the visualization is complete.

Using the name given to you by the Archangel Sandalphon, call your guide to you. Once the entity appears, it is important to ask if it is, indeed, the guide provided to you by the sephirah's Archangel. Once an affirmative reply is received, thank the entity and give it strength by drawing the invoking pentagram of earth (Malkuth's element) toward its figure. Visualize a powerful, flowing circuit of energy being drawn into and throughout the figure by the power of the pentagram.

If the guide is the one sent to you by Sandalphon, it will grow stronger and more solid before you. If the guide is not the one sent by Sandalphon, the power generated by the pentagram will cause it to dissolve. By using this magickal symbol, we are testing the power of our visions. This is not to say that you will be harmed if the wrong entity appears—there is nothing in these exercises that will harm someone exploring these higher realms. There are, however, other inhabitants of these realms that will occasionally try to take part in the exercises being performed. While not harmful, they will at times misguide or misinform us about the powers and workings of the realm we are within. By testing our visions and guides, we assure that we are working with pure powers and entities.

Once we are assured of having our proper guide, we may turn to the South of our temple and approach the door. Until now, many of us will have perceived this as a blackness extending into the realm of Malkuth. Now, draw the invoking pentagram of Earth toward the door, concentrating on the landscapes you saw in your previous visions. Slowly, the blackness will lift and you will find yourself looking out into Malkuth. Tell your guide that you are ready to investigate the landscape.

Follow your guide into the world outside the temple. First, look for sights that assure that you are within the matrix of Malkuth. Perhaps, since Malkuth holds such plants as willow and ivy, you will see trees on the hillside that resemble willow, with ivy trailing up their length. Look for symbols such as the magickal animals, planets in the night sky, or temples made in the precious stones and metals of the sphere (in this case, rock crystal). Once you see these symbols, test them by using the invoking pentagram of the sephirah's element (in this case, earth).

Do not act as a passive observer in this experience; you are a tourist in a strange land with a tour guide to show you the sights. Ask your host to explain the placements of the things you are seeing; go out and touch, smell, feel, look at, and experience the symbols in the new environment.

If you see any inhabitants of the realm, ask your guide to introduce you to them. After the initial introduction, test the inhabitant by asking for information like the name of the sephirah you are in, the vibratory names and colors, and even the meanings of those names. If you are satisfied that not only is an entity true to the realm, but it is knowledgeable about the landscape, offer it energy and strength with the invoking pentagram of earth. If the entity encountered gains strength, it is of the light and proper to your experience. If it does not belong, it will become distressed and disintegrate.

Rarely will you encounter anything strange, dangerous, or out of place along your journeys into the sephiroth. At times, however, you will encounter lower levels of life in these realms, or beings that for whatever reason are not native to the realm. Your guide will make sure you do not come across anything dangerous. Listen to your guide. If there is an area that you are requested to not explore at this time, or a symbol you are advised to avoid, ask your guide to explain. Later, when you become proficient at rising on the planes and testing visions, you may begin to explore these areas. Often they represent areas of subconscious functioning that you are not presently equipped to handle. Your guide, and your own intuitive feelings, will dictate what is proper.

If, however, for any reason the contacts you encounter distress you, simply thank the offending entity for its help and ask it to depart. If it still persists, imagine that your form increases in stature, perhaps taking on the astral form of a God or Goddess belonging to the realm. Ask the being once more to depart. If more force is still needed, draw the banishing pentagram of the element toward it and demand it to depart by the powers of the divine name of the realm. Return to the temple, descend back into the circle, and write an accurate record of the experience. Later, as balance is regained, you may try to interpret why the contact was distressing, and perhaps discover a subconscious block that you did not know existed.

Like any travel, rising on the planes can be exhausting. If you find that your energy levels are falling, or the visions of the landscape are becoming tiring, will yourself back into the temple. If you have the strength to go walking or flying with your guide, that is best. In an emergency, merely thinking about being in your temple will draw you back into it.

Once you are securely within the temple, begin to descend through the vibrations of color and sound into the circle. Close the space, and record your experiences.

To illustrate how rising on the planes works, below is an entry from one of my journals, dated August 27, 1991.

I've been working in my magickal temple of Malkuth exclusively for two weeks now, so I decided it's time for a change of pace; I went walking through the landscape of Malkuth. As usual, I opened my circle and used the vibratory rates to go into my temple. After intensive work within its boundaries, I find that merely thinking the name while in the Archangelic colors brings a strong, solid visualization of its boundaries. Turning to the North of my temple, just beyond the altar, I called for my guide, _____.

After using the invoking pentagram of earth to give him strength, we ventured into the sephirah beyond the confines of my temple. This time, the doorway in the South seemed to open into a great cavern—Malkuth teaches us about the inner workings of the material world, so I took this to symbolize that we were about to learn the more subtle, hidden workings of the realm.

Although the cavernous entrance was dark, there was light at the end of the tunnel. Remembering that a tunnel with light at the exit was not only a symbol of Malkuth, but possibly Yesod, I paused, and asked my guide to do the same. Gathering my strength, I drew a huge invoking pentagram of earth with my power hand; the image of a cavernous tunnel intensified and became illuminated by the bluish, flaming light of the pentagram. Satisfied that I was within Malkuth, I told my guide that I was ready to continue. We emerged at the top of a huge room with an opening to my right into the outside world, and a path that spiraled along the outer rim of the cavern into a mine below.

Below us were a number of inhabitants dressed in clothing made of citrine and black; these are part of Malkuth's planetary colors. They were mining various crystals: emerald, quartz, ruby, peridot, tiger's eye—the list goes on. Most of the crystalline structure I could not identify. Remembering that the precious stone of the realm was rock crystal, I once more tested the vision by vibrating the planetary, angelic, Archangelic, and Deity names of the sephirah. The walls of the cavern began to glow with an opaque light; I was within a great cavern of rock crystal. Confused, I turned to my guide for an explanation.

"Malkuth receives the powers and emanations of all other realms; this, the crystal cavern, symbolizes the intangible forces of the other worlds manifesting in the realm of Creation."

I asked for clarification—if crystals were the material focus for the sephirotic powers. I was told that as I gained entrance to the other worlds, I would learn this information. However, rock crystal did contain the essence of Malkuth.[3]

One of the gnome-like elemental inhabitants was drawn to us by the power of my invocations. Conversation with him was irrelevant; I asked him to depart. When he refused, I imagined that my stature was increasing in size, and my form followed thought. When he still refused to leave, I banished him with the banishing pentagram of earth, and he promptly returned to his work. My guide explained that the elementals here were of low intelligence, performing manual tasks to continue the flow of energy. In their present state, they were unaware of the higher workings of Malkuth.

Finding that my strength was waning from the expended energy, I informed my guide that I would like to return to my magickal temple. We returned via the tunnel; upon entering my temple, I thanked my guide and bid him to depart. Then I returned to the circle, closing it as I had opened it.

 I chose this entry because it illustrates some good points. First, even though I have visited Malkuth many times in my magickal journeys, I still stumble upon unfamiliar areas. These new regions usually correspond to one of the many life-cycles we go through, subconscious workings, or conscious learnings. The entry was dated at a time in which I was researching the Qabalistic uses of crystals; the information that I gleaned from this and my subsequent research led me into a new area of study. Also, even though I knew that I was within the energy structure of Malkuth with my guide, I still tested the initial vision with the invoking pentagram of earth. New territory and experiences can be confusing and even frightening at first; by testing my vision, I was strengthening my own belief and control over the new circumstances. And, this passage also illustrates the fact that not all entities of a given sephirah will be knowledgeable or helpful in our studies. Just because an entity derives its energy from a higher plane does not mean that it is any more spiritually evolved than we are.

After a few experiences with this method, we may move on to discover some of the higher secrets of the realms. Remember that we may walk, run, fly, or even bilocate on a plane. When rising on the planes, there is more within its realm than ground level. If we take to the skies, we discover different aspects of the realm we are in; likewise, as the above entry shows, if we go beneath the surface, we discover some of the inner workings. In realms that seem to consist of oceans, rivers, and lakes, we may even safely go below the water to visit the scenery there. In the magickal matrix of the sephiroth, imagination is the only limit.

Eventually, as we explore these realms, we will feel that we have experienced all we need at this time. Sometimes our guides will tell us that it is time to move on to the next world, learning what we may there before coming back to theirs. When that time comes, what are we to do?

---

3. It is important to remember that guides can only confer information that pertains directly to the sephirah in which they live.

The steps to acquiring entrance to the other realms on the Tree are the same as for Malkuth. First, we must prepare our sacred space. Then, after the circle is cast, we use the vibrations of color and sound to ascend the Tree of Life. There is one rule that must be followed in this regard: ascend the sephiroth in their numerical order. Begin with Malkuth, and once you have become firmly established in its realm, then you may begin to rise into Yesod. We go from sephirah number ten into sephirah number nine. Once we have established ourselves in the energy pattern of Yesod, we may begin to construct our magickal temple there, using the list of correspondences from Appendix One.

Within the temple of Yesod, we can begin to call upon the magickal image, a beautiful and strong naked man, to communicate the secrets of the sphere to us. From the magickal image and the Archangel, we may ask to see landscapes that we will be allowed to venture into, and be given a guide to safely take us to these areas. Always remember to use the invoking and banishing pentagrams corresponding to the element of the realm (in Yesod, that would be air) to test and strengthen the visions. Use the divine names to ascertain if the inhabitants you meet are helpful entities. And remember that as a stranger within a strange land, unless circumstance dictates otherwise, always act with courtesy and respect to those you meet.

Once Yesod is mastered, you may move into Hod, Netzach, Tifareth, Geburah, Chesed, and Binah in that order. Remember that once you begin to venture beyond Yesod, however, the travels become more mental than astral; it will take some time to move from a two-dimensional viewing experience to a three-dimensional interaction within the realm. Beyond the abyss, it will be all but impossible for us to venture, even in mind.

Progressing into these sephiroth on the Tree of Life will strengthen our magickal consciousness of each world as it exists both within the psyche and the Macrocosm. Learning the details of each realm's landscape, we continue to strengthen the reality of the Tree of Life within. We move into worlds where we may gain true mystical experience; we have access to entities and teachers, helpful forms who may instill magickal knowledge and secrets not recorded elsewhere. Our awareness, sharpened by our developmental work, may now be used to hallow the forces of light, life, and love that permeate all of Cosmos. We began by moving between the worlds of the seen and unseen to rise on the planes of consciousness; we end by moving between the worlds and calling on the powers of these realms to honor the God/dess in Her many guises, and change, create, and recreate the reality that we are presently living. Within the magickal realms, between the worlds, we are free to explore and take part in the ever-changing, re-creating consciousness of humanity.

CHAPTER SIX

CREATING MAGICKAL RITUAL

Power is latent in the body and may be drawn out and used in various ways by the skilled. But unless it is confined in a magick circle, it will be swiftly dissipated. Hence, the importance of a properly constructed circle—power seems to exude from the body via the skin and possibly from the orifices of the body; always, you must be properly prepared for ritual. The slightest dirt spoils everything, which shows the importance of thorough cleanliness.

The attitude of the mind has a great effect, so only work with a spirit of reverence. A little wine taken and repeated during the ceremony, if necessary, helps to produce power. Other strong potions may be used, but it is necessary to be moderate, as if you are confused, even slightly, you cannot control the power that you invoke.

—From my Book of Shadows

 08/29/93.[1] In my dream, I stand alone in the desert, the hot sun beating down upon me, draining me. Beside me is a vast winged figure; strong, masculine, muscles rippling beneath robes of scarlet. It is Khamael.

"You stand in the midst of my realm—the realm of might and power. Can you control that power?"

"I can!" I say.

"Then show me!"

The sun was hot, unbearable, so I began to conjure a breeze. Concentrating, I became enveloped in an orange light; it flashed—the air moved. "More," I thought, and a gentle wind began to stir, lifting sand, ruffling my hair. "More!" I commanded, and the wind grew into a gale force—I flung my arms into the wind, commanding it to rip across the desert. My aura exploded in violent hues of red and scarlet, and the wind unfurled across the desert. It was gone, rushing out toward the East.

Khamael gazed into my eyes, sorrowfully, and turned to face the West. I saw a huge sand dune rising over the horizon, twisting and writhing as it moved closer. Again, a slight breeze stirred the still air, becoming stronger as the wave of sand approached. I realized my error—I had not stilled the wind! I gathered strength, I concentrated; the wind again bore down on me full-force, its strength magnified

---

1. From my magickal diary.

threefold. An angry wall of sand loomed above me; I was ripped away, caught in the power that I had unleashed; rough grains of sand sliced through me; hot pain flashed within my body. I had lost control of the power!

"Stop," I screamed, but it was too late. I awoke in a sweat; the words still echoing in my head—"Can you control limitless power?"

 At the heart of Witchcraft is magick, the Craft of the Wise, the sacred art of molding reality to our desires. To the uninitiated, nothing seems more appealing, yet so unreal. For to use magick is to assert total autonomy over ourselves—our bodies, our environment, our lives— there is no part of our universe free of our control. We are empowered to sink deep into the dark womb of Earth, to rise beyond the illusions of physical existence, to dwell upon the spiritual reality of creation, learning its intricate workings. With our new perceptions of patterns and reality, we are enabled to reweave the intricate web upon which we build our lives, altering the inherent pattern of all things. With magick, we can change the world.

This art works according to the new view of reality we have adopted: the holistic view of Cosmos. In Chapters One and Two, we altered our perceptions of the material world, concluding that not only is the universe a part of self, it is a projection of self. Likewise, the matter that surrounds us is not concrete; it exists in the midst of change, full of empty space. The forms we sense are illusory projections of our minds. Our minds, knowing no boundaries, interpret Malkuth's illusions: through five senses, we receive a limitless number of distinct impressions. Each impression, each new sensory delight, is another subjective, mental interpretation of self. If the universe is merely another part of self, it follows that there is no limit to how we may alter its appearance, mechanics, or concepts.

At first, we can make only small changes in our environment, such as increased prosperity, a healing, drawing love; these basic workings are necessary parts of our training. Just as increasing magickal consciousness develops magickal power, so will practicing magick develop our consciousness. Remember the statement from Chapter Two, "To will a thing is to remember that you are not that thing." A lack or a conflict in environment symbolizes a problem in consciousness. To redefine the reality existing without ourselves, we must first redefine consciousness within; that consciousness, once developed, may be used to redesign our seemingly "external" world. By reweaving our environment, we are raising consciousness to new heights.

Spellcasting is necessary for magickal training; by viewing and manipulating the symbols of the Tree of Life, we learn more about its intricate workings. Each time we invoke a sephirah to create a change, we open our consciousness to its full power; that power moves through us unimpeded. We imagine the symbols, work with those symbols, become those symbols. At first, it may seem that the powers are difficult to mold; at times, it may even seem that they are difficult to manage. Repeated effort, however, allows us to move and merge with the powers from the higher realms with little effort. Each time we create and perform magickal ritual, we are developing the skills of consciousness.

Spells also help us understand the material world in which we live. As we begin to alter our present realities, we begin to realize the true nature of the human spirit—there is nothing beyond our capabilities, only our preconceived ideas about reality keep us from enjoying the fruits of existence. A person practicing magick will find a predisposition toward certain workings; one who is confident and filled with love will have no problem casting spells to draw appropriate suitors. Amplifying the inner vibrations of love and projecting them outward results in innumerable encounters. The same person may harbor feelings of inadequacy in other areas, such as prosperity. The repeated workings of a money spell may have little, if any, results, merely because the person employing it has not yet accepted that he or she deserves abundance. The magickal ritual soon becomes geared toward banishing those feelings of economic inferiority, rather than amassing prosperity. Once this is accomplished, money soon follows.

As we raise energy and create magick, we soon learn that the self is all-encompassing; it exists everywhere. Symbolically, our reality agreement mirrors life on spiritual levels; while in the body, we can only influence that which we make a part of ourselves. To move a vase, we must reach out with our arms, grab it in our hands, and move the object to a new location. If we wish to eat, we must reach our food; in turn, we can only use the energy stored within food once it has been digested and made a part of ourselves. Through magickal ritual, we can only influence things we can touch on spiritual levels: if we want prosperity, we must reach out and grab the influence that we desire; if we wish to draw love to us, we must first make that emotion a part of ourselves, and touch the minds of others with our power. The greater our realization of the self, the greater our power in magick becomes.

With this growth in power, the ethics of our working become increasingly important. In my Book of Shadows is this rhyme:

Bide the Wiccan Law ye must, in perfect love and perfect trust: Eight words the Wiccan Rede fulfill—ere it harm none, do as ye will. What ye send forth come back to thee, so ever mind the rule of three. Follow this with mind and heart, until merry meet, and merry part!

As we begin to study the magickal arts, we begin tapping into powers and realms that are denied the ordinary person; we learn methods that, if properly applied, cause the changes we decide are important in our lives. A new car, new clothes, a special familiar—all these things can be brought into our realities if we so will. There are no restraints on how we may work our magick, or what we may work for, as long as it does not harm anyone else.

Most people are familiar with the idea that if you harm another, you harm yourself, for you become the power that you invoke. So if I, in a moment of rage, were to will harm on another human being, I would first have to pull negative energies into myself, thereby disrupting my own energy pattern with powerfully destructive vibrations. The Rede teaches us more than this; the power returns to the sender threefold (the Threefold Law represented by the triple-edged athame). It may not occur the same day, it may not return to us five years later, but one day the power will come home to roost. Similarly, if we work for the good of others, magickally blessing and empowering the lives of those we love, those loving vibrations will return. Our new awareness that we have developed has taught us another reason to use this force only for good—everything in the Universe, from the most lifeless rock to the planet that we stand on, is a part of ourselves. If I were to lash out and attack a stranger, then I am willfully destroying myself. Would I mutilate my body, perhaps cutting off my own finger? Never! Why, then, would anyone consider harming another?

There is an old saying that a Witch who "cannot hex cannot heal." I say that if one can heal, one can hex—but only one aspect of the power is necessary: the healing. To cure cancer, the cancer must be eliminated; however, if the destructive energy is first invoked by the Witch performing the ceremony, the Witch, momentarily, must feel the effects of the power. Despite the rationalization, hexing and healing are not synonymous. True, the cancer must be stopped, the spread must be immobilized; invading disease microbes must be nullified lest the patient suffer irreparable damage and die. If energy truly runs in circles, to invoke the power to blast the disease out of existence ensures that the energy will somehow return threefold. And one can rationalize, again, that the intent to heal would cancel out the effects of the negative energy—but karma does not work that way. Simply stated, karma is the law of cause and effect. Everything that happens, every effect, has a cause. The resulting manifestation becomes the cause of something else; it soon creates a domino effect in which the results are ever-changing.

When using magick, it would be better to bind the disease from doing further harm, while strengthening the patient's energy field with powerful, healing currents to assist the body's healing process. Send out a stream of energy to bind the harmful effects of disease in another's body; you, in turn, will be bound three times over from doing harm to your own body, or perhaps the greater body that we all share—the Universe. Now the Threefold Law has an entirely positive effect on every aspect of life. Likewise, when one is faced with another person who is doing harm to others, the other may be bound, not cursed. You, in turn, may find yourself bound from performing the same harmful actions. If you want to harm others, you have no business practicing magick, an art of healing.

Before creating changes with magick, we must keep in mind that there are three basic premises to fulfill—knowledge, needs, and emotions are essential factors to our work. Knowledge implies a basic understanding of the Universe's hidden workings, an understanding that reality is malleable, based upon a pattern of energies. We must know how to discern the complex web of forces that entangle us; we must know how to invoke energies capable of changing these patterns. Our work dealing with the manipulation of consciousness has given us the basic knowledge to make these changes—all we need to learn now is how to construct rituals symbolic of our desires.

To work magick, there must be a central focus for the spell, a clearly defined goal to be held in the mind while invoking the power to create change. This goal expresses our need—magickal needs must be things we are not otherwise able to manifest. Works dealing with prosperity, love, and healing are examples of needs that may be filled with magick; however, it is a waste of power to use magickal ritual to attain these desires if we have not first tried to obtain them through conventional means. A true need is more than a passing whim; it is a necessity, something to be had at all costs. Need implies lack, and we cannot determine if we lack the qualities to obtain our goals if we have not first exhausted all our "normal" options.

Beyond this, the power of magick manifests through seemingly natural means. If we perform a ritual to obtain love, it will assist us in setting up loving vibrations. It may not, however, draw others to us—it will help us find and seek out others who are well suited to our personalities. Prosperity spells may assist us in getting raises at work; if we are actively looking for a new, better position, it may boost us toward an interview that results in higher income. Of course, there are times when results manifest in spite of our mundane labors: one may win the lottery, or by chance meet a stranger on the street who becomes our newest lover. If our need is sincere, if it is more than a passing whim, magick can assist our mundane actions.

For more difficult workings, such as influencing matters of vast economic or ecological proportions, one may argue that personal action is impossible, if not impractical. For anything that we desire to manifest magickally, we can begin the chain of events by personal action. Looking toward an impending cold spell, a farmer would not simply pray to the Gods that his crops be spared, he would react to the pending disaster by protecting his plants with plastic coverings and the like. Faced with drought, the same ingenious farmer might irrigate the crops with reclaimed water; having taken his only probable steps, he would then begin to work magick to bring needed rain. During wartime, magickal practitioners could become involved in a peace movement by writing letters, protesting invasions, organizing marches; to maximize their effects, rituals invoking peace could be planned.

A goal should also generate overwhelming emotions: if our goals are something we truly need, there is emotional involvement. The farmer whose crops are dying will suffer if either cold or drought destroys his plants; he feels misery, anger, anguish—these emotions begin to prompt him into action. A student who needs a 4.0 GPA to get into his intended department will become emotionally involved with his classes, and will study accordingly. A lonely person may suffer because of emotions, and these emotions can stimulate the process of finding love. Our emotions become driving forces; they are felt throughout the entire psyche, and if channeled properly, become vast reservoirs of power to energize our magick. Becoming emotionally involved with the outcome of our spells ensures that we are not merely acting on a whim; we go beyond wanting something to needing something. Having an emotional stake in our magick helps to guarantee success.

Once we have determined that these three necessities of magickal practice are met—we have the knowledge to create change, the need requiring the use of magick, and the emotions to empower our work—we may begin to cast spells. Spellcasting can take many forms, from the simple burning of a candle to the creation of theatrical rituals. The amount of preparation and work needed will depend on the strength of energy required. Now that the basics of magick are known, we can begin changing our realities.

THE BASICS OF POWER

Magick is the art of changing consciousness, and hence, reality: a spell is a focused ritual that molds our increased consciousness into a specific form. Raising consciousness to a designated pitch is an active process, yet the results of such activity are passive; once we reach our plateau, we rest and revel in the energies. The spell, then, becomes the climax of our ritual—we direct increased awareness toward a specific, practical purpose. Fueled by intense imagery and concentrated willpower, it becomes a set of directions that literally "spells out" what the power of increased awareness is to do. On deeper levels, symbolism is the language understood; we are, in effect, communicating with ourselves and God/dess while working magick.

Within the Tree of Life are ten sephiroth that equate with ten states of being. As we try to alter our present realities, we are merely altering our environment from a state of unbeing to a state of being. For example, if I were to desire knowledge of the art of alchemy, my present reality is obviously one that lacks these teachings. I want to have this knowledge, so I admit that this state of being does not exist in my present life. Knowledge is the function of the Qabalistic sephirah of

Hod. Increasing my consciousness to the realm of Hod, I open up a reality that offers new vistas of learning; however, knowledge in general is not my goal. Desiring knowledge of alchemy, I would design a spell initiating symbolic communication with this realm of power, drawing knowledge of alchemy to me. By doing so, I have changed reality.

The ten sephiroth have ten separate, generalized states of energy that are capable of producing a vast number of realities: the secret to casting successful spells, then, is to choose symbols appropriate to the work we are doing. For instance, Yesod is the sphere of the moon, and as such, it controls and regulates a variety of activities. Travel, tides, menstruation, love, illusions—all these are part of the work that the greater sephirotic power is capable of doing. Desiring to protect a loved one traveling in bad weather, I invoke the powers of Yesod to cast my spell; my symbols, however, must somehow represent my desires. Projecting Yesodic energies to the intended recipient will not do; these energies might help, or they might have some other influence. My desired outcome, protection during travel, must be symbolized. To do this, I chant to focus my mind, spelling out the power's purpose. I focus myself, perhaps with the glow of a single colored candle. Most importantly, I would visualize the desired effect occurring; mental imagery is our strongest method of detailing what the power is to do.

We now know the basics of magick—how it works, what it is based upon, and from where the power comes. Before beginning to work with this art, we need to understand the mechanics behind magickal power. We live in a Universe permeated by energy: the rivers, streams, trees, plants, and animals are conduits to power. Within ourselves, as within other energy forms, are connections with the greater tides of power, the Source of life. When working magick, we may draw off the power that exists within ourselves, realizing that in time, the energy we deplete will return naturally from other sources. Or we may draw off the energies of crystals and herbs, realizing that their powers will be replenished from the universal flow of power that surrounds each of us. We may even use the techniques of consciousness that we have already mastered, aligning our own energy centers with the greater concentrated stores of energy in Cosmos, becoming conduits and generators for the Cosmic flow itself. Then, we can use the symbols of crystals, plants, candles, colors, and vibrations to not only help raise consciousness, but also help spell out what the power is to do.

As Witches, many of us have learned to use what is called the Witches' Wheel, the eight paths to power: meditation, invocation, trance, natural substances, dancing, blood control, the scourge, and the Great Rite. These methods, when used in various combinations, serve to release the vast amounts of life-force that each of us has—within the magick circle, we can form this energy into a cone of power, released to draw our desires. These methods work, but after completion of the ritual, many need further rites such as wine and cakes to replenish expended energies. In some cases, such as with the great cones of power raised to avert disasters, like attacks by the Spanish Armada and the Nazi invasions of Europe (and, so I am told, against the recent dictatorial regime of Sadaam Hussein), the life-force expended by each individual Witch was so great, older participants lost their lives upon the cone's completion. An aging body, already depleting its own stores of power and slowly losing connection with the greater life-force of which it is a part, cannot withstand such sudden releasing of energies.

With those who are younger and more resilient, once the body's excess stores of power are depleted, subconscious functions begin to operate and replenish the expended power. At times, if the methods of releasing power are carried out long enough, exhilaration ensues; the legendary "second wind" kicks in as the body's energy systems automatically begin to draw from Cosmic sources. Through the practice of the Middle Pillar exercises and opening the sephiroth in the body, from the start of our rituals we can begin to draw off these universal centers instead of depleting our own energy first. We can use our bodies to channel vast stores of power from greater sources, leaving our own systems cleansed and intact, not depleted and exhausted. Through this form of magick we can each generate an amount of psychic energy equal to that of a traditional Witch's coven without any of the dangers. The key to safely generating large stores of power is to use the Witches' Wheel in conjunction with the Tree of Life. Learning to raise this greater power will take time; and as in the opening passages of this chapter, the greater the power, the clearer the mind must be to control it. Enflame the mind with power, yet keep it clear and focused with the Witch's Wheel.

No matter how much energy is raised, if we work at odds with the natural tides of life that permeate this world, our spells will never have any effect on the reality around us. Imagine that you are in a canoe that has been sucked into the rapids. Realizing that you are in danger, you need to get to the shore. The current carries you in a straight line down the river, while you decide to paddle straight for the shore. You quickly become tired; as a result of the conflicting currents, your canoe capsizes. This is an excellent example of working against a natural tide—by not focusing your intent to coincide with nature's, you accelerate, not alleviate, your immediate peril. It would have been far better to paddle at a slight angle with the current; instead of fighting the power of the angry, swelling river, you flow with it, modifying its force to carry you closer to safety.

In magick, we work with three tides: rising, full, and receding.[2] These are best symbolized by the phases of the moon. The rising tide of power is in effect while the moon goes from dark to full; hanging full in the night sky, the full moon represents the full tide of power. Its darkening crescent is the receding tide. During the three days and nights of darkness, all power is withdrawn into the depths of night; this is the time for shielding, meditation, and introspection, not magickal work. To translate into practical uses, the waxing moon is the time to work for new projects, beginnings, and change; the full moon represents the tide of power for completion, bringing all projects to fruition; the waning moon is a time for banishing and destroying bad habits and thoughts; also, this tide is good for meditation and scrying.

This is not to say that a spell aimed at increasing the growth of your plants should not be worked during the waning moon; magick for anything may be worked at any time. We merely keep in mind the focus of the tide, and work our wills accordingly. For instance, if I wish to bless my plants during the waxing moon, my spell would be aimed at increasing growth; during the full moon, my focus would be on fulfilling their natural growth and strengthening the plant. During the waning moon, I could focus on banishing the conditions that are retarding my plant's growth; during the dark moon, I could synchronize myself with the plant, searching for those things that are impeding its growth. Remember that you must angle your spell to work with the natural tide you are within, just as in our canoe example we angle the boat to work with the rapid's force.

---

2. This chapter gives the basics necessary for creating magickal rituals. Chapter Seven explores the magickal tides in depth.

The next step in creating change, after defining the natural tide we must work with, is to determine the proper reality we wish to create, and hence the natural state of being (sephirah) we need to invoke. In Appendix One, the general energy state that may be used for magickal working is listed for each sephirah—this is the basic feeling, or psychic reality, that each sephirah may be used to create. The magickal uses also listed give some of the general activities the form of energy may create. If you can't find an exact match for your work under the magickal uses of each sephirah, examine the general energy states and decide which sephirah best encapsulates the idea, or reality, that you wish to create. Once you have decided, it is time to create the symbols for the spell.

As an example, let us suppose that we have recently started a new business, and we want to create stability in our endeavors. Reviewing the lists in Appendix One, we find that Chesed best encapsulates our desire; we find under magickal uses that it deals with financial stability. Some of its other effects—expansion, growth, increasing prosperity—are aspects we would like to create through our business; stability, however, is the main focus. Let us assume that we are in the waning of the moon, so we must work with the idea of banishing any elements that will prevent us from stabilizing our business. Some of the correspondences that we may use to build our ritual are the minerals amethyst, sapphire, and lapis lazuli—as we are projecting this influence to our business itself, we decide to work with the amethyst: its deep purple color matches the Deity color. From the list of plants, herbs, and trees we may use agrimony, nutmeg, star anise, cedar, mint, and olive. We decide to use nutmeg, cedar, and star anise; they have distinctive aromas that we find appealing. Now, we need to find a way to focus and symbolize our desires.

Since we are working to create stability in the business itself, we may use some sort of material to create an image of the building; personally, I would create and paint a cardboard cutout, stuffing it with my chosen herbs before sealing it to ensure that the vibrations remain inside my business. Also, to help empower the herbs, I could place a piece of amethyst within the image. Using common knowledge, I realize that to have a stable business, I must create a firm financial foundation for it by drawing a consistent clientele; therefore, I attach my image to a larger amethyst cluster, showing that the powers of Chesed form the foundation for my work. The symbolism of my spell is complete.

MAGICKAL RITUAL

Now that the basics of spells are understood, we may begin to use the Witch's Wheel in conjunction with our Qabalah to create magickal changes in our environment. There are eight spokes to this Wheel, also called the eight paths of attainment. They are as follows.

Meditation

Most of the course presented so far has dealt with this path to power: circle casting, visualization, and magnetizing the aura are all forms of meditation. Whenever the mind is consciously stilled, relaxed, and open to new vistas of awareness, we are practicing the art of true meditation. In conjunction with Qabalistic magick, meditation is the simplest method of invoking the sephirotic powers. Focusing awareness on a specific sephirah in the body's energy field, and willing that energy to increase and fill the aura and magickal circle, will channel vast amounts of power for the Witch to use. As such, meditation is one of the most important paths to power; although seemingly passive, it serves to enflame the mind to the necessary level of consciousness for magickal working.[3]

There have been reams of material written about this subject from a myriad of viewpoints—transcendental, Eastern and Western techniques, progressive relaxation, biofeedback—all these are important to the subject of meditation as a discipline, but they are unnecessary to it as a magickal practice. For magickal practitioners, there are two necessary divisions to meditation: the asanas and breathing. An asana is simply a posture. In Chapter Four, we worked with the asanas of the magickal images. By positioning the physical body to match the postures of the magickal images, we entered a mental rapport with them. A posture is a method of enflaming and centering the mind on a specific concept. We may create asanas symbolic of our magickal needs. To enter rapport with a tree spirit, we can assume a posture mimicking the tree that the spirit inhabits. To draw love, we may assume a position symbolic of the love we desire. Molding the body to symbolize our desires while invoking the energy of the sephiroth through meditation is a powerful way of making magick.

No matter the position adopted, however, it is important that the spine, neck, and head be properly aligned—pretending that the buttocks form the base of our alignment, the entire spine must be at a ninety degree angle with our imagined base. This aligns the natural energy centers of the body, and opens an unblocked path by which our invoked energies may circulate. To develop proper posture, find a saucer and a cup made of an unbreakable material, such as plastic. Fill the cup about half-full with water, and position yourself before a full-length mirror. Sit comfortably with your legs crossed before you, staring into the reflection of your eyes. Try to align the spine, head, and neck so that they are at an exact ninety degree angle to the floor. Carefully, balance the saucer on the top of your head; next, place the plastic cup of water on the center of the saucer. Hold both in place while you reposition your body—use the centered weight of the cup and saucer to help you find an aligned position. Once your body is aligned properly, remove your hands and place them comfortably on your lap. Staring into the reflection of your eyes, try to hold this position for about five minutes.

As you try to hold this position, you may feel momentary disturbances from the balanced items on your head; even though they do not lose their balance and fall, with every breath you take, they do quiver. This is due to improper breathing—the next step to learning proper mediation technique is to concentrate on the flow of breath. Many breathing exercises have been delineated for attaining different states of consciousness; for magickal practice, however, it is only necessary to master slow, even, prolonged breathing from the diaphragm. The diaphragm is a muscular membrane that separates the organs of the chest from those of the abdomen; it forces air to move in and out of the lungs. To locate the diaphragm, run your fingers down the length of your sternum (the hard, central bone of the ribcage). Now, find the point halfway between your belly button and the end of your sternum; this is the location of the diaphragm. Breath a few times, and it will

---

3. Here, we will examine meditation as a path unto itself; however, as we study the remaining seven spokes of the wheel, meditation will be used initially to invoke the power of the sephiroth.

seem that the focus of the stomach's rising and falling is located here. This will be our initial point of concentration for meditation.[4]

Without the cup and saucer, but still staring into the mirror, align your body properly. Next, locate the diaphragm, and place your hand over its location. Close your eyes and breath in, concentrating on drawing in air from the diaphragm. Instead of forcing yourself to inhale, force the diaphragm to expand; when exhaling, force the diaphragm to collapse. Firmly resting your hand over this location will help you concentrate on the diaphragm itself, helping you establish a center of focus for your mind and breath. Once this is accomplished, begin to slow and strengthen each breath. Count silently how long each inhalation and exhalation lasts; as you begin to relax, extend each breath by at least one count. When you reach your limit, begin to hold each breath for at least half that count: for example, if each inhalation and exhalation takes a count of six, hold the breath still for at least the count of three. Continue to extend your breaths until you have reached a point where it is no longer comfortable; drop back to the previous count and continue in that rhythm.

Once proper posture and breathing are mastered, the mind/body complex can fall into progressively deeper states of relaxation. Opening up to the power of the sephiroth becomes easier, and with a forceful, yet relaxed, flow of breath, it becomes simple to move the channeled energies and mold them into our desires. Before working with any asana, whether it be one created to focus the resulting energies on a magickal desire, or a specific posture directed at molding the mind into a specific state of consciousness, the previous two exercises should be done before ritual to ensure that we can align the spine and regulate the breath properly. These two considerations lead to the success of any magickal ritual designed with this path of power as its focus.

Exercise One

Focus on an area in which you would like to create a magickal change, to cast a spell to alter reality. Using Appendix One, decide which sephirah best embodies your desires. Decide on a magickal posture that would sum up your need—if you cannot, either use the basic position given in the previous exercises for posture and breathing, or use the position of the sephirah's magickal image. Memorize the color of the sephirah needed;[5] review the list of correspondences for the sephirah. Also take into account the natural tide of life that is flowing now—dark, waning, full, or waxing moon. Decide on a visualization that would sum up the focus of your spell in conjunction with the predominant life-tide. Once all this is done, you are ready to begin ritual.[6]

Create sacred space. Stand in the center of the circle, opening all the sephiroth in your body. Once the energy is flowing, concentrate on the energy needed; focus

---

4. Another exercise used by vocal instructors to locate the diaphragm is this: Place one hand just above the navel and pant like a dog. The point at which the stomach "jerks" the strongest, the central location of the rising and falling of the abdomen, is the location of the diaphragm.

5. For a review of using the sephirotic colors to draw and repel energies to your reality, turn to the section on magnetizing your aura in Chapter Four.

6. Through the rest of this chapter, it will be assumed that the student keeps these three basics in mind: natural tide, sephirah, and symbolism. Working out these basics before the beginning of ritual will ensure success in all operations.

on each sephirah, willing the magickal color to flow throughout the aura, and hence, the circle. Continue this meditation until the energy flows freely about you, then move into the magickal asana you have chosen for casting your spell. Using proper posture and breathing, will the energies to flow and coalesce into your chosen symbol—the visualization of the outcome. Continue to meditate on the channeled energies flowing into your symbol. Once all the invoked energies have coalesced into your symbol, force the energized visualization to enter into the sephirah itself—will it to enter into the anatomical region of the body from which the energy came.

Return the colors in the circle and the aura to normal, and awaken to full consciousness. Close the circle, knowing that your need will soon manifest. The spell is complete.

Invocation

This path to power involves a variety of techniques, including chants, rhyming couplets, invocations of Goddesses, Gods, and elemental powers. We have already used several examples of this path of the wheel; in Chapter One, we learned to invoke the elemental powers to the magick circle, strengthening our own energies. We have learned to invoke various forms of the Goddess and God. In a sense, meditation with the sephiroth involves a type of invocation, for we are calling forth the Tree's energies. The concept behind this path to power can be summed up in the adage, "enflame thyself with prayer!" Focusing our minds on a single topic, we then speak a series of declamations, invocations, and chants to focus energy on a single topic—the desired results of the spell. Enflaming emotions with declamations of intent, the mind runs down a narrow path, taking the energies invoked with it to a time and place in which the energy may be manifested as our desires. The key to the proper use of invocations is to become emotionally caught up in them, concentrating all our efforts upon the eventual desired outcome.

Although we may choose this path to power as the focus of our ritual, a properly executed series of invocations may share aspects with the other spokes of the wheel: meditation, visualization, etc. This is a dynamic method of working; it is also one in which our words and symbols must be chosen carefully. The power, once enflamed, will latch onto the literal meanings of our words and symbols, so we must plan our invocations and symbolism carefully. When using this method, it is important to have worked out in advance our central symbols—here are a few ways in which we may design them.

Treasure Mapping

This technique for creating a new reality involves making a drawing or collage filled with symbols representing the outcome of our spells. When creating a Qabalistic treasure map, there are a few rules to keep in mind. First, the major color of the map should be that of the sephirotic color you are going to use. For a spell involving Netzach, if you are projecting energy to another person, use the Deity color (amber); if you are recreating your own reality, use the Archangelic color (emerald green). The best material to use for treasure mapping is poster board, as it comes in a wide variety of styles. If appropriate colors are not available, simply use white and paint it the desired color.

At the center of the treasure map, include either a photo or a drawing of the spell's recipient, with either photographs, magazine cutouts, or drawings of the intended effects surrounding it. The more symbolic the map is, the better it will communicate to your subconscious mind, and hence to the power you invoke, the results you wish to achieve.

Poppets

These make an excellent symbolic focus for the power you invoke when it is to be sent to another. Make sure that you construct the poppet out of material that is in the Deity scale of color, as this is always used to send the power to another. Inside the poppet, you may stuff hair, nail clippings, swatches of clothing, and photographs of the recipient to establish a magickal link; likewise, on the poppet you may sew the recipient's name to further enforce the magickal connection. While sewing the poppet, try to visualize the person whom it represents—it is not necessary to have a doll that resembles the recipient.

To further enforce the magickal connection between the spell's recipient and the symbolic energy, you may also fill the doll with herbs representing the sephirah, or other symbols such as shredded play money to represent prosperity, etc. The more symbolic the doll is inside and out, the more powerful the connection with both the recipient and the power will be.

Sachets

If you are making a sachet to project energy to another, create it in the Deity scale of color. If it is being given as a present to a friend to draw specific circumstances, or if it is for yourself, create it in the Archangelic scale of color. Stuff the sachet with appropriate pictures, crystals, symbols, and herbs. Perhaps sew a symbol representing the desire onto the outside of the cloth.

Forms of the Goddess and God to be invoked, elemental powers, if any, and the final rhyming chant or couplet spoken to emphasize the spell should be planned out in advance to eliminate errors. Ambiguities should be avoided. For example, in a recent prosperity spell that I worked, I used the following chant as the focus for my power, "Silver and gold will come to me soon, Goddess and God, grant this boon!" My spell was aimed at increasing my present prosperity, perhaps finding a better job or getting a raise at my present one. The results of my spell, due to the wording used, were not quite what I desired. The same night that I cast my spell, I found an old 1960 silver dollar that I thought I had lost. At the time, I did not make the connection between finding the silver dollar and the spell that I had cast. Two days later, while walking down a sidewalk near my apartment, I found a gold bracelet lying on the roadside. My work had indeed brought silver and gold to me, not the increased prosperity that I had desired. The next time I worked my spell, I redesigned the chant to "Increased prosperity I will receive; my present reality, I reweave!" This new chant helped bring the results I desired.

Exercise Two

Determine an area in your life that you would like to change. Since this path to power is complex, I will guide you with a spell that I cast to help me understand the spirit of sacrifice in our present day. Once your need is determined, search through Appendix One to find a sephirah appropriate to the work that you will be doing. For understanding the concept of sacrifice, I chose the sephirah of Tifareth; it deals extensively with spiritual sacrifice and the sacrificed gods.

Now, we must decide how to invoke the power of the sephirah that we will be using. The section on magnetizing the aura in Chapter Four is perhaps the best and easiest used method; however, invocations assume use of the spoken word. While magnetizing the aura to the desired color of the sephirah, we need a spoken invocation to enflame the mind and increase the amount of power being poured into the circle. For my invocation to Tifareth for obtaining understanding of spiritual sacrifice, I used the following:

> *Sacred power of Tifareth, mighty one called IAO; I invoke you to my magick circle. Come in all your power and all your might, bringing knowledge of the true meaning of sacrifice. I conjure thee, thou powerful and strong Archangel, Michael; bringer of light and life. I conjure thee, thou powerful and strong angels, Malachim, the kings of the light! Mighty IAO instill the knowledge of true sacrifice within. May thy Archangel Michael bestow upon me the spiritual understanding to use this knowledge aright, and may the powerful Malachim destroy the feebleness of mind and spirit that would keep me from using this knowledge aright in the material world. Come forth, powers of Tifareth—I invoke you by your names of power: IAO; Michael; Malachim.*

During this invocation, I envisioned the powers of Tifareth unfolding from the area of my heart in the Archangelic color of yellow, because I was drawing understanding of my concept to me. Every time that I said one of the Deity, Archangelic, or angelic names, I vibrated them, or said them in a sing-song manner. The final three repetitions of the names served to increase the force generated about myself.

The next step in designing a ritual with this path to power is to determine what Gods or Goddesses to invoke. For obtaining an understanding of sacrifice, I invoked Cernunnos in his form of sacrificed God, and used the traditional invocation to Him given in my Book of Shadows:

> *Great God Cernunnos, return to Earth again;*
> *Come at my call, and show thyself to men.*
> *Shepherd of Goats upon the wild hill's way,*
> *Lead thy lost flock from darkness unto day.*
> *Gone are the ways of sleep and night;*
> *Men seek for them, though their eyes have lost the sight.*
> *Open the door, the door that hath no key,*
> *Whereby men come to thee.*
> *Shepherd of Goats, answer unto me!*

While these invocations are spoken, it is important to imagine that the form of the God or Goddess you have chosen is beginning to merge with your own, much as in the assumption of an astral form. The next matter of importance is to write the actual spell, the rhyming couplet by which the power is bound to your chosen symbol. For my working, I used "The power of sacrifice will be known to me; this is my will, so mote it be." Once we have written the different forms of invocation, we may begin to work our ritual.

Begin by creating sacred space; omit the initial invocation of Goddess and God. Instead, replace it with the sephirotic invocation you have written, imagining that the energy flows ceaselessly from you into the circle. Once the energy is at its peak, begin to invoke the God/dess you have chosen, feeling that the force is merging with your own. Here is the true key to this path to power—you must feel that the divine force of the sephirah and the God/dess is vibrating within and without. Enflame the mind with the power of the invocations until divinity becomes a definite, physical force in your mind/body complex. Magick done once this force is felt is sure to succeed; magick done in the absence of this force very often fails.

Now, focus on the symbol you have chosen. Begin to chant your rhyming couplet, imagining that the energy raised is going within the object representing your desires. Keep up the chanting, losing yourself in the flow of power until all that your mind focuses on is the chant and the object. Once the power is exhausted, return your aura to its normal colors and descend to normal consciousness. Close the circle; the spell is complete.

Trance

The paths of meditation and trance are often confused; this is understandable, since prolonged meditation often leads to trance. Likewise, repeated chants in invocation can cause a trance-like state. The difference in definitions between meditation and trance is subtle, but the difference in results is great. Meditation is reflection and contemplation. Relaxing the body ensures that the mind soon follows, and the resulting state of consciousness enables us to transcend the material boundaries of Malkuth. From this heightened state of awareness, trance might ensue if we focus on one principle, such as a chant, color, or vibration. In meditation, we open up to awareness of the higher realms; in trance, we narrow consciousness to one specific principle.

A single burning candle, a repeated rhythm, a soothing yet monotonous voice—all these are ways to induce trance. Once in this twilight state of consciousness, we could describe our actions with one of three terms: hypnotic, cataleptic, or ecstatic. If a hypnotic state results from trance, the mind becomes open to the suggestions of other people, entities, or forces. During catalepsy, the body remains motionless and unaware of its surroundings while the consciousness soars free of physical restraints. Ecstatic trances are the result of overwhelming power; possessed by the energies being channeled, a person rocks, chants, dances, or sings ceaselessly, driven by the inner vibrations filling the psyche. During all three types of trance states, we are expressing a very active spoke of the Wheel. Magickally, this activity may be used in three ways:

1. In opening to positive suggestions, harmful thinking is restructured. Bad habits, poor self-image, and destructive behavior may be released, and replaced by positive affirmations of life and hope. It is unwise to open the psyche to the suggestion of an untrained person; this type of magick is best worked under the tutelage of a God, Goddess, or angelic presence. It is also the type of trance needed for channeling.

2. Projection of consciousness allows us to travel directly to the sephiroth, seeking out places of power to create change. Chapter Five explores this method

in depth. It is useless for casting spells if the power we need lies beyond the ability of our souls to rise.

3. By narrowing our consciousness to one specific vibration and becoming ecstatic, we channel the consciousness of energy into physical channels. This movement of the body, brought about by the overwhelming force of power, encourages more power to flow through us. Focusing on a single, lit candle in the sephirotic color we are using, while chanting a two or three syllable chant is enough to bring about this state of ecstasy. In extreme cases, another form of channeling is brought about, typically known as divine possession. A God or Goddess, perhaps even a highly evolved entity, will enter into the entranced Witch and begin to dance, speak, or otherwise move in a symbolic fashion.

Exercise Three

The path of trance lends itself to many uses; the most important are the destruction of bad habits and the development of healthy ones. Reviewing the lists given in Appendix One, any bad habit one might have exists as a vice in one of the sephiroth. This vice shows imbalanced activity of the sphere. Also listed is a virtue— what the destructive habits can be turned to once the energies of the sephiroth are balanced. Remember, the key to destroying bad habits is to balance the energy of the sephirah within the psyche so that the virtue of the sphere may arise. If looking over the lists, you are not able to find a sephirah that deals exclusively with the vice you wish to destroy, then determine which realm the unbalanced energy belongs to by looking over the general energy state.

To destroy a bad habit, begin trance work when the moon is waning. Select a candle in the Archangelic color of the sephirah to symbolize that you are trying to draw balanced energy into your life; likewise, choose a symbol that represents your bad habit. As an example, pretend that the goal of trance is to quit smoking; there is nothing in our virtues and vices that deals with such an activity. But by reviewing the general energy states of the ten sephiroth, we find that Geburah deals mostly with destruction. Smoking, we realize, is a destructive habit that we would like to give up. To further reinforce our selection of the sephirah, we see that tobacco, the main ingredient in cigarettes, is one of the herbs listed as a correspondence of Geburah. By constantly smoking, we are inviting unbalanced Geburic energies into our matrixes.

Geburah's Archangelic color is red, so we would use a red candle to draw balanced energies to ourselves. To symbolize smoking, I could either use a single cigarette, a pack of cigarettes, or some loose tobacco. Now, I have the basic symbols of my spell gathered and prepared. The next step is to decide how to induce trance. When working alone, the easiest method is to concentrate on a single candle flame, and chant. For this example, the affirmation "I will quit smoking, I will quit smoking," would do nicely. Or, the chant may take the form of a spell: "I will quit smoking soon; Goddess and God, grant this boon." It is important that the affirmation be simple and repetitive with a minimum of effort.

Once these basics have been determined, create sacred space. Begin with a simple meditation inviting the powers of Geburah to fill the circle. Light the colored candle, and begin the chant designed to induce trance. Staring at the candle's flame and repeating the chant will soon focus your mind on the task at hand. Balanced energies will be drawn to you as you reaffirm with your mind that the bad habit will soon be destroyed. As you are overcome with trance, you may feel warmth in your body and heaviness in your limbs; perhaps your sight will seem to narrow until all you can perceive is the single candle flame. These are normal signals that your consciousness has narrowed into a trance-state. Just as you have entered trance naturally and slowly, so will consciousness eventually widen on its own. Once this happens, relax for a few moments, feeling the balanced energies returning to your aura. Destroy the symbol of the bad habit before closing the circle and make an effort to avoid repeating the destructive thoughts and habits.

During periods of balancing, it is important to spend some time every night during the waning moon entering trance and working with the affirmations. As the influx of balanced energies loosens the hold of the bad habit, it is time to create a new, empowering thought or habit to fill the void that is created with the loss of the destructive one. In the example of quitting smoking, during the waxing moon I might desire to replace the old habit with a new habit of energy-raising breathing, using the powerful energies of Geburah to instill energy (the virtue of Geburah) into my consciousness. While entering trance during the waxing moon, I could use the chant: "Energy will increase soon, God and Goddess grant this boon." As my old force of habit tries to compel me to reach for a cigarette, I could begin a few deep breathing exercises to fill my mind/body complex with energy instead of smoke.

The point to instilling a new, healthy habit during the waxing moon is to replace the void left by the loss of the old habit; this new habit should take advantage of the balanced energies filling the psyche. The old habit may once again take hold in the void; the energies of the sephirah may again become unbalanced. By replacing old habits with new ones, we reinforce the power of replacing unbalanced energies with balanced energies, making our personal changes more complete and lasting.

Exercise Four

Trance may also be used magickally to create needed changes in the environment. After deciding upon a magickal need, go through the lists in Appendix One to find a sephirah that embodies your desire. Obtain a candle in the proper sephirotic color—Archangelic if you are creating change for yourself, Deity if you are creating change for another. Into the wax of the candle, inscribe the chant that you will be using; other symbols, such as runes representing your desires, may be used instead if you so choose. The final item you will need is a straight pin; if possible, obtain one with a colored, plastic ball on the end that matches the color of your candle. This pin will be used as a cue to the subconscious mind that trance should end; stick it into the candle roughly one quarter of an inch below the wick. When the flame burns to the pin, your consciousness will widen once more.

Cast the circle; before beginning work with the candle and chant, spend a few moments empowering your aura and the circle with the sephirotic colors. Light the candle and begin staring into its flame, repeating the empowering chant in an even voice. It is important to center your mind on both the candle and the chant; as the mind begins to focus, the power will begin to channel itself into the form of your desire. Continue this focusing of consciousness until the flame reaches the pin. As it falls from the wax, allow yourself to regain normal consciousness. Return the remaining power to your aura; finish the Tree of Life meditation by returning all energies to their starting point. Close your magick circle; the spell is complete.

Natural Substances

My Book of Shadows dictates that it is wise to incorporate "things that have life" into spells. Magickal practitioners of all ages have studied and guarded the lore of trees, herbs, and crystals; today, it is difficult to find a new-age shop or even a mainstream bookstore that does not carry titles about this system. Natural magick, as this genre is often called, enjoys mainstream popularity. As a path to power, the use of natural substances such as herbs, crystals, trees, and plants can become one of the most important reality-altering methods for the Witch. Everything in the universe is composed of vibrations; Qabalah teaches that the symbols found in Malkuth, and hence, Earth, all have their point of origin in another spiritual realm—a sephirah from the Tree of Life. By collecting items linked to a single sephirah, the sephirotic powers gathered increase geometrically. A living talisman is created: if imbued with our desires, each symbol in the resulting mixture molds the energy it channels into our desires.

Malkuth is a realm created by the action of the other nine sephiroth—all the energies of the Tree somehow merge and become one vast Universe. All thoughts, emanations, and creations find completion here; Cosmos is the fruit of this sacred Tree. To be created and sustained by the Tree of Life, it logically follows that everything in this world can be traced to a point of origin somewhere in the branches between Kether and Yesod; anything encountered on a daily basis may be used as symbolic of some sephirah. If I take a trip to the ocean, I can use this vast body of water as a symbol of Binah in its form of Mara—the bitter sea, primordial Mother of life. The sun above becomes Chokmah, the Supernal Father, while the sand below my feet represents Daath, the abyss that separates the Supernals from the rest of the Tree. Sitting beside a lake under the light of the full moon, I am experiencing the power of Yesod upon the landscape. More importantly, each herb, plant, tree, crystal, or other substance found in nature can be traced to a part of the Tree because of its vibrations. Through their existence, they channel and renew the vibrations of each sephirah in our world.

Within the natural world, these symbols are randomly distributed to keep the power flowing smoothly: deep below our lake might lie vast amethyst geodes; the vibrations of Yesod and Chesed merge together in a spiritual symphony, creating vibrations unique to that locale. If various natural symbols of a single sephirah are amassed, however, the power of their combined vibrations increases geometrically. If these natural substances are gathered and empowered in a place symbolic of the sephirah being invoked, wonders ensue. Desiring to enhance my own beauty, I might obtain a clear quartz crystal and some damiana, empowering each with my magickal goal. Alone, each carries a weak vibration; together, empowered for a single purpose, their powers entwine into an ever-widening spiral. If empowered at a locale that receives large quantities of Yesod's vibrations, the resulting cone of power becomes a tidal wave of Yesodic vibrations. The talisman resulting from our work molds the sephirotic energies into our desires.

Using natural substances, then, is perhaps one of the most powerful paths to power contained in the Witches' Wheel. By taking different items from nature, symbolic of the sephirah with which we work, we create vast channels of power; that power, in turn, may be molded to our desires. "Things that have life" become our most magickal tools, the most important weapon in our arsenal to create desired changes.

Exercise Five

Deciding upon a magickal need and a state of being, review the list of correspondences for the sephirah you are going to use. Choose three or more crystals and herbs (odd numbers are said to be the most pleasing to the Goddess) to incorporate into your spell. You may wish to sew a small bag to contain each of the items; it is important to have this bag in either the Archangelic or Deity color of the sephirah—the color you choose depends on the work to be done. Prepare the incense and/or perfume you will be using. Once all of your materials are prepared, assemble them in your ritual space.

Cast the circle. Open the sephiroth in the aura, concentrating on the one that you will be using for your work. Fill the circle with the sephirotic powers; gather your incense or perfume in your hands, directing the invoked energies to flow through the mixture. Once the incense is lit, imagine that the rising smoke is drawing more power into the magick circle. Continue the visualization until the circle is filled with power.

Now, begin to work with the materials gathered for your spell. If you are using a crystal, empower it first. Holding the crystal in your power hand, begin to sense the sephirotic powers within it. Feel how it resonates with the energy gathering in your circle; let it share its energies with you. Visualize your desire in your mind; with your breath, force it to flow from within your mind and into the crystal. Spend a few moments visualizing a symbol of your need resonating within the crystal's structure. Place it in the bag on your altar.

Having empowered the crystal, take each herb or other substance in your power hand, directing a visual image of your desire into it. Once all the items are properly imbued with your desires, place them inside the bag. Repeat the initial visualizations, ensuring that all the materials in your bag are vibrating with desire. Close the circle; the spell is complete.

Dancing

At the heart of magickal ritual are the ecstatic states—anything that causes the mind to transcend ordinary reality becomes a path to power. Proper breathing produces and moves power, for the mind relaxes, losing its grip on mundane reality. Through intense concentration and invocations, the mind shifts to a state wherein sephirotic energy may be channeled into the circle. Trance focuses the mind into a narrow beam of force, causing the existing vibrations to focus on a magickal goal. Producing power, all these paths are ecstatic states with one thing in common—they channel energy through consciousness; they are refined mental techniques. An old Witch belief is that magickal power not only flows with the mind, but it also exudes naturally from the body. Anything that quickens the body releases power.

Dancing quickens the body, and energy is produced in large amounts; during magickal ritual, if the body is consecrated to a specific sephirah, a substantial amount of power is generated. Physiologically, the pulse rate increases; breathing becomes rapid and uneven. Heat and moisture exude from the pores; if enough people are present during the dance, the room's temperature rises measurably. In a small space containing many people, the results of this exertion become more evident as the temperature and humidity rise to an uncomfortable degree. Internally, a multitude of changes occurs as stored glucose is released into the bloodstream zooming through the body at lightning speeds—energy exchanges occur at a fantastic rate; oxygen is whisked to cells crying for more. An increasing demand is met with an increasing supply. The brain itself becomes charged with a flurry of electrical activity; neurons fire ceaselessly, and as physical exertion increases to exhaustion, natural endorphins are released into the body to dampen the increasing discomfort. Ecstasy occurs!

Following the release of heat and mechanical energies are psychic energies; to a trained psychic, the aura may be seen to flash and gyrate in an endless display of colored eruptions. Every physical movement prompts the aura to expand as the etheric energies move, deplete, and replenish in accord with the physical processes. As heat radiates into the room from a moving body, excess energy from the aura begins to radiate outward. As moisture evaporates into the air, so do the more subtle energies of the body; magickally, the moisture and heat represent the moving of fire and water from the body to the circle. Heavier breathing results in the flowing of the element air, while the body itself establishes all these occurrences through the element of earth—Malkuth. Dancing becomes a celebration and generation of the life-force itself.

Just as dancing in a small room will measurably increase the amount of moisture and heat in the atmosphere, so will dancing in an enclosed circle measurably increase the amount of power. For magickal needs, this psychic energy will not serve to empower our spell; we need a specific type of energy for each spell that we are working. By consecrating the body beforehand to a specific sephirah (magnetizing the aura), the psychic energy generated will be that of the sephirah desired. Consciousness is increased by raising awareness to the level required; a specific sephirah is invoked throughout the body's anatomy. Then, through methods that have already been mastered, the entire mind/body complex is forced to vibrate with these energies. Because the power fills the circle, it in turn causes the body and mind to continue vibrating at the required pitch; the more power channeled, the more power that can be channeled. Once consciousness is increased to its zenith, dancing will quicken the body's tempo, and hence, the amount of power present in the circle.

Dancing becomes a passage to power. A vortex swells within the circle; fueled by intense imagery and movement, this vortex rips through reality, slicing open the thin veil between the worlds. A tidal wave courses through consciousness; energy moves in amounts that increase geometrically within the sacred space. Moving through limitless space and eternal time, our circle fills with the etheric energies generated, threatens to burst with the power; when the magick threatens to rip apart the reality of the circle, when our own energy systems cannot withstand the ever-increasing onslaught of force, we collapse to the ground. The power, having become a self-sustaining field, moves on in spite of our release—it gushes into the unseen realms to bring our desires to fruition.

Exercise Six

As usual, begin by establishing your magickal need: from this, determine the sephirah you will be using. It is important that the magickal colors be determined beforehand; for attracting a new reality to yourself, use the Archangelic color; if you are projecting the energy to another person, use the Deity color of the sephirah. Begin to create the magickal circle; once it is cast, begin to open the Tree of Life in the body's energy field. Concentrate on the sephirah that you will be using, and force the center of action to vibrate to the proper pitch. Once you have the appropriate energy present in the anatomical location, magnetize the aura. It is important that you feel these energies throughout the body and circle. Continue magnetizing yourself until the energies are at their peak.

Now that the energies are present, hold a firm image of the desired outcome in your mind. For this type of working, it is important that the visualization be a simple image of the outcome. It must be simple, for the body is the center of focus for this type of spell, and the mind will be caught up in the physical ecstasy. The simpler the visualization, the easier it will be to hold in your mind. Likewise, the image should be only that of the desired outcome; this power will be extremely active—results are likely to manifest quickly. By visualizing only the outcome, and not the steps needed to achieve results, you ensure rapid success. With this visualization firmly in mind, begin to move. See yourself flowing through a world of pure color and vibration; feel that the powers are increasing, channeled into the circle by the movements of your body. Allow yourself freedom of expression; do not be afraid to move your arms and legs in wide, sensual rhythms. If a part of your body is not involved in the dance, you are not dancing correctly. The secret to success is to move; realize that the God/dess forces invoked to your circle take pleasure in movement.

Soon, your breath will become more forceful; your pulse will quicken and you will start to sweat. Pick up the tempo of the dance; accentuate the movements, dancing faster, gaining speed. Focus strongly on the spell; let your movements become symbolic of your desires. As the dance becomes more heated, more emphatic, the body will generate more power on both physical and etheric levels—having consecrated the physical vibrations to the sephirah before beginning the dance, all energies mediated now will be of the sephirah desired. Move until your body begins to express discomfort: once your breathing is labored, your sweating is profuse, and your pulse feels as if its ready to rip out of your skin, fall to the ground, letting the power wash over you and into the unseen realms. For a moment, the room may continue to spin, and you may feel that the power still pours from your body; all this signals success, for the dance has become a living vortex of power. Let it flow as it will before closing the circle; your spell is cast.

Blood Control and Bindings: Use of the Cords

Of all the paths contained within the Witches' Wheel, no one technique is more geared toward mystical attainment than this. Through mastery of blood control and bindings, we can desensitize our physical senses one by one, causing them to lose focus on the physical world, turning within to the body's inner workings. Over time, as sensory loss becomes more complete, the mind, unable to exist without some sort of stimulation, begins to create its own illusions, much like those of a dream state. Through passive observation of this process, we learn more about the mind's inner workings; released from physical input, we can turn awareness totally within, fully examining the contents of the mind. Or if we desire, we may begin to dwell on various principles, meditating on the individual sephiroth. Without the body's constant monitoring of the external world through the physical senses, our sensory environment becomes centered on our own inner realities.

Traditionally, this path is worked within a student/teacher relationship; someone who has mastered the basics of power and altered consciousness would bind the student in such a way that the body would be deprived of sensory input. The eyes are firmly blindfolded; the ears are padded and covered so that sensory stimulation is muffled. With the eyes and ears restrained, the powers of clairvoyance and clairaudience would be enhanced; these senses, deprived of outer stimulation, would turn inward, focusing on inner levels. The feet would be bound, and the student in turn would sit on his or her heels; the entire body would rest on a large pillow so that it is cushioned from the hard floor. This position, comfortable at first, would begin to lead to slight discomfort as the regions below the waist were deprived of full blood flow. This, plus the pinching of the nerves, created numbness, facilitating the illusion that the student may move beyond the physical body.

The cord used in these operations was traditionally red, symbolizing the blood that is life; it would be braided out of three smaller cords to represent the triple Goddess of Maid, Mother, and Crone. Its is nine feet long, symbolizing the number of months involved in the gestation of a child. After the feet were bound, the cord would be brought up and tied snugly about the wrists, securing the hands behind the back. The resulting effect would be that as hands are bound, inner perception is increased. Thoughts that cannot be conveyed in either words or images are often released through the hands; merely watch a conversation and this soon becomes evident. Binding the hands serves to force increased mental perception. The only two senses that cannot be bound are taste and smell; through the administering of the sacred meal while in this binding, the sense of taste could be used to consecrate the student's body to the magickal working, while smell was manipulated by incenses symbolic of desires. As the blood began to slow, the body's sense of touch would be desensitized by the cramped, unchanging position.

This method does present danger; that is why the path of binding is so little presented in texts on Craft practices. If the blood becomes too still, the body suffers, possibly leading to tissue damage. At the first sign of shivering or complaint of chill, the teacher would immediately loosen the bindings for the aspirant until some semblance of comfort was regained. It was extremely important for the teacher to know the basics of physiology; likewise, the student would develop an implicit trust and love for the teacher, as this binding reduced one to a helpless, fetal state. If the technique is not perfect, disaster ensues.

When using this method of sensory stimulation alone, these dangers are not evident. A person cannot make his or her own bindings so tight that the body cannot move; therefore, if the blood becomes too still, even while in trance, the body's subconscious functions are able to operate and shift the position enough to reestablish proper blood flow. Sight and hearing may be completely cut off by the solitary practitioner; blood control and hand binding will be done mostly by willpower.

As stated earlier, this path is used mostly for development of "the sight" or peering into the astral realms. When using this path, we can easily invoke sephirotic powers to ourselves, and then either project ourselves into the realm, or we can enter the pattern awareness of our adverse circumstances, pulling it apart and putting it back together again.

Exercise Seven

Before using this path to power, we must prepare our cords. Obtain three slim silk or cotton red cords, each about ten feet long. You will also need a measuring tape of at least nine feet, and a needle and red thread for securing the cord once it is braided. Cast the magick circle, invoking the elements and the God/dess. Once you are secure within its boundaries, tie a knot in one end so that the cords are firmly secured together, and in silence, begin the braiding. This in itself is a magickal act, for as we overlap the cords, our own energies become bound into the spirals. After the entire length of the cord is braided, tie a knot in the remaining end. Below the first knot, sew the three cords together so that once the knot is cut away, the three cords will remain braided. Measure nine feet from the area of the sewing, and then sew the remaining end so that the cords are secure. Cut away the extraneous cord—it is now complete. Using the ritual given in Chapter Two for the magickal tools, consecrate the cords for magickal work. They are now empowered for use.

For scrying into the various sephiroth, we will need several additional tools: a large, cushioned pillow upon which we may rest; a thick blindfold; a set of pads for the ears; and an additional length of material to hold the ear pads in place. It is important that the pillow be large and comfortable so that the lower legs are not pressured by the floor; also, it is important that the bindings for the eyes and ears be thick enough to block stimulation, yet are not too uncomfortable. Experimenting with different materials will help you find what is right.

Before beginning the ritual, decide which sephirah you would like to scry into. Memorize the Archangelic color and the Deity name, for we will be using the power of vibrations to help draw the sephirotic energies to ourselves. Next, prepare an incense for the sephirah to be used to help bind the sense of smell to the energy we are invoking; likewise, have the materials on hand for the celebration of the sacred meal. Once all is gathered, create sacred space. Light the incense, and celebrate the sacred meal.

Begin by binding the eyes and ears so that you can neither see nor hear. Once the bindings for these senses are comfortably in place, double up the cord so that it is in two equal lengths; beginning with the folded end of the cord, loosely tie your feet together. The binding should be firm enough to hold your feet together, but not tight enough to cut off circulation and become uncomfortable. Seat yourself on the cushion; your body should be resting on your heels and lower legs. Wrap the cord loosely, yet snugly, around your waist—with the remaining cord, secure your hands behind your back. It will be impossible for you to tie them together, but twisting the cords around your wrists will secure them snugly. Keeping the head, neck, and spine aligned, begin to relax your body and breath until you feel that your blood is beginning to slow. If the sensations become too uncomfortable, simply move your body slightly until you find a comfortable position.

Now that your body and senses are bound, your awareness will begin to turn inward. Relaxing in this state will result in a few mild hallucinations; you may hear sounds that do not exist in the material world; in the darkness over your eyes, you may begin to see momentary visions, flashes of people, places, or things that do not exist in your environment. This is the state of mind that we need for our work. Begin opening up the sephiroth in the aura, and then narrow consciousness to the sephirah with which you want to work. Expand the Archangelic colors throughout the circle; once the energies are firmly established, vibrate the Deity name. Although the body cannot perform the physical actions, it would be wise to use the method given for vibrations in Chapter Four, for by doing this, we invoke greater amounts of energy from the Macrocosmic sephirah. This influx of energy will establish a greater connection. The vibration itself will not be heard, but felt reverberating throughout the circle. By now, the sensation of having a finite body should be replaced with a feeling of expansion.

Concentrating on the colors and symbols of the sephirah, plus vibrating the Deity name, will begin to change the visual and auditory hallucinations that we have been sensing. Pictures or scenes will unfold before us. Unlike the visualizations we are used to, these will seem three-dimensional, almost like a dream. But with the mind awake and the body stilled, these visions will not be dreams, but actual experiences of the relevant sephirah. By willing our minds to move, we can fly through these scenes and landscapes, viewing the complexities of the world we have conjured before us. Remember, though, that these are visions—our minds have opened up to the energy level required, and are now sensing landscapes and areas of the other worlds. When your mind becomes tired or cloudy, the visions begin to fade, or your body sends signals of discomfort, will yourself back into full rapport with your body by concentrating on your feet. Loosen the bindings on your hands, release your eyes and ears, and unbind your feet. Spend a few moments returning to full consciousness.

Partake of the sacred meal once more and close the circle. The ritual is complete.

The Scourge

This is another neglected path to power; this is unfortunate, as the scourge is a powerful method for purification and charging of people, places, and things. The use of this tool becomes a powerful method of enflaming the will and directing magickal energies. When made by the Witch, the handle should be the length of the fire wand—from the inner crook of the elbow to mid-palm in length—and it should have eight red, soft cords attached to one end. Its color scheme is quite simple; the handle should be painted black to represent the womb of darkness, and on the base (the end without the cords), it should have the symbols of Taurus and Scorpio painted in white [See Figure 6:1]. These two symbols represent the Horned One in His forms of waxing and waning year; painted on the black handle, they signify the God rising in all forms from the womb of the Goddess. Red is the color of life, and of the blood which the scourge excites.

It is of the utmost importance that the cords of the scourge be long—at least twice the length of the handle—and extremely soft. Silk cords would be the best for this purpose. When used as a whipping tool, the purpose is to enliven and excite, not harm, the person or object being struck. The number and length of the cords causes a loud "whooshing" and "whipping" sound as they flail through the air. The expectation of pain, the sound of the scourge being whipped through the air, and the subtle brushing of eight silken tails upon the skin are symbolic of the forces of nature in our lives. It reminds us that even the most horrible circumstances, the most inevitable catastrophes, really can not hurt us. The scourge, then, is the true kiss of the Goddess: to learn, we must suffer, but in the end even the sufferings are nothing.

This method of enflaming the mind is meant to be worked in a partnership, enhanced by the use of the cords. The blood, forced to be still by the bindings, is excited in the body parts which are struck by the scourge. While forced to sit still during scourging, the mind is enflamed, leading to wonders of consciousness. Through its power, we learn to trust and love our coveners unconditionally—voluntarily reduced to a state of virtual helplessness, we realize that those with whom we work will not harm us. In the hands of an experienced Witch, the scourge can even be used to draw the soul out of the body, a wonder produced by careful, rhythmic stroking up the back toward the head.

Unfortunately, these effects cannot be produced by the solitary Witch; although we could, while unbound, use the scourge to strike our own bodies, this would be a mockery of the symbol's power, for it supposes purification at the hands of another. How, then, may we use the scourge, without defiling its symbolism? We may use it to purify, subdue, command, and enliven symbols created for our magickal workings.

Before using the scourge in this manner, there are a few basic rules we must remember to follow. First of all, it is said that it is not proper manners to make an offering of less than two-score to the Goddess; a score is twenty, so when using the scourge to purify, channel energy, and sanctify the material basis of our spells, we must remember to offer a total of forty strokes to the Goddess. Also, keep in mind that as we are using sephiroth in our magick, we must somehow group our strokes to have numerical significance with the realm of power. For instance, if working with Yesod, the number of the sephirah is nine, and nine goes into forty four times, with a remainder of four. That would give us four series of nine strokes or nine series of four strokes; each set would be preceded with four to purify before empowering. This same line of reasoning would follow for each of the remaining sephiroth. Figure 6:2 gives a chart to be used when basing the magick of the scourge on a perfect prayer of forty.

THE SYMBOLS FOR THE SCOURGE

TAURUS

SCORPIO

Represents the Horned God, the power of fertility, and the Sabbat of Bealtaine.

Represents the God as Lord of the Underworld and Death; the Sabbat of Samhain.

Figure 6:1

Obtain a length of wood not more than one-half inch thick; its length should extend from the crook of the elbow to mid-palm. Sand it until the wood is smooth, and paint it a deep, rich black. Allow this to dry overnight. Next, paint the symbols of Taurus and Scorpio with white paint on the base of the handle. Remember that this symbolizes the power of the Horned God rising from the womb of the Goddess.

Next, obtain enough red silken cord to cut into eight tails for the scourge; each tail should be twice as long as the handle. With red thread, sew the ends of each cord so that it does not unravel, then glue one end of each cord on the handle of the scourge. Dry the tool overnight, then consecrate it with the ritual given in Chapter Two for the elemental tools.

Once the scourge is complete and consecrated, it is ready for magickal work. As with the other paths, decide upon a magickal goal and sephirah to use. Scourge magick works on the premise that a symbol is purified and charged by lashing, so it is important to use some type of physical symbol to manifest the desire. For example, let us assume that we are working a spell to draw a familiar to us. The sephirah that embodies this desire is Binah. We have decided that we want our animal helper in the form of a cat; therefore, we fashion a small cat statue out of clay. As always, it is best to create your own magickal symbols for use in spells; however, if you lack artistic ability, a picture of a cat would work just as well. In my statue, I would include herbs that belong to the sephirah of Binah, perhaps some cypress, hyacinth, and myrrh. These would be placed in the clay before the statue was prepared, to incorporate the vibration of Binah in my work.

I must also use the basic numerology behind the scourge in my ritual. The number for Binah is three; a perfect prayer to the Goddess is forty. That results in thirteen divisions with a remainder of one. To begin charging my symbol, I would purify it with a single lash; to empower it, I have two choices: I can either use thirteen sets of

PERFECT PRAYERS FOR THE SEPHIROTH

Sephirah	To Purify	Sets of Lashes
Kether	Not used	Not used
Chokmah	Not used	Not used
Binah	One lash	Three sets of thirteen
Chesed	One set of ten	Three sets of ten
Geburah	One set of eight	Four sets of eight
Tifareth	Six lashes	Six sets of six
Netzach	Five lashes	Five sets of seven
Hod	One set of five	Four sets of eight
Yesod	Four lashes	Four sets of nine
Malkuth	One set of ten	Ten sets of three

Figure 6:2

three lashes, or three sets of thirteen lashes. The second choice, three sets of thirteen lashes, is easier to keep track of, so I decide on that pattern. I now have a perfect prayer with the scourge.

Once the symbol is prepared and the sets of scourgings are decided upon, the actual method of working is quite simple. First, create sacred space, and open the sephiroth in the aura. Concentrate on the sephirah you will be using, channeling the necessary vibration (Archangelic or Deity) into the circle. For drawing a familiar to me, I would use the Archangelic color of black. Place the symbol in the center of the circle and begin with the initial purification—administer the number of lashes allowed for driving out any unwanted energies from the symbol. Now pause, willing the energies of the sephirah to enter into the scourge. Once it is charged with power, begin with the first set of empowering lashes; every time the scourge strikes the symbol, more power flows into it. Pause between each set, imagining that the scourge draws in more energy from the circle. Once the total of forty lashes has been given, the symbol is cleansed and charged; finish with the words, "It is done; so mote it be!" Return the remaining energy to your aura, then close the Tree visualization. Banish the circle, knowing that your need will soon manifest.

The Great Rite

Laden with sensual forces, the Great Rite is more than a sexual act. It is a conception of reality, a hallowing of the movements that began our Universe, the primal stirrings of the Great Goddess—it is birth; it is life; it is death—and as reality involves all levels of the Tree of Life, this focusing of magickal force reverberates throughout all planes of existence. As a path to power, Witches make no excuse for its use, as sex is another of the natural creations to be enjoyed in our realm; therefore, we are uninhibited sexually. As a sacrament, sexuality puts us in touch with the essence of existence, our own core of being. It is holy to the Craft, and as a holy thing, sexuality is not to be profaned. We love whom we will; we honor the Goddess, the God, within. Knowing no boundaries of flesh, transcending the appearance of outer forms, knowing that God/dess lies within each individual, our love is expressed regardless of sex or preference. In honoring another, we honor all else; promiscuity, then, is to be avoided, for to focus our love on one individual is to create a laser-force of desire, one that can permeate even the thickest material reality.

As a path to power, the Great Rite is normally worked in a partnership: man and woman, man and man, or woman and woman; the energies of two are alchemically joined as one force, and this force is used to empower the spell. Unless this form of magick is used by two with whom intercourse is a normal part of the relationship, however, the energies raised become dangerous: magickally, sex involve the pairing of opposites on all planes of existence. Two who are practicing this form of magick may be unprepared for the spiritual linking taking place—and when all levels of being are forcefully thrown together within the confines of the magick circle, instead of merging the higher realms, they clash.

When following the solitary path, however, there is no danger in enacting the Great Rite. The Great Rite can be one of our most powerful tools. On inner levels, we are both Goddess and God, male and female; during moments in which we honor ourselves magickally, we are paying homage to the essence of divinity that lies within ourselves. The powers of sexuality are the powers of self. Honoring our own sexual powers is an act of worship—one that can generate enough power to pierce the veils of the unseen worlds, giving us access to unlimited amounts of power. Within the magick circle, between the worlds of realities, we can build a sexual vortex and rip the worlds asunder. Focusing our minds on one specific goal while raising these energies, wonders occur. Instead of a cone, a tidal wave of power is created—we are swept away in vibrations of pleasure that course through us; reality merges and melds into our moans of pleasure; we recreate; we aspire. At the climax of our ritual, the forces invoked explode on all the planes.

There are no set rules to this sacred art; but as usual, the basics of magick must be taken into consideration. Obviously, when caught up in sexual ecstasy the mind will be enraptured by sensual pleasures; therefore, it is important that all symbolism used in the ritual be simple. Before beginning the ritual, we must sit down and decide exactly what it is that we wish to manifest in our lives, and create a simple sigil or symbol to empower the energy that will be raised. The easiest way to do this is by using the sigil wheel given in Figure 6:3, based upon what is called the Rose-Cross. By narrowing our desired goal into a single word, that word may be plotted out on the sigil wheel, giving a geometric figure upon which the mind may be centered during ritual. To help remind us of the purpose of the rite, and to help attune the energies that are invoked into the magick circle, we may also place copies of this sigil at the four cardinal points of the circle, and on the ceiling, so that no matter where our focus turns, there is something to keep us centered on our work.

As a path to power, sensuality can become one of the Witch's strongest tools, for through its use we tap into the same power that began our Cosmos. We transcend the physical; space and time melt away; the final veils separating realities come crashing down about us as we become caught in the rapture of eternal ecstasy. Through this final path to power, we become one with the God/dess.

THE SIGIL WHEEL

Figure 6:3

Exercise Nine

Begin by deciding the purpose of your ritual, the spell that you wish to cast. Reduce this to one single word, and by using the wheel of sigils, plot out a geometric character to represent your desire. Obtain five pieces of poster board in the relevant sephirotic color; on each draw the colored sigil in the opposite sephirotic color. For example, if I were to do a ritual for protection from enemies, I might interpret this by the word "defense." The sephirah that I would choose for my work would be Geburah (might), and since I am attracting these defensive forces to myself, I would choose a red medium upon which to draw my sigil [Figure 6:4]. The sigil itself would be drawn in orange. These symbolic reminders of my desires would be placed in the North, East, South, and West of my circle, plus one on the ceiling of my ritual space, so that no matter where I turn, I will see a reminder of my magickal desires.

Create sacred space, invoking the sephirah needed by magnetizing the aura. Once the sephirotic energies fill the circle, begin to imagine that the sigil is transposed over your aura in the Deity scale of color. Now, begin to pleasure yourself; focus not only on the area of the genitals, but see and feel your entire body. Erotic imagery may be used, as long as the actual symbol of your desire is kept somewhere in the back of the mind; as you fantasize, you might occasionally wish to glance at one of the sigils placed within the circle to focus the energy raised. As the stimulation builds, allow yourself to reach orgasm—it is important that once orgasm is reached, you focus yourself on both the visualization of the symbol chosen and the word upon which the sigil is based. Let the power go. The spell is complete.

THE SIGIL FOR THE WORD "DEFENSE"

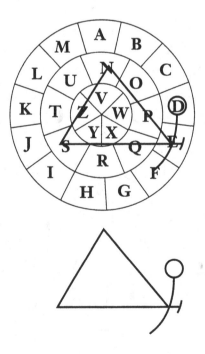

Figure 6:4

In mastering the powers of the Tree of Life and using them to create magickal ritual, we must learn one basic premise: the life-force is to be honored in all its forms, whether they be friends or foes, humans or animals, physical or ethereal. Our world is composed of balanced forces, powers that blink rapidly in and out of existence, a vast rolling, swirling sea of energy that moves in invisible, yet powerful, tides of motion and force. Energy must coalesce, mold itself into an impermanent form before it can again melt into nothingness. Controlling all these forms and forces is the power of God/dess—the ultimate forms of masculine and feminine energy—creating cycles that underlie manifestation. Through the realms of spirit we can attune ourselves to the cycles of nature, to the original, sensual union of opposites. Successful magick demands that we destroy our present views of the world and reality, laying ourselves down on the great altar of the universe; we must annihilate and release our unnatural hold on the forces that permeate our very structures, allowing them the freedom to coalesce into something new and beautiful. Merge with the natural tides of life that suffuse everyday existence; learn the dance of life that began in the far distant past and will continue into the more distant future—only then will we as Witches be able to wield the powers of life; only then will we be able to merge with the tides of life. Our next chapter takes us on the first steps of that dance.

CHAPTER SEVEN

DISCOVERING THE TIDES OF LIFE

THE QABALAH OF A SUNRISE

March 20, 1994—Spring Equinox. Alone, in the final fleeting moments of night, I stood on the banks of New Smyrna Beach, where the edges of the continent lose their solidity to the sandy shoreline, constantly eroding and rebuilding into the ceaselessly churning ocean. All was lit by a crescent moon that curved upward like two horns; against the backdrop of a sable sky, with small points of light spiraling into the deep vacuum of space, I could see the shadowy outline of the horizon's edge, blending into the night. The tide rose about my feet, the sand slipped away beneath me and left me with constantly unstable footing. I began to sink into the shoreline; losing my footing as sand gave way to water, I shifted my weight lest I fall into the cresting, crashing waves. Beckoning me, pulling me, the undertow bade me to enter the ocean, the great womb of life—Mara, the bitter sea, called to me.

I gazed into the inky blackness; the velvet extended outward and up in a never-ending spiral of twinkling stars; it seemed as if the darkness bent into a great arch above our world. The Milky Way stretched above me, a great white smear of light across the heavens. I tried to imagine an earlier era, a time when science had not yet reduced our world to so many lifeless equations, a time when all the Earth was conceived as a voluminous life-form ruled by powerful Gods and mighty Goddesses. A time when everything was considered holy: our bodies, the animals, the trees, the Earth, the sky. As I reflected upon the inherent inviolability of life, it was not hard to imagine that the sky above was, indeed, the Goddess Nuit arched into infinite space, the great Goddess of the primal darkness from whose breasts poured the milky stars. Gazing at the crescent moon, the Horned Goddess, I raised my arms high above my head in invocation and sent a vibration spiraling out into Cosmos, "Ay-huh-yay." It engulfed me, moved through me, and crashed out into the night.

I envisioned the great, dark sky as the anti-existence before time, and the crescent moon became the symbol of Kether, the Horned Goddess from whom the primal movement began. A brisk wind was blowing from the Eastern ocean; I opened my eyes and watched as the far reaches of night began giving way to the first stirrings of reds and oranges—the sunrise was beginning; the Great Supernal Father of Chokmah was birthing from the dark womb of the

Goddess. Scintillating lights massed in the Eastern sky; fold upon fold of changing, luminous light suffused the horizon with new, glowing life. As the darkness washed away, my voice ascended into the auroral glow, "Yod-heh-vau-heh." The forces of the Supernal Father descended and rushed to merge with me.

The sunrise sent pinwheels of mauve and apricot exploding over the horizon into blood-red ribbons that angrily unfurled throughout the void, the newly-born God engaged in the primal birth-scream, then deepened into the vibrant glow of newly emerged daylight. Suddenly, I could see that the ocean itself was filled with life; seagulls dove into the rhythmic waves, soaring away with fish hanging from their beaks. Below swam a school of dolphins, bounding above the waves before gracefully arching and plunging through the surface. I walked waist-deep into the water; the salty waves crashed into me, trying to force me back on land, while the undertow beckoned me deeper. I could feel the forces of Aima, the bright Mother, pushing me toward life, and Ama, the dark Crone, pulling me into the womb of darkness. All around me was Mara, the bitter sea, the churning, relentless womb of creation. I chanted, "Yod-heh-vau-heh ay-low-eem," as the waves crashed into me, answering my call.

I had touched the powers of creation!

We have come a long way in our magickal training: the Tree, planted within the soul, has taken root and grown into a giant that bridges sky and earth. We began our studies by piercing the heart of the Qabalah—the Tree of Life—and reclaiming its God/dess concepts as our own. Having grasped the fundamentals, we began to work with the powers of the Goddess and God in their myriad forms, transforming our bodies into vessels of power. Now, having experienced the forces of the Tree of Life individually, we shall begin to work with them as they filter into our home, Malkuth. The energies of the various sephiroth may be experienced in a linear fashion, from Kether to Malkuth, but once they manifest in our realm, they begin to merge in a new way. The daily, lunar, and yearly cycle are all patterned after the flow of creation throughout the four worlds.

Until this point, we have used the emanations of God/dess to enhance our spiritual consciousness. Beginning with the awareness that we could slip between the worlds of the seen and unseen, we used the concept of a circle to ground us between realities. Slowly, we worked with the concepts of consciousness individually, moving into a state wherein we could invoke the powers of the sephiroth to us. We caused these emanations to vibrate within and without, slowly ascending the planes and strengthening ourselves magickally. But for the Qabalah's magick to become a part of our lives and fully enhance our spirituality as Pagans and Witches, we must find a way to incorporate its teachings into our seasonal celebrations—the Esbats and Sabbats.

Qabalah as a unified whole expresses the cycles of nature. Earlier in this text, we explored how Cosmos, and all within, began with the first stirrings of the Goddess. From Her first sensual awareness of Self came waves of energy that extended through the void of nothingness, merging and mutating into the various sephiroth. New worlds of power were conceived; new forms and faces of the God/dess emerged from primal darkness. As we encountered each new realm or evolution of power, we were propelled closer to the source.

Reinterpreting the traditional symbolism, seeking to find its core, we were presented with a Cosmos birthed by the divine feminine, and cultivated by the eternal love-play between Goddess and God. The final realm, Malkuth, became receptive ground for the myriad concepts of the Tree of Life. In a sense, Malkuth is a magickal mirror that reflects the occurrences of the other realms; like a mirror, it often becomes a polarized opposite of what it reflects. Kether, the pure spiritual realm, becomes mirrored in Malkuth as a pure realm of dense energy, or matter. The linear journey of divine energy is reflected, also; within the confines of this realm, the line of power that travels into and out of our realm is seen as the sacred circle. The forms and faces of the Goddess mix and merge in a pattern we can only describe as circular, since it continues to repeat in our world.

Already, we are familiar with the forms and faces of the Goddess; we can trace their symbols to their point of origin on the Tree of Life. Using this knowledge, we shall apply it to our traditional rituals of the Esbats and Sabbats, examining each part of our spirituality in full until we can come to a holistic view of the interplay of energies found in the world of Malkuth, especially the Earth, upon whose breast we live. Although we shall focus on the changing tides of Gaia, remember that the primal forces shaping the Tree also merge throughout the Universe; however, we shall focus on the shifting tides of our lands and seas for now. The easiest way to begin is with the daily cycle and the four worlds presented by the Tree of Life.

Throughout this chapter, we will analyze the material that we have already mastered. In conjunction with the text and exercises, we will again use the magickal journal we began in Chapter Five. At various points, you will be asked to record your thoughts on the material presented. In some places, a daily plan of meditation will be given in conjunction with the various earth tides we will be studying. We begin here with the first entry in our journal.

Journal Entry

Once again, read the opening passage to this chapter, "The Qabalah of a Sunrise." Read this passage until you are able to visualize the scene as I saw it; enter a meditative state and visualize each occurrence. Spend some time outdoors in the early morning, watching the sun as its light breaks the horizon; if possible, plan an outing to an Eastern shore to view the scene from a location similar to mine. Once you can visualize a sunrise over the ocean, analyze the symbolism presented in connection with the world of Atziluth, the initial creative impulse presented by the Supernals (Kether, Chokmah, and Binah). Also include an analysis of the Goddess Nuit in connection with the Veils of Negative Existence. In the magickal journal, record all your thoughts, feelings, and an analysis of the sunrise. Try to match the symbolism with the creative processes of Atziluth; refer to Chapter Three if you need to review the material covering Kether, Chokmah, and Binah. Finish this exercise before reading my interpretation below.[1]

---

1. In some instances, your interpretations may differ from mine; at times, you may totally disagree with my logic! When investigating philosophical/spiritual concepts such as these, there will never be one absolute truth—your answers, if well thought out, are just as valid as mine.

Analysis of a Sunrise

Qabalah is a system that rewards constant practice and meditation. If you tend it with love and devotion, it returns the energy threefold. If you rise to meet the powers of the Tree within their own realms, those energies descend to invigorate the body. As you incorporate these energies into the psyche, they expand and propel you higher to the God/dess. Realizing that all nature is part of ourselves—there is no division between what lies within and without—if we look into nature, we will find that the Qabalah permeates everything around us. Our universe, the material world, is the result of the primal stirrings of the great Goddess; She awakened to Her own existence, and all creation followed Her movements. Magick, the sum of all existence, the basis of our world, began to flow. Fragmenting, coalescing, undulating in the eternal rhythm of life and death, the power of the Tree of Life moves through us, through the Universe; it merges into our world. Each new day, every sunrise, sunset, even the pulse of the Earth are controlled by the powers flowing throughout the Tree of Life. If we honor the tides, the cycles that move throughout our realm, we create rituals that honor the forces sustaining life.

It follows that if we examine the natural phenomenon occurring during a sunrise, we see the symbolism presented by the world of Atziluth (Kether, Chokmah, and Binah). A sunrise begins a new day; likewise, the world of Atziluth begins a new cycle of creation. While the world is still enveloped by darkness, the arched sky above represents the Goddess Nuit, queen of infinite space; the heavens represent the Veils of Negative Existence. Hanging high in the night sky, the crescent moon becomes the symbol of the Horned Mother, about to birth the first form of the God. As the sun bursts forth from below the horizon, we see the sacred birthing of the Supernal Father, divine son and lover of the Goddess. Binah becomes the ocean below, absorbing the energy of the sun, echoing the primordial origin of life.

Remembering the material presented in Chapter Two with the four worlds, Atziluth is the realm of the initial creative impulse, the first desire of the Goddess to create. Before Atziluth there is nothing, only the veils of negative existence symbolized by the Goddess Nuit, Queen of infinite space. The sky is filled with thousands of small, twinkling stars—the milky substance poured out into the Universe as the Goddess begins Her quest to become self-aware. Gazing at Herself in the curved mirror of space, Nuit draws upon Herself, concentrating Her light and energy until the concentration of power develops into the first sephirah, Kether.

Symbolizing the first movements of the unknowable Mother is the crescent moon, gently curving upward into the sky like the curving of two horns.[2] Kether's magickal image is that of an ancient Horned Mother in full view—in the moments before the sunrise, we have the symbol of the great Mother surrounded by curved space and the Goddess Nuit. They hang ever close to each other, yet separated by the eternal reflection of not-being before being. Ever seeking, ever yearning to know each other, their magickal passions set up waves of orgasmic force that send energy spiraling into the Cosmos.

Finally, the tension that lies before sunrise is broken by gentle wisps of light emerging over the horizon—the powerful Supernal Father bursts forth from the

---

2. Remember that the moon is the planetary influence of Yesod; however, the moon also symbolizes the feminine forces permeating our world. Therefore, during the phenomenon of a sunrise, this symbol may represent the unknowable feminine forces of Kether.

womb of darkness. Fading under the power of the sun, the stars dissolve from sight; anti-existence replaces pure force. The sun rises higher in the sky; its power is reflected in the ocean's surface. Chokmah has projected its energy outward and inward, and the projecting forces are received by the womb of the ocean. Mara, the bitter sea, takes in the light energy and molds it, creating heat. Somewhere in the distant past, in a similar scene, the forces combined the chemicals contained in the saline, creating the first stirrings of life as one-celled organisms.

Crashing onto the shore, the incessant waves and rising tides represent the forces of Aima, the bright, fertile Mother. Those who have been resting deep within her womb, awaiting birth, are propelled from the depths to the shores of life, and these children emerge. But as Aima gives her progeny life, Ama, the dark one, gropes for those who cannot escape her grasp. The powerful undertow leads back into the primal womb of darkness; those not strong enough to resist its relentless pull are caught in her vortex—pulled back within her—to perish and become ready, in time, for new life.

If we learn to observe the pattern, an eternal cycle of creation and dissolution, we can recognize the primal powers of the Tree of Life at work. Creation itself has a pattern; the chart given in Chapter Two [Figure 2:3] shows that there are, indeed, four steps to creation: the worlds of Atziluth, Briah, Yetzirah, and Assiah. Each world contains a sephirah from each of the three pillars (Mercy, Severity, and Mildness), giving each realm of power a masculine, feminine, and central focus of power.

Diagrams, however, enforce a two-dimensional, linear view of the system. Within the Tree of Life, an energy circuit is created, one that begins with Kether, flows to Malkuth, and then returns to its point of origin, Kether. Originally, in the great movement that began all worlds, the progression of power was, indeed, linear. One manifestation of God/dess led to the next, and soon ten realms of being were created. Energy, however, cannot be destroyed, and for there to be balance within the system, the power within Malkuth must return to its point of origin to be reused and recycled. Returning eternally to its source, this cycle of energy begins to manifest as a magickal circle.

For the Tree of Life to become a living, central part of our Craft, for it to be a valid system for Witches, Neo-Pagans, and Goddess-worshippers, we must learn to seek out these life-tides and merge into the powers that control their rhythm. We must find ways of expressing the Qabalah through our Esbat and Sabbat rituals. So far, we have used the new realms of power hidden in the branches of this sacred Tree to transform our consciousness, propelling us closer to the elusive source with each new ritual. Ours, however, is a spirituality based upon Gaia, Mother Earth, and the symbols that flow and transform with the shifting seasons. We must trace the steps of the divine dance of the seasons and tides, learning to merge and become one with the patterns. Once we can feel them not only flowing without, but within, we can begin to celebrate rituals in their honor.

THE FOUR WORLDS: THE DAILY CYCLE

Stated simply, Witchcraft is a spiritual system based upon the cycles of nature. By cycles, we refer to the repeated occurrence of a specific phenomenon—in life, birth and death are parts of the same cycle. Every year brings the four seasons: spring, summer, fall, and winter. Traveling with a rhythm throughout the night sky, the moon grows lighter and darker. Perhaps the shortest recurring cycle within nature is the daily cycle, the fluctuating patterns between sunrise and sunset. The term "cycle" comes to us from the Greek *kuklos*, which translates as "circle." Thus, whenever we say we are basing our spirituality upon the cycles of nature, we imply that our beliefs are based upon the eternal, unifying concept of a magickal circle.

In trying to merge with the patterns, we must first discover a starting point, some initial pulse in the cycle that implies a beginning. This concept is due to linear thinking and the reality agreement called time; however, individual moments, the relentless ticking away of seconds, minutes, and hours is nothing more than an anatomical quirk deriving from basic physiology. We believe that energy impulses travel from sensory organs to the brain, covering a vast amount of internal space in a few nanoseconds. Chemical impulses leap between individual neurons; these brief delays in electrical/chemical transmissions become moments, frozen flashes of time. Remember that the five senses of touch, smell, sight, taste, and hearing limit us to stimuli important to our survival in our present energy forms—if we open on deeper, intuitive levels, the quirk of time disappears; space melts into a meaningless concept. A rhythm is a pulse, a rising and falling pattern of energy, repeating until it changes form, melts into something new. As we move through the daily cycle, for the sake of convenience, we will work with the creating and ebbing flow of sunrise and sunset, and the fluctuating highs and lows between them.

At first, each point within the pattern will be seen as an individual event: we will move from the East, to the South, to the West, and then to the North. (Figure 7:1 illustrates the daily cycle with the cardinal points of the circle.) Brief adorations, commemorations of the solar event, will be spoken in connection with the cycle. As time progresses, we will begin to see the individual points becoming patterns, a greater cycle. Soon, we will come to the conclusion that there is no separation

THE DAILY SOLAR CYCLE

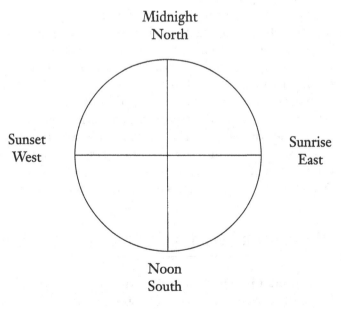

Figure 7:1

between sunrise and sunset, for each will be known as a single step in a sacred dance. As we perform our daily adorations, the pattern of nature will imprint itself into our consciousness, slowly pushing us upward into a great, powerful spiral that will expand into the greater cycles of Cosmos.

Obviously, this greater awareness will not occur from a single observation of the solar cycle; we were born into the cycle of Cosmos, and have spent our entire lives losing the inherent rhythm. Our first few attempts at relearning the steps will be awkward—as the day progresses, we will constantly glance at watches and clocks, making sure we do not miss any part of the rhythm. Slowly, however, the reality of this cycle will be imprinted in our awareness, and our internal clocks will begin to signal that another phase is about to commence. Linear observances will become circular consciousness, and intuitively we will merge into a pattern that was begun long ago, and will continue until the end of time.

Adorations of Light

Even within the traditional Craft, it seems that the power and the pageantry of a newborn day is overlooked as too common an event to commemorate. Who can deny that, when the lonely hours of darkness are broken by wisps of sunlight unfurling across the heavens, ecstasy occurs? The psyche, thrilled by the vibrancy of the color palette splashed throughout the sky, awakens to sensual pleasures. There is nothing trivial within nature; every part of the natural rhythms of God/dess deserves an occasional ritual to honor the tide of power. Early in the morning, just before the darkness of night melts into the light of day, stand outside, facing the East. Watch as the sun emerges from below the horizon. Greet the newly-risen forces: "Hail unto thee, morning sun in thy rising; hail unto thee born from the dark womb of night—symbol of life, giver of strength, primal masculine force of Earth. Hail to thee from the abodes of darkness!"

Who can deny the strength and vigor of the sun at noon, when its virile power unfurls upon the Earth? Heat, life, and light comes to their zenith; its power relentless in the sky, none can deny its effects upon all. We bask in the light; we hide from its heat. As noon approaches, once again greet the sun outside, facing the South. Say, "Hail unto thee, mighty forces of light, power, and strength at its height; sustainer of life, giver of strength. Hail to thee who rides in the Southern sky, rising from the abodes of early morning!"

In the evening, as the sun descends to the womb of darkness, so, too, does our strength begin to ebb; the light decreases, and with it we begin to slow down. As the daystar skims the horizon, watch in silence as darkness grows around you—feel your own strength ebbing. The sky glows deep fuchsia and violet, the colors of death and dreams. Watch as the sun sinks below the Western sky, and say, "Farewell O sun, ever returning light. Farewell unto thee as thou descendest from the light of day into the darkness of night, returning to the womb of Earth from whence thou came. Farewell to thee, from the abodes of day!"

Midnight comes, and with it arrives a strange, in-between time of night. Devoid of solar light, the night is alive with thousands of twinkling stars. Yet inwardly, something stirs. Magick and mystery surround the world; although the sun sleeps in the land of dreams, it stirs silently, preparing to be reborn and grow in strength until it rises once more in the Eastern sky. The depth of night is no more than the first stirrings before light. Rise and walk outside to face the North, the place of darkness and mystery, the home of the God/dess. Say, "Hail unto thee, sleeping sun. Hail unto thee, who awaits rebirth in the Eastern sky, now lying dormant in the realm of mystery. Sleep, dream, gather strength, for we await thy first stirrings at the sunrise. Hail from the womb of night!"

Without beginning, without ending, the solar cycle continues, eternally rising and setting over the Earth's sky. More than just a cycle, it becomes the daily renewal of the life on our home, the Earth Mother, partner to Gaia. We tap into this cycle, slowly reaffirming this revival; as the dance once again emerges within us, we move slowly into awareness of the larger cycles of life that move throughout our lives. The dance flows eternally, the music plays forever; we affirm our place at the center of the circle. Our daily cycle, then, becomes the melody upon which we build our magickal symphony.

Progressing with these daily adorations, it becomes apparent that the cycle commemorates more than the passage of the sun; the basics of our Craft spirituality are applied to the cycle of a day. Since we began these rituals with the rising of the sun in the East, we shall begin with analysis of the rising of the Young Stag. Our Horned God, Lord of Life, is conceived as being born from the womb of the Goddess. Young and fresh, he arises from the darkness of the womb, full of force and vigor, growing quickly in strength with the passage of time. This is the springtime of his youth; the God follows the steps of the Maiden Earth, playfully pursuing her in a sacred dance, awaiting consummation.

Between the East and the South, the sun grows in strength: so too, does the power of the divine child grow. As the sun rises to its height of strength in the South, their passions grow, and he becomes her Consort and Lover. He lays above the Earth, in the sky, and gives all his strength to continue the rhythm of life on the planet below. His masculine power heats her body; but as he is at the height of strength, he is also at the beginning of death, for now he begins to wane in power, slowly moving from his height in the South to his demise in the West.

Here, at the Western gate, the sun sinks below the horizon, descending into the realm of night. So, too, does the Horned One sacrifice himself to the Earth. With his last rays, our once mighty Lord of Life gives all power to her so that life may continue; that force is poured upon our planet, and he moves beyond our world, into the land of dreams.

Here, he becomes Lord of Shadows, the giver of rest and peace. All that dies on earth, all that passes out of this life and into the next, joins with Him to become young again. He sleeps, dreaming sacred dreams of his eventual rebirth into our world from the womb of the Great Mother. Eventually, the darkness of death cannot hold him; the strength he gave at his height of power earlier has also provided him with the power to emerge again from the womb. He is reborn as the Young Stag, future Consort and Lover to the great Goddess. The circle of life continues, and all is replenished with new life.

Journal Entry

Just as the phenomenon of a sunrise has its basis in the world of Atziluth, so the other points within the daily cycle share their symbolism with the three worlds of Briah, Yetzirah, and Assiah. Respectively, they intersect with the times of noon, sunset, and midnight. Before continuing with the material in this chapter, spend some time contemplating the four daily adorations you have performed; if necessary, review the material presented in Chapters Two and Three about LVX, the cycles of life, the four worlds, and the individual sephiroth. Write your own brief interpretations of the connections between the four worlds, and the four parts of the daily adoration.

Throughout the second and third chapters of this text, we studied the concepts of the four worlds of creation within the Tree of Life. The first world, Atziluth, lies at the top of the glyph, representing the initial creative impulse; Kether, Chokmah, and Binah were the sephiroth contained. As the desire to create became the idea of creation, we entered the world of Briah: Chesed, Geburah, and Tifareth. Desires and ideas led to the building of the Universe's foundation, Yetzirah, through the realms of Netzach, Hod, and Yesod. Finally, the world of Assiah emerged from the energies of the Tree, and Malkuth was born. Through these four worlds of creation, all in Cosmos was brought from primal chaos into order; through these four worlds, we also find that the inherent order of nature survives. The energy of the Tree, although evolving in a linear fashion, must return to its point of origin and be recycled lest creation grow stagnant. Through this return of energy from Assiah to Atziluth, linear forces begin to circulate in a cyclic fashion. Translated into the forms of Malkuth—more specifically, Earth—these flowing forces become the changing patterns of the solar and lunar cycles.

In Chapter Two, we discovered the forces of LVX, the life-energy that exists in limitless amounts throughout Cosmos. As we created our sacred space, we worked with the elements in the order of fire, water, air, and earth; this is the progression the elements follow through the four worlds in the Tree of Life. Our logic for this progression was simple: we were using magick to create, and as original creation followed this process, so should we in our magickal operations. The Universe is one vast, living energy structure containing a myriad of smaller energy patterns derived from this primal light; as microcosms of the Macrocosm, we, too, could invoke LVX and use it to create smaller energy patterns based upon our own.

As we began to work with the Archangels, angels, and elementals, however, we began to work with the traditional pattern of deosil progression. We met with Auriel in the North, and moved around our circle until we ended with Gabriel in the West. The same pattern of casting the circle was used to generate LVX, but as we moved on to the elements and the tides of life, we asserted that the natural cycle of evolution must be followed. In understanding how the four worlds of creation became the cycles of change on Earth, we must first understand how we came to this alteration of our workings.

Creating the magickal circle is synonymous with creating our own personal magickal Cosmos. We separate ourselves from mundane living, which symbolizes arising from anti-existence. Before entering the sacred space, we realize that we are without true spiritual focus; once within the circle, we have become more truly ourselves. In Appendix One, you will find that a magickal circle is one of the symbols of Malkuth; fire, water, air, and earth merge to give us a new body, a new focus, and hence, true spiritual life in our own mini-cosmos. Once created, it becomes a power-filled structure birthed by the same forces and energies that brought our greater Macrocosm into being.

Once created, however, the circle becomes a structure in itself; the energies merge into a pattern that spirals from North, East, South, and West. This pattern continues until we again step toward the outer limits of our Cosmos, hurling the invoked forces of LVX back to the proper realms. So it is with the realm of Malkuth: once the powers of LVX are brought to the physical realm, they, too, move in a cycle. As long as this Universe exists, the four divisions of the Tree will focus their energies on Malkuth, and those powers will dance the spiral dance of Cosmos.

This still leaves us with the necessity of determining how the four worlds translate into Malkuth. Obviously, the cycle of Tetragrammaton only works during the actual process of creation. If you remember the Middle Pillar exercise given in Chapter Four, once invoked, the energies of Tetragrammaton quickly become Pentagrammaton, the formula of a symbol (such as the human body) given life with the LVX energy. Now, we have an important key to understanding the operation of the Tree of Life's four divisions in Malkuth—life is a cycle of energies and patterns. Energy, in any form, flows in a predetermined fashion; there are two points of rest, where two extremes of energy are in total balance: a point of high activity, or positive power; and a point of low activity, or negative power. Figure 7:2 shows the linear flow and motion of energy. Beginning with a point of non-activity, a balance between positive and negative charges, a wave of energy increases in strength and motion until it becomes positive in polarity. The energy then descends to another point of resting before it becomes negatively charged. This action repeats, and energy moves through space.

It is important to remember that the periods of non-activity in the motion of energy are not periods of neutrality, but points of balance. Being in balance, however, they still have a preordained motion: every high point in our cycle eventually becomes a low point, which again becomes another high point in the cycle. While moving into balance from a positive polarity, we may also say that energy is not merely in balance, it is balance carrying a disposition for a negative potential: this point of balance will soon give way to a negative charge. Likewise, as the energy moves into a balanced position between negative and positive potentials, we may also say that this point of balance carries a disposition for positive energy. Periods of balance become points of major activity, or turning points within the centers of action within the energy's motion. Energy, then, moves in an eternal circle, a rhythm much like that of the daily solar cycle. In Figure 7:3, the motion of energy is merged into a unified whole by connecting the two equal halves of our graph.

Now let us analyze the four worlds of creation in terms of receptive and projective powers, high and low points of activity. Within Atziluth, the focus of power

THE LINEAR FLOW OF MOTION AND ENERGY

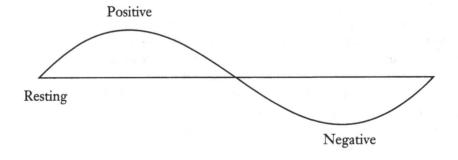

Figure 7:2

is contained in Kether; the archetype of the Great Horned Mother is the central, balancing focus of this world. Atziluth emerged from negative potential, so for energy to form and begin moving throughout the void of space, the initial world must take on a positive charge. Traditionally, we are taught that the feminine forces are receptive and negative, yet, on inner planes, the opposite can easily occur. Kether becomes impregnated by the negative veils of existence; however, as the great forces of Kether are functioning as birthing energy, projecting outward into the next sephirah, this realm represents positive potential.

Logically, we may draw comparisons between Atziluth and the sunrise. In terms of practical force, the world of Atziluth generates an urge to create; a mental/spiritual affirmation to begin building a Universe is conceived. Although this is the beginning of Cosmos, Atziluth represents emergence from a negative state before a flurry of activity. Within our magickal circle of the daily cycle, we may best attribute this to the East, the sunrise. The sun emerges from a negative potential (absence of light, total darkness) and begins its climb toward its height of power and activity in the noonday sky (positive polarity).

Now that we have determined an initial location on our daily cycle, the rest of the system falls into place. We may assume that the area of the South represents the world of Briah. In searching for symbolism to test this hypothesis, we could first allude to the fact that Atziluth is a resting potential emerging from a negative potential, the Veils of Negative Existence. The next stop along our graph of energy's movement and potential would be a realm of pure positive polarity, represented by the sun at the height of its power. The sunrise moves toward the noonday sun, just as Atziluth moves toward creating the world of Briah. Tifareth is the harmonizing force of Briah, and although it lies within the Middle Pillar, its symbolism is solar

THE CIRCULAR FLOW OF MOTION AND ENERGY

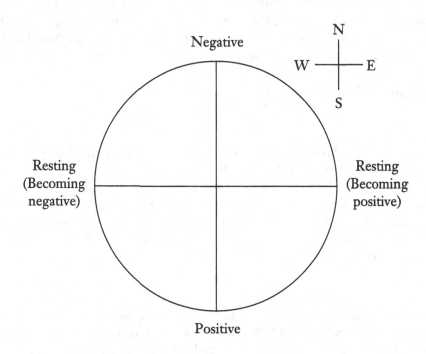

Figure 7:3

and masculine—the powers of Briah are balanced in the image of the sun. Also, Tifareth reflects the powers of Kether, which means that the world of Briah would need to remain close to its point of origin. Being the height of creative power, the forces of Briah merge well with this point on the circle.

Now, we move to another resting potential in the West of our circle, or sunset. Following our previous model, we would have to assume that the world attributed to this area would be Yetzirah; again, we must check our symbolism to make sure the assumption is correct. We have gone from a period of contemplation, an idea to create, into a realm where the initial planning was done. Within Briah, the basics of Creation were planned, so all that is left is to build the actual foundation. This flurry of spiritual/mental activity begins to wind down until the actual foundations for the Universe's physical foundation are set. Once done, there is little left for the creative forces to accomplish beyond fleshing out the creation; once again, we find ourselves at rest when the foundations are in place. Within Yesod, the harmonizer of this world, we find the realm of material foundations. If it follows that the noonday sun is the height of our cycle, and thus positive, we can also assume that the North would be the place of negative potential. This makes the West the ideal location for the world of Yetzirah.

The negative resting potential moves into the North, the place of total darkness. Left only with Assiah, we must place this world here. If we delve into the symbolism of Malkuth, the heart of this creative world, we find that this is, indeed, a negative and receptive potential. All that was begun in the world of Atziluth flows until it is absorbed into this realm. All ideas, concerns, and emanations are imprinted into the fabric of reality. Assuming that this final negative potential initiates another cycle in the motion of energy, we must also assume that the negative charge carries positive potential; if we look beyond the material of Malkuth, we find that all energy permeating the realm does, indeed, return through the Tree of Life to the realm of Kether within the world of Atziluth. During this period of rest in the creative cycle, the energy prepares to move again to a resting state with a positive predisposition, and the travel of energy begins anew throughout Cosmos. The energy travels through the void of space in an eternal, immortal circle.

Adorations of Light, Part II

Atziluth

Just before the sun breaks the horizon, stand outside, facing the East. Close your eyes, and imagine that the sephirah Kether glows brightly above the crown of your head. Vibrate "Eheieh." Let the light descend from Kether into Chokmah and Binah—feel the power of Atziluth within yourself, your own primal assertion, "I am." Imagine that the power flows from within yourself, reaching out to the Eastern sky. As the sun breaks the horizon, utter the adoration for the East. Close with silent meditation.

Briah

At noon, go outside and face the South. Breathe slowly and deeply; become aware once more of the realm of Atziluth that was awakened earlier in the day. Allow the light to flow from the realm of Kether and into the sphere of Tifareth in your heart; vibrate "IAO." Imagine that the sephiroth of Chesed and Geburah open in the aura, and allow shafts of light to connect all the spheres. Feel the energy within Briah; let it flow outward to the South. Utter the adoration for the noonday sun, and close with silent mediation.

Yetzirah

Just before the sun begins to sink in the horizon, walk outdoors and face the West. Close your eyes and visualize the sephiroth that were opened earlier in the day. Allow the light to descend from Tifareth into the area of the genitals, where it becomes the sephirah of Yesod. Vibrate "Shaddai el-Chai," feeling the powers growing within yourself. Imagine that the realms of Hod and Netzach open within the aura; meditate on the growing powers of Yetzirah within yourself. Let the power flow outward, into the area of the Western sky. As the sun begins to sink below the horizon, utter the adoration of sunset. Close with silent mediation.

Assiah

Rise from sleep at midnight; face the North and visualize the energy from the previous three worlds opened in your aura during the day. Allow the energy from Yesod to descend into the area of the feet, Malkuth, and vibrate "Adonai ha-Aretz." Feel the power of Assiah vibrating within; allow the energy to flow outward and meet the Northern horizon. Say the adoration for the North, and close with silent meditation.

Lunar Cycles

Most have been taught that the Goddess has three phases—Maid, Mother, and Crone—that coincide with the changing cycles of the moon—waxing, full, and waning. From the first crescent in the night sky until just before the full moon, the Maiden reigns; the adventurous, young Goddess who brings enchantment and mystery to the Earth. She belongs to herself, yet is eternally pursued by her Consort, the Young Stag. Then, as the moon becomes full and ripe over the Earth, she becomes the Mother, Creatrix of life, lover to the Horned One. The Mother Goddess turns her power over self into power for the race, belonging unselfishly to the children emerging from her womb. She screams the birth-ecstasy, and the whole world reverberates in its power. Reclaiming her essence, belonging to herself once more, the Goddess' light begins to shrink in the sky as the archetype of the Crone emerges. Aged and wise, her bleeding womb dries up; she bleeds from the heart for love's sake. Her Consort, the Horned One, becomes the Lord of Shadows as he descends to the depths of the Summerlands, leaving her to guide the children of light through the darkness. By her own power, she descends into herself to arise anew as the Maiden Goddess.

Remembering the material that was covered in Chapter Three of this text, these are the archetypes found in the sephirah Yesod, sphere of the moon. Within the realm of Yetzirah, the triple Goddess of nature holds all power, becoming young or old as it pleases her. She rules the magnetic/astral tides governing creation, molding them to create the forms of Cosmos. Drawing her inspiration from Netzach and her science from Hod, she weaves a complex web of life and death; a web that holds the basis of all cycles and seasons. Within the Supernals, also, we find a much earlier, more primal form of the triple Goddess. Drawing inspiration from the realm of Saturn, she manifests as Aima, Maya, and Ama: the beginning, duration, and ending of time. Both forms of the triple Goddess are valid; both are necessary to the complex manifestations within Assiah. If we analyze each sephirah separately, we can find some aspect of each that corresponds to one of these three Goddess-forms.

We know there are four major points of activity in the daily cycle: sunrise, noon, sunset, and midnight. These four points of activity coincide with the four points in the magick circle, and they also coincide with the four worlds of Atziluth, Briah, Yetzirah, and Assiah. Within the phases of the moon, we also find that there are actually four phases involved in the monthly cycle, not three: waxing, full, waning, and new (dark). The triple Goddess, however, has been placed as changing form and face with the cycles of the moon—the dark moon becomes an in-between time when the mystery of the Crone grows young again and becomes the Maiden. While properly sychronizing these three faces of the Mother with the tides of the moon, we have reduced an astrological cycle of four to a cycle of three, with the fourth tide of the moon becoming an in-between phase. While this is true, in part, the dark moon also implies another face of the Goddess, and a deeper mystery.

Let us think about this briefly. In all traditions of the Craft, the phase of the Maiden ties in with the waxing moon, the Mother with the full, and the Crone with the waning. Astrologically, the full moon only occupies the space of one day; however, to the naked eye, it appears full for a total of three days—one day before the astrological event and one day after. Likewise, the dark moon appears devoid of light for not only the astrological event, it also appears this way the day before and the day after. When celebrating the full moon, most covens allow for the three-day period of seeming fullness; magickally, it makes sense that the dark moon should be observed for an equal length of time. If the moon lies in darkness for a period of time equal to that of the full moon, it should also embody some form of the Great Mother.

"The Legend of the Descent of the Goddess," a short myth from my version of the Gardnerian Book of Shadows, is given in Appendix Two. While this myth is not presented to initiates until the second degree, it explains the "Fourth Face" of the Goddess, the part which lies eternally unseen by humanity. In the myth itself, it alludes to the three days and three nights in which the moon lies in darkness, hidden from the face of the Earth. This secret fourth face is also acknowledged by Dianic and Feminist Witches as a special place of feminine power. Also, in the section on Malkuth in Chapter Three, we learn a bit about the Goddess descending into herself through the Horned Passage (which lies in Malkuth) to see what she has become, regenerating both herself and the inner forces of our realm by her secret rites of power.

If we extend our concept of the lunar cycle to include four phases, not just three, we again have a cycle that includes the four worlds of the Tree of Life; it also connects intimately with the placements of the daily cycle within the circle of the four worlds. Figure 7:4 shows the cross-circle diagram with the placement of the four worlds and lunar cycles. Obviously, the daily cycle is an expression of the masculine forces; likewise, the lunar cycle becomes an expression of the feminine forces of creation. As we experience these two cycles, solar and lunar, we begin to experience ways in which the masculine and feminine opposites of the Tree of Life can be balanced within the same realms. For example, in our section on the daily cycles, we learned that the East corresponded to the world of Atziluth, and although the elemental energy in the realm on the Tree of Life is fire, in Malkuth, the initial impulse to create, the desire to exist, begins activity for the entire cycle. In Cosmos, the initial desire to create is full of life and vigorous strength; in Malkuth, it is internal darkness stirring toward light—the time of creation. Therefore, the waxing moon easily corresponds with the East and Atziluth.

Journal Entry

Meditate on Figure 7:4, analyzing the connections between the point on the circle, the world from the Tree of Life, and the lunar connections. In your journal, write about the symbolism of the four worlds in connection with the four points of the lunar cycle. Also, try to conclude how the cycles of the moon coincide with the cycles of the sun. Finish this exercise before continuing with this text.

Figure 7:4 places the lunar cycles at their proper points on the magick circle. In the East with Atziluth, the waxing moon is fixed as the cycle is beginning. Moving to the South and Briah, we come to the tide of the full moon. Yetzirah, in the west, corresponds to the waning moon, while from the North, we approach the mysteries of Assiah and the dark moon. Remember, also, the fixed daily cycles: sunrise in the East, noon in the South, sunset in the West, and midnight in the North. Remember that each world represents a focus of action; with Atziluth, we have the idea of creation, progressing until we end with Assiah, the actual creation. Each cardinal point on the circle represents some aspect of the Cosmic cycle, and as a focus of power, some part of our divine mythology.

When investigating the symbolism of the solar rhythms, we began in the East; likewise, we shall use that as our starting point. We begin with the waxing phase of the moon, the period of the Maiden, and her place in the cycle of Cosmos. This aspect of the Great Goddess represents the life-force beginning throughout the Earth—it is a time of freshness and purity. New beginnings are strewn throughout

THE FOUR WORLDS AND THE LUNAR CYCLES

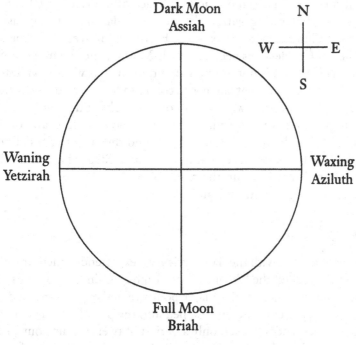

Figure 7:4

the planes of existence; the virgin earth is prepared to received new life. The Maiden belongs only to herself, although she is constantly pursued by the Young Stag across the sky and Earth. He seeks to know her, become one with her; seductively, she leads him in the first steps of a sacred dance that will leave the earth soft and plowed beneath their feet. A magickal tease, She arouses the life-force within him, preparing him to project his power into her, making her the Mother. This stirring of energy, then, belongs to Atziluth, where the tides of life are beginning to rise.

Waxing slowly in the night sky, the crescent begins to hang full and ripe over the horizon; the Maiden becomes the Mother. Her Consort, the Horned God, becomes entangled by his own passions: the power erupts from him in an ecstatic consummation of the sacred dance—he gives his power over to her. As his longing for the Goddess reaches its height, when she can no longer elude the rising tide of life stirring within herself, the love-chase becomes the sacred marriage. By his strength, she becomes impregnated, and this force pours out and sustains the world. The Goddess is at the height of her power. The full moon, as a symbol of this force, rises to its zenith in the South. The power here belongs to the realm of Briah.

Having reached the height of their power, their passions soon begin to recede; the God, having given her his strength, dies in the embrace—he descends to become the Lord of Shadows. The Mother's power, too, begins to change. Growing old in the night sky, the full moon begins to lose its lunar light; it returns to a crescent, ever darkening as it moves through the heaven. She becomes the Crone Goddess—Goddess of Wisdom, Destroyer of Nature; she is both the grave and reaper who gathers the last strength from her Consort as he falls limp in her embrace. The God descends into the land of dreams, sent into the next world as the Crone Mother wisely spreads the fruit of her harvest to her children. This dissemination of force belongs to Yetzirah, where the power is molded into the forms found in Malkuth. As the sun sinks in the West, as the moon shrinks in light, they both head for the Western gate of the magick circle.

Our Horned Lord is no more upon the face of the Earth; he has withdrawn into the underworld, resting within the womb of darkness, the breast of Gaia. Alone, the great Goddess withdraws to the Earth, and moves in darkness through Malkuth. The sky Goddess has become Earth-Mother, and she mourns, ever seeking her other half. But he is not found without, for he has withdrawn into her; the Goddess, seeking to know what she has become, follows him through the horned passage of death into her own womb. Without the light in the night sky, the Earth is thrown into darkness for three nights while the power withdraws to the innermost realms of Malkuth; she meets him, there and they create rites of power that makes her the Maiden once more, and he the Young Stag reborn from the primal darkness of Earth. We are within the realm of Assiah, the mystery of the North, and the eternal midnight of magick and mystery.

Adorations of Night

When we began to work with the daily cycles, we experienced them through a simple set of exercises called the "Adorations of Light." Using the periods of sunrise, noon, sunset, and midnight as the major points of activity, we stopped our mundane routines during these times and tapped into the prevalent tide of energy. The daily cycle, however, encompassed only a period of twenty-four hours; in one day, we were able to follow the cycle through its high and low points of power. The cycles of the moon, however, cover a more complex rhythm of nature, for they involve not only the changing forms and faces of the Goddess, they also include the dynamic interaction of energy between the moon and sun, Goddess and God. On physical levels, the moon changes its forms because of its dynamic rotation and interaction with the sun; on spiritual levels, the Goddess changes form as she changes her level of involvement with the Horned One.

This cycle involves roughly twenty-eight days. Owing to this more complex rhythm, the adorations of the lunar cycle will be more complex than those of the solar. We will begin our adorations in the East with the Maiden: by obtaining a lunar calendar or an almanac, you can find the next new or dark moon, and then count two days away from that date. Begin your lunar adorations on that day. Next, determine the date of the full moon, and count backward two days. That will be the last day you will perform the adorations for the Maiden.

For example, suppose that the next dark moon occurs on September eighth. We allow the day before the dark moon and the day after as a complete phase; therefore, the Maiden does not begin her reign in the night sky until the first appearance of the crescent two days after the eighth, on September tenth. The calendar would list September ninth as the first quarter of the waxing moon; magickally, however, the Goddess would still reign in the land of dreams. We would begin our work with the Maiden on September tenth.

The full moon in this example would occur on September twenty-third. Allowing the day before and the day after the full moon to represent one complete cycle, we would do our last adoration of the Maiden two days before the full moon, on September twenty-first. Therefore, we would mark September tenth through the twenty-first as days for the adorations for the Maiden.

Logically, we would use September twenty-second through the twenty-fourth as the days of adoration for the full moon. The second day after the full moon, September twenty-fifth, would begin our first adoration to the Crone. Looking ahead, we find that October seventh is the next dark moon. Two days before that, on October fifth, we would perform our last observance to the Crone. The three days of the dark moon, the sixth through the eighth, would mark our observance of the dark moon.

This may appear complicated at first; in truth, determining the days of our cycles is quite easy. Simply find the dates of the full and dark moons, and mark off the day before and the day after each as belonging to those phases of the Goddess. The remaining days belong to the waxing and waning moons. For simplicity, it would be wise to obtain a magickal almanac and mark out the days of the cycles a few months in advance. By doing so, we obtain an intellectual view of how our cycles run, and we can plan our activities accordingly.[3] Once the cycles have been marked on the calendar, it is important to wait until the first day of the Maiden before beginning these adorations. Also, due to the complexities of these exercises, it is not necessary to perform them every day, although that would be advantageous. These cycles of nature occupy a large amount of linear time, and if we honor the pending cycle on at least three separate occasions every week, we will begin to align ourselves within this greater circle of Cosmos. During the periods of the full and dark moon, perform the adorations at least once.

---

3. The dates given in this exercise were determined from the 1991 edition of *Llewellyn's Magickal Almanac*. It is put out every year by Llewellyn and is one of the best on the market.

The Waxing Moon

On the morning of the first day of the Maiden, seek out some secluded spot in which you will not be disturbed. Face the East as the sun comes up; greet this sunrise as the first stirrings of the Young Stag. Raise your arms to the sky in invocation, and say, "Hail to thee, powerful Young Stag; hail to thee who has risen anew from the primal womb of darkness. Begin thy search, begin thy seeking; your partner, the Maiden, lies waiting in darkness. Begin now the sacred dance that leads to new life and birth." Spend a few moments meditating on the reborn Horned Lord, fresh and full of desire, as he begins searching for the Maiden Goddess.

As the day progresses, use the other points on the daily cycle as times of quiet introspection and meditation about the Maiden Goddess and Young Stag. At noon, as the sun ascends to its height in the South, quietly compose yourself for a few moments and meditate on the rising passions of the God, seeking to find consummation with his other half. Feel his force growing and yearning for the other part of himself; realize that as the eternally unpenetrated virgin, she eludes even his most powerful desires, teaching him the ways of feminine enchantments. As the sun begins to set in the Western sky, meditate on how he descends beyond the realms of day, searching for her. As the cycle approaches the midnight hour, the point of greatest darkness and mystery, begin casting your magick circle. As usual, begin the tracing of its boundaries from the North, the place of darkness and mystery.

Once within the sacred space, face the East to greet the Maiden Goddess. Say, "Hail to thee, young Maiden hanging in the night sky; giver of enchantment and mystery. You call, and the Horned God rises; you beckon, and he follows. Through your sacred dance along sky and earth, the fields become fertile, the seeds are sown, and all life becomes fresh and new. Hail to thee, loveliest of all Goddesses." Spend a few moments within the circle, meditating on the power of the Maiden—both over herself, and the God. Close the circle.

The Full Moon

On the first day of the full moon, rise in the morning to greet the Eastern sky as the sun rises. Use this time to quietly meditate on the rising of the Horned God to meet the Great Mother, merging into a dynamic union that brings all the Earth's creations into the full tide of fertility. Again, as the sun ascends to its height in the Southern sky, greet the orb at its height of power and say, "Hail unto thee, Lord of Life, as you meet the Mother at her height of power. Dance the eternal dance of life that shall lead to your death, and life again; sacrifice yourself in her arms that all may live. Great Father, sacrificed God: We hail you and bless you as you give yourself freely to her. Blessed be!" When the sun finally sinks below the Western horizon, use this part of the cycle to meditate on the impending union of Goddess and God—the sacred marriage.

As midnight, the time of darkness and mystery, approaches, create your sacred space. Once safely within, approach the South to greet the Mother as she hangs full over the horizon, and say, "Blessings to thee, bright, fertile Mother; I honor you as you give yourself over to your Consort, the Horned God. Blessings to thee, powerful Horned One; I honor you as you give yourself to the Mother. Dance the sacred dance; perform the rites of power that shall bring fertility to the land. Hail to thee as you bring new life to our world." Spend some time within the circle, facing the South, meditating on the growing tides of life all around. Close the circle.

The Waxing Moon

As the Crone Goddess begins her rule in the sky, seek out a quiet place in nature just before the morning sunrise. Use this time as a period of silent meditation; concentrate on the qualities of the Horned God as he begins his descent into the Land of Youth. Likewise, meditate on the concept of the Mother as an aged wise-woman, keeper of all mysteries. During the day, pause also at noon for silent meditation. As the sun begins to set in the West, however, pause facing the sunset and say, "Farewell to thee, mighty God; you have given your strength over to the Mother, and now must descend into the Land of Dreams. Rest, relax, grow young again; the time will come when, once again, you will rise to new strength in the Eastern tide of life. Hail and farewell."

As midnight approaches, seek out a secluded spot in which you will not be disturbed; facing the North, begin to cast the magick circle. Once you are safely within its boundaries, walk deosil to face the West, imagining that the Crone Goddess comes to the circle, attending to the passing of her Consort. Address the ancient Mother, and say, "Hail to thee, ancient Mother; farewell to thee, Horned Lord in thy passing. The Mother carries you against her breast; she watches over you as you descend from her grasp, into the dark womb of the Earth. I call to you, dark queen, Grandmother, rain-bringer—most feared of all the Mother's forms. Let us share in thy wisdom, let us feel your power in our lives. Blessings to you as you gather thy lover's harvest, spreading his bounty across the Earth. Blessed be." Remain in the circle, meditating on this aspect of the Goddess—the powerful Crone. Take some time to feel her strength and wisdom. Close the circle.

The Dark Moon

As the moon disappears from the night sky, we begin the reign of the dark Mother. Seek out a quiet space in nature where you will not be disturbed; do this early, just before the sun begins to rise above the horizon. If you choose, this cycle is the one to use for cleansing and purification; spend some time fasting and abstaining from all but liquids. Mundane habits and addictions, such as drinking and smoking, should be avoided. In some traditions, it is taught that as the symbols of power are totally withdrawn from the night sky, it is wise to shield all personal power, limiting magick to passive forms of meditation. Due to the static, seemingly lifeless, yet powerful pulses of power emerging from the darkness of the moon, it is wise to respect this tide of life. All vestiges of magick that permeate our world at this time are mysterious and subtle, yet extremely powerful and essential to the continuation of life in our realm.

Whatever fasts and observances you choose during this tide should begin with the morning and sunrise. At every point of the day—sunrise, noon, and sunset—set aside some time to meditate on the concepts of the dark moon; review the "Legend of the Descent of the Goddess" given in Appendix Two of this text. As midnight approaches, the time of mystery and magick and the point of the dark moon, create sacred space. Once you are safely within it, turn to face the North and say, "Hail to thee, Dark Lord of Shadows; lying deep within the darkness of the Mother's womb, you rest and await rebirth. Hail to thee, Goddess of Life; searching for the Horned Lord, your other half, your mysterious other self, you have descended into your own womb by way of the Horned Passage. Within your holiest of places, you find yourself, you meet yourself, creating rites of power to continue the cycle of life upon the

Earth. Blessings to you both, as you dwell within the North, the place of power, mystery, and the gestative realms of Night."

Silently, read the mystery of the Goddess's descent, imagining that each scene of power is being played out before you. Feel the tide of power that is represented by the North, rising thickly about you, dawning mysteriously from the depths of the Earth and permeating our world like an invisible gauze, a web, that sustains and holds life in its present form. Once your mediation is complete, close the circle.

THE GREATER EARTH CYCLE: THE SABBATS

Early in my magickal training, I was first exposed to the belief that the Esbats, held in honor of the lunar cycle, revered the patterns of the Goddess, while the Sabbats, the solar celebrations, were held in honor of the God. Daily rhythms were not experienced, nor was there much blending of the two archetypes throughout the Esbats and Sabbats. But there is another view that is being embraced by the modern Neo-Pagan movement, a view that also expresses the holistic view of the Qabalah: the cycles of the sun and moon espouse the cycles of both Goddess and God, although during each cycle one holds prominence. Perhaps this is the Craft growing up, moving into a deeper understanding of the complexities of the natural world in which we live. Under this new world view, the patterns of the day may be used to trace the primary cycles of the Horned God, the lunar phases the patterns of the Goddess. As they blend into a unified whole, we begin to see how the phases of Goddess and God merge into a static union that can only be expressed as God/dess.

If we follow the next step in our investigation of the natural cycles in conjunction with the Qabalah, we arrive at the Sabbats. Through our new viewpoints, we find that the Sabbats become more than solar festivals; the cycles as a whole depend upon more than the sun. The yearly cycle is aimed at expressing the changing tides of fertility on Mother Earth, Gaia, and as such the yearly cycle is the slowest, summing up the slower tides of power that penetrate our planet within Malkuth, governing the changing seasons accordingly.

There are eight Sabbats, four major and four minor. The major Sabbats are Imbolc, Bealtaine, Lughnasadh, and Samhain, while the lesser Sabbats are the equinoxes and solstices. Our major Sabbats are centered around the tide of fertility that controls plants and animals alike; the lesser Sabbats deal with the waxing and waning of light upon the Earth.

Figure 7:5 illustrates the turning of the wheel of the year in accordance with the four worlds of creation. As commemorations of the waxing and waning of solar light, the Equinoxes and Solstices have been plotted alongside the cycles of sunrise, noon, sunset, and midnight. They line up on the diagram as follows: Spring Equinox—Atziluth; Summer Solstice—Briah; Autumn Equinox—Yetzirah; and Winter Solstice—Assiah. The greater Sabbats have been placed between these cycles of increasing light and dark, commemorating how the cycles of fertility upon Gaia depend on the ebbing and flowing of the God's solar strength. Bealtaine falls between the East and South; Lughnasadh is between the South and the West; falling between the West and the North is Samhain; Imbolc lies between the North and the East. When followed about deosil, just as in the daily and lunar cycles, we are following the evolution of the four worlds within the realm of Malkuth.

Review the sections comparing the four worlds to the daily and lunar cycles; also, review the material that you wrote in your journal concerning these conjunctions. Using Figure 7:5 as a guide, plus any personal knowledge you have about the Sabbats, try to determine why the four Equinoxes and Solstices are placed at the cardinal points of the circle-cross diagram. Remember that the daily and lunar cycles represent the cycle of the year in miniature; the same themes presented by those rhythms will also be present in some form during the Sabbats. Work on your analysis before reading the following material.

As we began our study of the daily cycle, we began working with patterns of light; in the morning, we found the first stirrings of light in the Eastern sky, manifesting as a sunrise. The sun rose in power during the day, ascending toward the Southern sky until the zenith was reached in the South—this was the time of the noonday sun. Every high point is the beginning of a low point; likewise, the sun began to sink in the sky until it reached the West, where it disappeared from sight in the natural phenomenon of a sunset. Throwing the world into darkness as it sank, the sun traveled in darkness through the Northern quarter, until it was reborn in the East with the new day. This cycle repeated daily; as it did, it went through the eternal cycle of the four worlds: Atziluth, Briah, Yetzirah, and Assiah. Interpreting each world as part of a cycle of life-energy, we were able to place them at the cardinal points of the circle, allowing us to determine the aspects of the Horned God at every time of the day.

Soon, we began to work with the moon and its four phases of waxing, full, waning, and dark. These, too, we placed at their points within the magick circle:

THE YEARLY CYCLE AND THE FOUR WORLDS OF CREATION

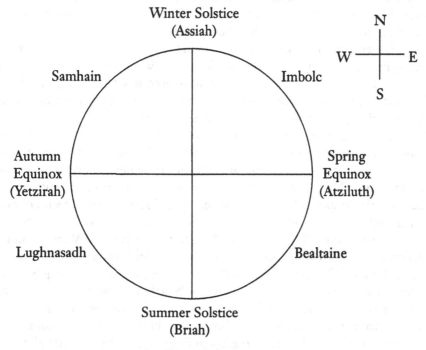

Figure 7:5

the Maiden in the East, the Mother in the South, the Crone in the West, and the dark Mother in the North. Suddenly, we found that we had the basis of the Craft's spirituality laid out before us—from the pursuit of the Maiden by the Young Stag to the decline of the Horned One in the arms of the Crone. In the span of twenty-eight days, we were able to move through the entire divine cycle; yes, it was simplistic, but it was effective.

Expanding our concepts derived from the daily and lunar cycles is the wheel of the year: the Sabbats. Now, working with a cycle of roughly 358 days, we can work out the complex relationships between Goddess and God in full, honoring them in a myriad of guises that can be found throughout Malkuth. As before, we can place this cycle of seasons on the circle-cross diagram, using the Sabbats that commemorate the changing cycles of light and darkness as the major turning points. These Sabbats are the Equinoxes and Solstices. Although called the lesser Sabbats due to their simple nature, these are actually the turning points for the year, the area in which light and dark weave into a complex web that controls the impending tide of life. So far, we have taken the East and the world of Atziluth as beginning any single cycle. We shall begin our investigation of the Sabbats and their connections with the four worlds in the East, with the Spring Equinox.

Spring Equinox

As the sun moves into the first zodiac sign of Aries, the season of spring begins. By looking at the chart in Figure 7:5, you will find that the Spring Equinox has been placed alongside the realm of Atziluth, along with the Maiden, Young Stag, and the sunrise. Spring encompasses all these concepts, for the Earth has been renewed with youth, strength, and vigor. The Earth has become the Maiden, filled with freshly plowed fields, newly born animals, and a burst of wildflowers. The greenery that withered during the time of cold and darkness has returned refreshed; the world seems centered around rituals of renewal. Every major world religion has established some sort of festival in conjunction with this time, commemorating the resurrection of gods and youthful beginnings.

It seems that the world is caught up in the idea to be creative; with the increasing light, nature's activity increases. In Europe, where increasing darkness leads to the icy chill of winter, the Spring Equinox becomes a time of planting seedlings indoors in preparation for outdoor planting around the time of Bealtaine. Older mythologies speak of some sort of rising of the Goddess-force; in our mythology, the Goddess arises from her own womb, having descending into the darkness of the North and Assiah in search of her other half, the Horned God. As the Young Stag is reborn from her womb, she, too, arises from within herself, bringing new life to the Earth above. Our celebrations at this time focus on the increase of life and light that comes with the spring. Night and day may lie in balance now, but with our yearnings for the return of life, the light increases, becoming the ruling force at this time.

Throughout all traditions of the Craft, it seems that Vernal Equinox celebrations are filled with references to the Maiden's return to Mother Earth; in turn, the Earth becomes fresh and fertile once more. The Young Stag, rising in strength after his birth from womb of the North, fills the world with his light and life—creation themes in all their glory. Therefore, we begin our next cycle of the sacred circle in the East with the Spring Equinox. As the cycle continues, as the life force on the Earth begins to grow in intensity, we move deosil along our path, until we arrive in the South with the festivals of Summer Solstice.

Summer Solstice

In the South, we come to the world of Briah, and the tides of the noonday sun and full moon. Now, we can add the correspondence of Summer Solstice, the longest day of the year. It marks the height of the light on the face of the Earth; having risen anew in the East with the Spring Equinox, the sun's powers have grown in strength through Bealtaine, culminating on this day. This festival marks the time when the days begin to shorten, reminding us that progression into the autumn and winter of the year are inevitable. Just as in the cycles presented to us by the moon and sun, this is the time when the God, in all his blazing strength, plunges his masculine core into the depths of the Great Mother; he gives his strength over to her so that life on Earth can continue. With that transfer of power his own life-force is depleted, and he plunges within her, beginning his descent into the land of dreams.

Many people light bonfires on this date to commemorate the passing of the sun. At sunrise, the pyres are built, and they are tended all day, well into the night. As the last vestige of the day is extinguished, so, too, does the height of strength that was represented by this festival wane. But at the height of the sun's power, we have a lusty Sabbat; the night becomes filled with passions that match those of the burning fires. Dances, parties, and lovemaking continue into the night, the participants seeking union with the height of power that has erupted in this Southern tide of life.

With the strong, solar symbolism—the longest day, the height of the sun's reign, the beginning of the descent to darkness and the dark womb—this period belongs in the South with the world of Briah. By giving his power over to the Goddess, the Horned God takes his first, most powerful steps into creating the energy that will build and sustain all future forms of Malkuth. As he dies in the embrace of love, he takes his first step toward the Western quarter, and the festival of the Autumn Equinox.

Autumn Equinox

In Figure 7:5, we see that the Autumn Equinox has been placed in the West, aligning it with the cycles of the setting sun, waning moon, and world of Yetzirah. From our previous studies of natural cycles, we know that this is the world of foundations and rest. The astral counterparts of all created things have been finished, and all that awaits is the final projection into the world of Assiah, the energy realm that contains what we call matter. Here, the dark queen, the Crone Goddess, rules; she watches over the passing of the Horned Lord of Life into his form as the dreaded Lord of Shadows. As such, she harvests the last vestiges of his strength, distributing his dying force over the Earth so that all may live.

As we begin to study this Sabbat, we learn that the Autumn Equinox is a time of harvest: the last seeds planted during spring have reached the height of their cycle, and now that the fruits of our labors are ready, we begin to harvest them lest they begin to decay. The increasing darkness requires that we begin to take stock of our surroundings. The cold winter is coming; we must prepare. The grain is ripe and must be harvested. Our plans are coming to fruition; we must examine our present situations and prepare for the reaping what we have sown.

Themes of wisdom also permeate the thinking behind this Sabbat; we descend into the darkness of self to learn about the secrets we have hidden within. In operations such as these, we invoke the Crone Goddess of wisdom into ourselves, asking guidance for the future. We harvest what we have worked for, laying down a firm foundation that shall carry us through the increasingly darker and colder months that lie ahead. As such, the Autumn Equinox is a fitting Sabbat to place at this part of the magick circle with the world of Yetzirah. It also leads to the next point on our circle, the Winter Solstice.

Winter Solstice

Arriving at the North of our circle, we come to the gates of Assiah; with this cardinal point, we also have the correspondences of midnight and the dark Mother. Already we have learned that this part of our circle represents a twilight, in-between time of night; the Goddess, having passed through her own horned passages, arrives deep within the dark womb, the eternal land of rest and youth. Within it, she finds her other self, the Horned Lord of Shadows, her own final manifestation of self. Magickally, they unite their powers into one final, creative whole. From this union he is reborn as the Child of Light, and she becomes young again, rising on the Earth as the Maiden once more. These subtle stirrings of power deep within the heart of the Earth sustain life on the physical realms when it seems that all life has been withdrawn. Magickally, Yule embodies the same concepts; it rightfully belongs here as a manifestation of Assiah's powers.

At first, it may seem that there is a conflict here. The Goddess descends as the Crone of Wisdom, regaining her youth as she enters the Land of Youth. Meeting with her other self within her own womb, she becomes Maiden once more, yet gives birth to her Consort as the Divine Child of Light. In Goddess traditions, the concept of the Maiden does, at times, become synonymous with virginity; however, it is the Earth that resurrects the Lord of Life at the Winter Solstice. During the Autumn Equinox, he descended into the Earth-womb as the Crone Goddess watched over his transition; she too descended into her own womb. Using the power to become Maiden once more and to give birth to her Consort, she emerges from the womb young and refreshed. He, however, must be reborn, as he died in the Mother's arms before descending. (Remember the mystery of blood presented with Tifareth in Chapter Three of this book.) To continue the life force, to continue his own evolution, the God must sacrifice himself to be reborn.

As the original Creatrix of Cosmos and the divine womb of life herself, the Goddess lives eternally, changing form and face by her own power. She becomes Maid, Mother, and Crone with the changing of the moon's phase. To renew herself, she merely withdraws along the path the God has forged for her through the Earth, revitalizing herself by the power of their passions. He is reborn; she is renewed. As such, Yule also becomes a time of rebirth for hope, as the birth of the God and renewal of the Goddess' strength paves the way for new life, light, and warmth upon the Earth. The growing season shall soon be renewed. Within the dark of the earth lie seeds, fallow, frozen within the ground; as the Lord of Light begins to take his proper place in the Eastern sky, his power warms the breast of the Mother Earth, allowing the dormant seed to grow. The cycle of Assiah returns to the East and the initial impulse to create; the seasons and cycles of Earth continue in a dance that leads to life after life.

Now that the Solstices and Equinoxes have been explored in connection with the four worlds of the Tree of Life, we may begin to examine the four greater Sabbats: Bealtaine, Lughnasadh, Samhain, and Imbolc. These festivals are placed between the cardinal points (see Figure 7:5). So far, our work with the natural cycles has involved those cycles that could only be divided into four major points of activity, such as sunrise, noon, sunset, and midnight. In our work with the daily and lunar cycles, this allowed us an easy division to overlap with the four creative worlds; in examining the yearly cycle, we were also able to place the solstices and equinoxes neatly in conjunction with the four worlds. Now it seems that there is a problem with the process: eight astrological turning points must be placed with four creative worlds. Already we have determined the correspondences for the worlds themselves; there are still four other Sabbats that must be interpreted. The question is: how?

The key to understanding the remaining Sabbats and their places in this cycle is to interpret them as in-between times during the year; and as such, turning points of major activity. Until now, we have worked with the divisions of the four worlds, and the simpler cycles with which we have attuned ourselves dealt only with the full manifestation of the worlds' forces. As we study the yearly cycle, we arrive at a more dynamic view of the Tree's function in Malkuth: we are able to experience the ways in which one world interacts and melts with the next, sending its power into the next stage of manifestation. The greater Sabbats become points of extreme activity, combining the symbols of the previous world with those of the next, marking how one realm of power evolves into the next manifestation of nature.

Journal Entry

Spend some time thinking about each of the four greater Sabbats: Bealtaine, Lughnasadh, Samhain, and Imbolc. Realizing that these are times of activity and transformation, determine how each incorporates the symbols of the two realms. If you already are familiar with the symbolism of each Sabbat, analyze its meaning in context with its place on the circle-cross diagram. If unfamiliar with their individual symbolism, try to logically deduce the symbols that would be derived from their placement between the four creative worlds. Finish this exercise before continuing with the text.

Bealtaine

At this point in our yearly cycle, the solar light is at its midway point; it is stronger than at the Vernal Equinox, yet has not reached its zenith at the Summer Solstice. This midway point between the two major solar cycles is a flurry of sexuality; the Young Stag, in pursuit of the Goddess, begins the sacred marriage—their passions become consummated in a frenzy of lovemaking. The virgin Earth Maiden has become pregnant with all life;[4] she is not yet the Mother, but she is no longer the

---

4. This may seem an aberration from our earlier work with the cycles of life presented by the daily and lunar phases; however, the yearly cycle presents a more complex interplay of energies between the union of Goddess and God, moon and sun. Through the yearly cycles, we will be able to not only investigate the turning points of activity presented by the four worlds of Atziluth, Briah, Yetzirah, and Assiah, but we will also be able to see how the energies of one world mingle and merge into the energies of the next.

For example, the daily cycle of the sun and moon each presented us with four major points of activity. These points of activity allowed us to pair them with their counterparts in the four worlds, and the cardinal points on the circle. Now, we also have four Sabbats that represent major turning points on the circle—the Equinoxes and the Solstices—and we have four Sabbats that represent the merging on energy as it moves from one major point of action to the next—Samhain, Imbolc, Lughnasadh, and Bealtaine. With these extra points of action plotted on our circle-cross diagram, we may now see in depth how each of the four cardinal centers of action melts into the next.

Maiden. Our Goddess belongs to the power that she is birthing, and not to herself. Some have called this celebration the First Flowering, because of the appearance of wildflowers and the earliest vegetables ripening. We begin to see the first rewards of our plantings during the Spring Equinox—our shoots have emerged from the warming ground; our previous plans are beginning to take shape; the Goddess allows herself to captured by the God, and the world trembles with their passion.

Of all the Sabbats, Bealtaine perhaps carries the strongest sexual symbolism. Youth is a time of strong energy and spring, while the Summer Solstice is seen as a time when the masculine forces of the God are at their height and begin their decline in power. Now, however, the God is at his sexual height, impregnating the Goddess with his passion. In this role, he becomes Lord Priapus, the male erection personified. Their union is for both procreation and pleasure; already impregnated, they continue their union and yearning for dissolution with each other well into the Summer Solstice. Tall, bright bonfires are lit in offering to the forces; fire begins with a spark (spring) and increases in heat and power (Bealtaine), until it reaches its height, and thus, begins its decline (Summer Solstice). Maypoles, symbols of trees and phalluses, are erected at festival sites and danced around, evoking the raw tide of fertility that threatens to sweep the land.

As a frenzy of rising fertility and unashamed sexuality, Bealtaine marks well the in-between tide that runs from the East and to the South, from Atziluth to Briah. As the initial desire to create flows into a flurry of actual creating, the world becomes caught in the mixed tide of power and passion. Thus, Bealtaine properly belongs in the Southeast.

Lughnasadh

As we continue our deosil travel around the circle-cross, we arrive between the South and the West; the Sabbat here is Lughnasadh. Summer Solstice has come and gone, and with its passing, the God's strength has been plunged into the Goddess. Within her, it begins to flourish and grow; the grains planted at the Spring Equinox ripen, preparing for the harvest. The Crone Goddess, who rules in this time of the year, becomes the reaper of grain, harvesting the bounty that was poured out from the passionate union of the Goddess and God. There seems, as this is one of those complex, in-between Sabbats, to be two faces of the Goddess at work here: neither one has yet established dominance in the scheme of the year. Gaia is still very much the Earth Mother in her forms of Ceres and Demeter—the fruits of her womb are ripening. The Goddess in the decreasing light of the year is the Crone, reaping the harvest and tending to the dying God.

Lughnasadh is a time of birth, as much as it is a time of death. Weakened by his union with the Goddess, the God has descended into her womb, only to spring forth as the newly grown grain. He is a dying God, however, as the grain is quickly harvested, and his essence spreads to the humans reaping the fields. Often, this Sabbat is called Lammas, translating into "loaf-feast." This is the first harvest festival in which the grains are gathered, ground, and made into a sacred loaf, the bread of life, which is used during the Sabbat to commemorate the rebirth of the God into the grain, and his new sacrifice into our bodies to keep us alive.

Dealing with the recurring themes of the Earth Mother giving birth to her Consort as the newly reaped grain, the God's death as the grain is harvested, and the Crone Mother supervising the reaping of the first harvest, Lughnasadh is a celebration dealing with the mutation of Briah's energy into that of Yetzirah. As such, it belongs here in the Southwest of the circle.

Samhain

Of all the Sabbats, none has as much universal appeal as Samhain, also known as Halloween. On the circle-cross diagram, we arrive at this Sabbat in the Northwest of our circle; it occurs after the Autumn Equinox, and is referred to as the third harvest festival. Samhain is another of the in-between Sabbats, suffused with the symbolism of the worlds of Yetzirah and Assiah. In the Craft, these two worlds are called the realms of the seen and unseen, Assiah representing physical manifestation, and Yetzirah being the astral planes. The veil between these two realms is extremely thin at this time of the year; spectral sightings and similar occurrences are common.

At Samhain, we deal with powerful, complex symbolism. All remaining vestiges of the Horned God's strength have been harvested during the last two festivals, and at the West, the Crone Goddess watched as her Consort sank below the horizon, deep within the Earth Mother's dark womb. Now, he is no more the Lord of Life; he is ever the Lord of Shadows, bringer of peace and rest. Having completed his cycle of birth, life, and death, he is now fit to await the souls of the dead, offering them comfort and peace while they grow young in the Land of Youth, awaiting rebirth on the Earth.

The Crone Goddess grows lonely, yearning for her other half, desiring to know what she has finally become. She follows the setting sun, entering the depths of the Earth by the way of the Horned Passage, the secret knowledge that the God has come to own. Once descending into the land of youth by her own will, she slowly grows young again. One can only marvel at the comparisons between this and the Changing Woman of the Apaches, who walks over the Earth, growing older until she meets herself coming the other way, still young and fresh. There, she merges with her other form and becomes renewed by her own power.

Likewise, as the Goddess descends to meet the Horned Lord of Shadows, she becomes young by her own power, within her own womb. Once she meets what she has become, she loves herself; alone within the depths of her being, the Goddess is able to understand her other self. As the two mingle as one, the Horned God begins his first steps to rebirth at the Winter Solstice in the realm of Assiah; the Goddess begins her magickal renewal that shall make her eternally young, giving birth once more to the Horned God.

Imbolc

In the Northeast of our circle, we enter a space between the worlds of Assiah and Atziluth; the energy of manifestation is returning to the primal archetypes from which it emerged. This Sabbat is called Imbolc, and its imagery is strong and varied. We deal with the concepts of the growing Divine Child, stirring on the face of the Mother, strong, yet not strong enough to manifest in the sky as a powerful orb of force. We find the Crone Mother who has once again become young—the tempting Maiden who instructs the Horned God in the mysteries of enchantment and life. We also see the first signs of spring, for the Horned God in his youthful aspect becomes the lover of the virgin Earth; even though the Earth Mother just birthed the Horned God, she still lies cold and unpenetrated beneath his feet. So many symbols, so much to merge in this static, changing tide of earth and sky.

Most traditions rely on the symbolism of Brigid within this Sabbat. Brigid is very much a triple Goddess, manifesting three faces at once; she is a fitting Goddess for this time of the year. As the wise Crone, she rules over the dark, barren Earth. As the divine Mother, she is the caregiver of the Young Child who has just been born. As the Maiden, she is the unyielding, cold ground below our feet, awaiting penetration by the Horned God, bringing the land to its first stirrings of spring.

In many traditions, Imbolc is celebrated with the creation of "Brigid's Bed." A corn doll is dressed in white to represent the Goddess, while a phallic wand is dressed in multi-colored ribbons. Both are placed together in a basket filled with hay; followers dance and say, "Brigid is come; Brigid is welcome!" Three deosil progressions around the bed and three repetitions of the chant are performed. If a fireplace is available, a roaring fire is lit, and the bed is ringed with candles. The scene is left undisturbed throughout the night; in the morning, if an imprint of the wand is found in the ashes of the fireplace, or the bed is otherwise disturbed, the invocation has been successful and the incoming tide will be one of prosperity and good fortune. Honoring the first stirrings of spring, and the growth of the Divine Child into the Young Stag, Imbolc properly belongs between the worlds of Assiah and Atziluth.

WORKING WITH THE TIDES OF LIFE

Everything in Cosmos moves to the rhythm of the four worlds; as Witches, we work to tap into this cycle of life. Our exercises so far have put us in greater rapport with our true, natural life-cycles; however, modern life has robbed us of our ability to live in this preordained pattern. The closer we can come to its realization, the more we use the daily adorations regularly, the more it becomes apparent to us that the cycle represents more than the constant renewal of the Tree's energies in our own world—the cycle also represents the repetitions of consciousness. Our minds, our thoughts, and our emotions run in a constantly connected circle of energy—each thought begins from the one previous to it, and directly affects the next. There is no such thing as fragmented or unconnected energy, as all in the Cosmos runs in an ever-connected cycle. Surprising? It shouldn't be! If the Tree of Life teaches us about constantly connected cycles, if it runs in an eternal spiral of energy that builds from the pulse previous and into the energy following, it only follows that the same cycles would be repeated within our own patterns. The Tree of Life exists within ourselves as it does our world; the energy manipulates our consciousness as it does the world without.

Using this knowledge, we may begin to use the cycles of energy presented by the four worlds of the Tree in conjunction with the daily cycle to increase our understanding of self and spiritual Cosmos. So far, we have applied ourselves to an intellectual understanding of the material presented in this text, along with various exercises to open us to the energies of the Tree of Life. But this practice will do little to implant the seed of wisdom, the intuitive understanding of the Tree of Life, in our souls. We need a systematic method based upon the Qabalah's wisdom to open us up to the intuitive concepts that we desire to understand. That method may be found as we work with the four worlds.

If we reinterpret the power of the Four Worlds of Creation in terms of mental abilities, it again becomes apparent that we are working with four parts of one cycle. The world of Atziluth begins our cycle with the development of an idea. From the vast depths of memory emerges some abstract thought, an idea that we wish to analyze. That abstract idea becomes a focal point in the mind, and we begin to concentrate all our energies on its analysis. This focusing of the mind is representative of the world of Briah. Then, we apply our thoughts to their purpose, we begin to flesh the idea into a coherent, logical train of thought. Yetzirah is symbolized here as the foundation of new thoughts. Finally, the idea becomes replaced in the depths of memory, having been analyzed and recreated into something new. This is the mental function of Atziluth. Another way of looking at the creative cycle of consciousness is to say that experience emerges from the depths of consciousness until it develops and intensifies. Then, it reaches its maximum potential by becoming the foundation of a new train of thought, then fades into the depths of memory where a new cycle is soon begun.

Using the concept of the daily cycle in conjunction with the four worlds of creation, we can create an exercise that maximizes the benefits of the cycles of consciousness. There will be four steps to this exercise. First, we will begin by rereading the material presented in the previous chapters of this book. Within each chapter, we will pick out the main points, topics that sum up major issues. For example, the material in Chapter One was about the magickal circle and the patterns of energy that flow through our Universe. As one of the points in my list, I might jot down the phrase, "Patterns, once altered, are never truly the same again."

By making a note of this passage in my journal, I am telling myself that I want to arrive at a more complete, intuitive understanding of the principle behind the passage. Also, we may sum up the main idea of any exercise or text passage as a focal point for the work in this exercise. We can even pick out some of the symbolism presented about the sephiroth in Chapter Three as a meditation topic. For example, wanting to know more about the sephirah of Yesod, I turn to Appendix One in the back of the book and find that ginseng, mandrake, and quartz crystal are all correspondences of Yesod, and frame my statement as, "ginseng, mandrake, and quartz are all within Yesod's domain." The contents of the phrase do not matter, as long as it is short and easy to remember.

Now, we shall spend a few more days following the daily solar cycle until we feel the connections not only between the passing of day and night with the four worlds, but the nature of our own, fleeting consciousness. Having established a strong rapport with the changing cycles, pick one of your major topics from the list you created to "sleep on." Write it on a slip of paper, repeat it to yourself, and place it under your pillow for the night. The next part of the exercise, then, is to fall asleep with the topic somewhere in the back of your mind, to be slept upon and given to the deeper levels of the subconscious functioning.

As you arise in the morning, instead of performing your normal adoration, pull out the slip of paper and glance at it once more. Enter the state of pattern awareness, and silently meditate while repeating the topic. This meditation does not need to be lengthy; merely impress the topic upon your open mind. You may find that as you meditate, your sleeping mind may have already formed some strong images or thoughts about the topic; these, however, should be ignored for now as you concentrate on the phrase itself. It is important that information you glean from deeper levels of awareness be allowed to simmer through all creative phases of the mind.

Spend the rest of the day until noon not thinking about the phrase, until it is time for the noon adoration. Instead of reciting the normal adoration, face the South and call to the Goddess and God, asking that they will help you gain better understanding of the phrase that you have chosen. This invocation need only last a few seconds before you return to your normal routine. If you allow the conscious mind to now forget about the topic, the subconscious will take over the analysis.

That evening, as it becomes time for your evening adoration, write the phrase at the top of a sheet of paper in your magickal journal. Begin to free-write your feelings on the subject; as the words begin to flow, you will find that the subconscious mind has discovered reams on the subject. Write as long as you can, then go back over what you have written. Reduce the material to only one paragraph, and then to only one sentence. Try to find a single word that sums up the material. Then, use the word as the title of a brief essay on another sheet of paper, use the single sentence as the main thought of your day's work, and finish out one paragraph that sums up the meaning of the material. Consider the evening adoration completed.

As you free-write, you may find that in the original material you wrote, there will be many brief passages and phrases only distantly related to the subject at hand; a few of these might be thoughts you will wish to explore another time. Put these notes at the bottom of your previous list. Before going to bed that night, pick item number two from the original list, to begin a new cycle of magickal analysis.

Having begun with just ten items on your list, you will find that as time passes, the list can double or even triple in size. This is a result of the work your own subconscious mind will perform, slowly allowing you to see where the gaps in your present knowledge lie, or even the direction you should follow in your studies on inner levels. Eventually, however, as the list continues to grow longer, you will need to lay it aside and move onto the next chapter. This exercise may continue indefinitely, not only with the material in this book, but with material presented in other magickal texts to which you may feel drawn. Using this cycle of consciousness will help you to more intuitively understand any material you are studying.

The cycles have been examined; the flowing and ebbing of the four worlds of creation can be felt both within and without. We have begun with the smallest cycle, the turning of the day, and ended with the greatest cycle that exists—the flowing of our own consciousness. We have renewed and centered ourselves; our life-force now flows in synchronization with the greater tides of life. Caught up in the sacred dance of life, we can now open our minds and souls to celebrate each point of the magickal circle called reality. We are prepared to dance the spiral dance of existence; we are prepared to celebrate the turning of the seasons.

CHAPTER EIGHT

HONORING MOON AND SUN

Upon my path, there stood a Tree
  growing forth from the veils of mystery.
Within its spheres, glowing with might,
  was the power of our Goddess' love and light!
From its heart, the realm of nature's harmony
  grew a circle, bright, pure luminosity.
Soon ... I heard a soft echo of power
  moving through space from the mystic hour
  in which all worlds were born.
From these vibrations of sound, I found my sight;
  and I saw, I knew, the paths of day and night:
The rhythmic dance of life and death.
  I entered trance; I held my breath ...
Before me were all mysteries unfurled
  as I stood alone, in another world,
Before the Tree of Life.

The Wheel begins ...

—From "The Wheel Turns On"
Hillary Jones, Faery High Priestess

Life is more than an unconnected series of events that begins with birth and ends with death; we have seen this with our work throughout this book. Life is a journey, a great, magickal adventure that leads us through realms of experience; as we begin our travels from spirit to flesh and back to spirit again, we flow with the greater tides of Cosmos. Moving through time and space, we descend through the horned passage of life and death, becoming human, becoming whole; that, however, is but the first step on a journey that takes us through life after life. As the tides of moon and sun run through our veins, we become caught in the magickal dance that whirls us through new vistas of awareness. Eternally connected with the greater tides of Cosmos, yet constantly asserting our individuality from the greater source, we become spiritual centers of action for the creative forces. As Witches, we sense the impending tides of life, merging with and honoring them through magickal rituals. We honor ourselves, as well as the God/dess within.

The celebrations in this chapter are based upon the material mastered in Chapter Seven. They are practical illustrations of Qabalistic concepts, not to be used as sacred scripts, unchanging from one ritual to the next, but as skeletons, basics that can and should be changed at will. In my group, the basic structure of our Esbats follows the guidelines given in our initiation ritual. Within that structure, however, are limitless ways in which we may rewrite, recreate, and renew the rituals to keep them from growing lifeless in what is to be a living, evolving spirituality. Perhaps the best way to approach these rituals are as suggestions for beginning your work; memorize the structure, the invocations, and the basic script. Once memorized, begin working with the ritual, and remember that if a word is stumbled over, or if in the midst of a powerful invocation, a spontaneous chant erupts from you, that's fine. In the end, it is the power that is felt within, the imagery that is evoked, that makes our rituals performances of divine drama.

With this in mind, let us celebrate![1]

THE ESBATS

The Waxing Moon

(To be enacted two days after the new moon, when the first crescent appears in the night sky.)

Seek out a secluded spot in which you will not be disturbed; ideally, a location outdoors in full view of the moon, although a quiet room will do nicely. This tide of life honors the newness of the Goddess and God, Young Stag and Maiden; therefore, any ritual of cleansing that you perform before the actual ritual will help commemorate the tide of newness you are invoking within yourself. Prepare an herbal bath filled with eucalyptus, jasmine, and lavender; burn some sandalwood incense, and surround the bath with white candles and soothing crystals. Wash yourself in the warm waters of the bath, surrounded by fragrances that soothe, cleanse, and arouse. Feel the powers of renewal awakening within yourself.

Before beginning the ritual, prepare the altar with your full set of ritual tools. To this add a flowerpot filled with earth, and a few seeds symbolic of your future desires (turn to Appendix One of this book. Decide which sephirah contains the energy symbolic of your needs, and choose your plant accordingly). Add to this an incense or perfume from the sephirah you have chosen; also, if you feel it is necessary, choose a name of a Maiden Goddess and God from the realm that you will be using. Once all the materials are gathered, stand in the center of your ritual area and say:

> *Tonight is the night of the waxing moon; the first crescent of the moon appears*
> *in the night sky, and with it, the Maiden Goddess _____ arises forth from*
> *the underworld, made anew by her rites of power. Her Consort,*

---

1. There are many versions of the lunar and solar rituals published; all are in tune with the natural cycles of the year, and all may be used in place of the rituals here. My ritual work draws off many sources, from the sketchy Esbat and Sabbat rites given in the original Gardnerian Book of Shadows, to the more recent rituals of Alexandrian, Faery, and Feminist paths. No matter what one's tradition, or the magickal terminology used, all expressions of the natural year follow the cycles of the Tree of Life.

_____, *also bursts forth from the womb of darkness, reborn by the power of the Great Mother. I come within this sacred space tonight to honor them, their tide of newness, and to create newness in my own life. Blessings to the powers of the Maiden.*

Cast your circle and invoke the Goddess and God. Lift the seeds in your power hand; hold them above your head in invocation and say:

> *Powerful God, gentle Goddess, bringers of change, sowers of seeds, rising freshness and purity of the Earth, I invoke you. Lend your powers to these _____ seeds; bring needed change into my life as I sow the first seeds of my new reality. As the crescent rises in the night sky, I plant the seeds of change. I plant the seed of (essence of desire). May the powers of the moon bless my spell.*

Spend some time visualizing your desired reality. Do not worry about the steps you will take to create the needed change, merely create a strong image of the needed results. Once you have firmly built this in your mind, will the image into the seeds. Take up the pot of earth and say:

> *Blessings be to this virgin earth, symbol of the Maiden. Blessings be to these seeds, symbols of her Consort. May they grow in strength and wisdom as the moon grows full in the night sky; may they grow in fire and passion as the young Goddess is pursued by her Consort. Blessings to the crescent moon.*

Plant the seeds in the flowerpot, pouring your energy into them as you do. Begin to dance, chant, and sing to the seeds, willing them to grow, asking the Goddess and God to help them grow. Once you feel the spell is complete, partake of the sacred meal. Close the circle.

The Full Moon

(To be enacted when the moon hangs full in the night sky.)

At the tide of the full moon, all passions upon the earth rise to their pitch; the Goddess and God, ever seeking, ever yearning, meet in the sacred marriage. Their union sends waves of force and power across the land and sea, and all becomes caught in their web of orgasmic pleasure. The tides roll ceaselessly, the winds whip through the night air, and we, as Witches, feel their energies spiraling through Cosmos. If for no other reason, we honor the tide of the full moon because of its hypnotic effect upon us: we feel inspired, giddy within its soft, tenuous light. Even though we may be alone in our rituals, we know that somewhere, someone is celebrating with his or her own rituals of power. We are never truly alone when we bask in her soft glow.

Prepare the ritual area with the usual tools: dagger, chalice, pentacle, wand, and athame. For the sacred meal, add moon-foods, things that remind us of the magnetic orb traveling through the night sky: milk, white wines (keep the red for the traditional repast), crescent-shaped cookies, phallic and cervical fruits (bananas, pears, peaches)—anything that serves as a reminder of the fertility sweeping the Earth. Once everything is gathered together in your ritual area, begin entering the altered state of pattern awareness, and say:

> *Tonight, I enter the sacred circle to honor the Mother Goddess of all life, and her Consort, the Horned God. As the moon grows ever-full in the nighttime*

sky, as it hangs low and ripe over the horizon, so is the flood-tide of fertility released upon the Earth. The Mother beckons, the God follows, and together they dance the sacred dance of life and death. Blessings be upon the Great Mother of all living!

Create your sacred space, invoking the Goddess and God in whatever forms you have chosen to honor tonight. No matter the form chosen, no matter what pantheon you select, it is important that the forms be in rapport with the energies of the full moon: the Mother archetype and her Consort. Standing in the center of the circle, raise your arms in invocation to the God/dess, and begin to chant the Deity names slowly, drawing out the vowels for three or four seconds each, letting your voice vibrate. As the chanting grows in volume, filling the circle, shorten the length of time you spend pronouncing the consonants until the chanting becomes one long string of vowels; the consonants become separators between sounds rather than sounds themselves. Allow the chant to live; change the pitch, tone, and length of vibrations. Begin to move deosil around the circle, visualizing the colors of your need spiraling from within your aura to fill the circle.

Let the deosil movement become a dance; visualize your need forming within the circle. Dance ecstatically, letting the energy writhe and undulate around you. Begin to chant, "I am Goddess; I am Horned One; I am Goddess and one with Mother Earth." Repeat this until your voice can no longer keep up with your breathing— once the energy is at its peak, just before your own is ready to fade, fall to the ground and announce, "It is done!"

Charge the food for your moon-feast as in the sacred meal from Chapter One. Honor the God/dess within with food and wine. Close your circle.

The Waning Moon

(To be performed after the last night of the full moon.)

For this ritual, gather implements to be used for scrying: a mirror, a crystal ball, a bowl of water, a pool of ink—anything that you can use to enter a trance state and peer into unseen realms. Prepare your ritual space with all the usual implements of athame, pentacle, dagger, chalice, and wand; to these add a small drum. For the ritual of the waning moon, it is best to perform a special ritual cleansing, imagining that all negative influences are being washed away, banished, by the bathwater. Once you are properly prepared, enter the ritual space and say:

> *This is the time of cleansing, of renewal; the Horned One has passed for love of the Mother—his life-force has been poured out upon the Earth so that life may continue while He descends into the land of dreams. The Goddess as sacred Crone, bringer of wisdom, lies in shadows, reaping the last vestige of the Sacred Harvest. Those with the Sight, and the wisdom to understand, can peer into the shadows and learn from this magickal tide of life. I walk between the worlds tonight so that I may see, so that I may listen, so that I may learn. I come to honor the Crone of Wisdom.*

Create the magick circle, invoking the Crone and Lord of Shadows. Settling into the center of the circle, facing the West, begin to tap the drum, establishing a very slow, but strong rhythm. Staring into your chosen scrying tool, chant:

Dark Goddess, Death Goddess;
Crone Goddess, Bitch Goddess;
Snake Goddess, Horse Goddess;
Earth Goddess, Moon Goddess;
Death Bringer, Sleep Giver, Wise Woman, Aged Crone;
Old Woman, Dream Weaver, Dark Mother we've all known.
Wish Giver, Wisdom Bringer, Night Woman, Dark Queen;
Grandmother, Rain Bringer, Mother all men fear to see![2]

Repeat the chant until trance ensues; slowly cease both drumming and chanting and begin to scry. The secret to scrying is not to stare at the object; rather, you
must look into it. As trance begins, if you feel the need to close your eyes, that's
fine—many use the object to promote trance before seeing mental pictures. Once
you are done, partake of the sacred meal, then close the circle.

The Dark Moon

(This tide should be celebrated when the moon fades from sight.)

In the dark of the moon, we find true magick and mystery. This is not the magick
with which we are familiar—the forces here do not lend themselves to creation, but
rather recreation. As the moon has waxed and waned in the night sky, the Goddess
and God have flowed through their various creative forms. Now, in absence of the
lunar light, we find that they have descended into the depths of the Earth, the primal womb of night. The life-force is withdrawn; as it fades from the Earth, we find
new power emerging, emanating from the land around us. With this power, we
may not do a whole lot of practical work; this is a time of meditation. This is the
tide of total rest and recuperation—a time of shielding in which we honor ourselves, and the growing life-force within.

To honor the dark of the moon, cast the circle without words; as you create sacred
space, silently visualize the powers you wish to invoke. Read the Legend of the
Descent of the Goddess (Appendix Two contains this in its entirety). Then sit in
silent meditation, feeling the life-force that rises from the Earth to greet you. And
again, silently, close the circle.

THE SABBATS

Winter Solstice (Yule): Late December[3]

Prepare the altar with seasonal decorations: holly, mistletoe, and pine branches. If
a fireplace is available, prepare an oak fire, with a larger log on the hearth to
become the Yule log. If a fireplace is not available, place a large, yellow taper in the
cauldron, with a chunk of oak before it. Begin the ritual in darkness, and say:

2. I wrote the words to this chant in 1992; it is used in the song "Crone Chant" from the 1992
Earth Tones Studios release *Alexian: The Mother, The Magick, The Music.* Inquiries for ordering
this album, or receiving a catalog, should be sent to Alexian; % Earth Tones Studios; 49 Alasaya
Woods Blvd. #324; Oviedo, Florida, 32765; (407) 366-5013.

3. The dates of the Equinoxes and Solstices vary from year to year; consult a good astrological
calendar for the exact dates.

*As the Solstice arrives, the darkness reigns—it is supreme. But nothing
remains without change in the tides of earth and sky; every low becomes another
high, and every high, a low. Having descended to the depths of night, the wheel
must turn; we must move on to the tides of lengthening light. Within the cauldron, the magickal womb of rebirth, awaits the spirit of the Dark King, Lord
of Shadows; he sleeps, and dreams the dreams of rebirth. In these moments of
eternal night, all the world stands still; silently, Nature awaits the birth of the
Divine Child. The Crone Goddess, queen of night, waits and watches, preparing for the mysteries of midwifery, and the Mother, the dark womb of creation,
screams the primal birth-pangs. We tremble at her cries, awaiting the renewal
of nature's spirit. Blessings to all on this magickal night!*

Light the altar candles and begin to cast the circle. Invoke the Goddess and God.

Take the cauldron with the yellow taper in it from the altar; place this in the center
of the circle. Begin a wordless chant; build a vortex of sound and energy throughout
the circle, and as you do, take sprigs of holly and mistletoe from the altar, decorating
the cauldron with them. When the decorating is complete, take up the piece of oak
from the altar, and begin to dance a deosil dance around the circle, chanting:

Queen of the moon, Queen of the sun,
Queen of the heavens, Queen of the stars,
Queen of the waters, Queen of the Earth,
Bring to us the Child of Promise!

Repeat these lines until you begin to feel giddy. Drop before the cauldron; light the
yellow taper within it. Place the oak inside the cauldron, before the taper. Listen,
silently, for the birth-scream of the Mother. Continue the invocation as you kneel:

It is the Great Mother who gives birth to him,
It is the Lord of Life who is born again!
Darkness and tears are set aside
    when the sun shall come up once more!

Try to feel the strength of the newborn God radiating from the cauldron—spend a
few moments feeling his strength:

Golden sun of the mountains, illumine the land;
Light up the world; illuminate all.
Sorrows be laid, and joy to the world.
Blessed be the Great Goddess, without beginning, without ending—
Everlasting to eternity![4]

Begin to chant, "IO EVOE! Blessed be!" Send the energy from the chant into the
cauldron, to the burning candle, the symbol of the Divine Child. Build up a wordless chant, a cone of power; let it wash through you. Once more, start a fast, deosil
dance around the circle, chanting and singing the words, "IO EVOE! Blessed be!"
When giddiness ensues once more, fall down before the altar, and partake of the
sacred meal. Close the circle; however, allow the candle to burn throughout the
night. If you previously prepared the fireplace, place the Yule log on top of the fire,
and let the candle remain burning on the hearth. In the morning, all remaining

---

4. The chant used throughout this ritual is adapted from the Winter Solstice Sabbat given in my
version of the Book of Shadows.

pieces of oak should be gathered (especially that within the cauldron—wax and all) and placed on the altar. It is said that the remnants of the Yule fire can bring luck to the household all year.

Imbolc (Candlemas): February 2

Before beginning the ritual, prepare the items to be used for "Brigid's Bed." Obtain a basket filled with hay, a homemade doll dressed in white, and a phallic shaped wand. A few small tapers should be on the altar with candleholders for each; these will be used to create a circle of light around Brigid's Bed. All these supplies should be gathered and placed on the altar. Once everything is prepared, begin a slow, deosil dance around the space to be used as the circle, saying:

> *Thus I banish winter; thus I welcome spring.*
> *I say farewell to what is dead, and greet each living thing!*
> *Thus I banish winter, thus I welcome spring.*

As you complete each round of the circular dance, think of old, outworn things, ideas, and circumstances you would like to rid yourself of during the coming tide of light. Having exhausted your mental list, stand in the center of the circle and say:

> *Now is the first stirring of light and warmth; the Divine Child, born at Winter Solstice, grows in strength and vigor. We who were there at the birth can now see that the days are growing longer; the icy chill of winter is beginning to soften into the warmer tides of Spring. No longer the Child, but not yet the Stag, the young God stirs; he runs across the frozen breasts of the Mother in search of his other half, the Maiden. She rests and waits; the Mother stirs and wakens beneath his footsteps. I come tonight to honor the first stirrings of Spring upon our Mother Earth!*

Cast the circle, and invoke both Goddess and God. Place the basket in the center of the circle; in this, place the representation that you have created for the Maiden Goddess. Begin to chant the name, "Brigid (Breed)," emphasizing the vowels, letting it build into a wordless chant that spirals out into the night. Raise the energy level by intensifying the volume of your voice; imagine that all energy descends and merges into the basket.

Become silent. Walk to the altar, taking up the phallic wand in your power hand. Begin a slow, deosil dance around the perimeter of the circle; each circuit takes you closer to the basket in the center of the circle. Visualize firmly that the wand is the God; his symbol of power and growing strength. As you dance the spiral dance, chant, "She burns for you, she yearns for you," again and again, until you reach the basket at the center of the circle. Place the wand in the "bed," and again dance, faster, chanting, "Brigid has come; Brigid is welcome. The Horned One has come; the Horned One is welcome!" Pick up the tempo until the dance becomes too fast, and you become dizzy. Drop before the basket, and light the circle of tapers around it. Partake of the sacred meal; close the circle, allowing the candles to burn throughout the night. In the morning, if the basket seems to have been disturbed, the coming tide will be prosperous for all in the household, for Brigid has, indeed, been welcomed into the house.

Spring Equinox (Eostara): Late March

On the day of Spring Equinox, plan a quiet outdoor excursions to nearby fields, forests, and orchards. Spend the day collecting wildflowers and blossoms to be used in the celebration at night; try to collect a variety of flowers with long stems. As the time for ritual approaches, set up the altar with the full array of tools. At each point within the circle, lay flowers before the Watchtowers in their respective colors—green for North, yellow for East, red for South, and blue for West. Decorate the altar with the remaining flowers that you have collected; you may also wish to place some sort of potted plant on the altar to commemorate the growing tides of life with the Spring Equinox.

Once you are prepared, center yourself and say:

> *In this tide of the year, Spring returns; the tide of planting, joy, new beginnings, and freshness. In the prime of his youth, the Horned God as Young Stag runs across the fields of Mother Earth, eternally in pursuit of his other half, the Maiden Goddess. Young and refreshed, she arises from the Lands of Youth, eternally eluding the advances of the Horned One. Where they run, the chill of winter gives way to the warmth of spring; they laugh, and fresh rains pour upon the land. May we find peace and joy in the approaching tides of spring. Blessings to Mother Earth!*

Create Sacred Space, and invoke the elements to the circle. Then return to the center, and invoke:

> *O mighty Maiden Goddess, bringer of freshness and spring, I invoke you and call upon you. Return, O return to walk upon the frozen fields of our Mother's breast, bringing sweet rains and soothing breezes. Mighty God, Young Stag, smell the sweet scent of desire upon her breath; even as she runs from your advances, She beckons you to follow! Blessings to you—Maiden of spring and Young Stag of desire!*

Begin to dance, building a wordless chant as you do. Dance around the circle, imagining that the energy you build is released into the world, encouraging the plants, trees, and flowers to bud into new life. Celebrate the sacred meal, and close the ritual.

Bealtaine: April 30

Before the ritual, create a phallic wand: a branch of oak tipped with a pine cone will do nicely. Decorate it with several colored ribbons, and let these hang loosely from the base of the pine cone to about twice the length of the wand. Lay this in the center of the altar, surrounded by the ritual tools representing the four elements. Have not only the normal supplies of wine and cakes for the sacred meal on hand, but also a few additional fruits in a basket beside the altar for the sacred meal. Once everything is prepared, take up the phallic wand in your outstretched power hand, and dance around the circle, singing:

> *Oh do not tell the priest of my art, for he would call it a sin;*
> *But I shall be out all night, a'conjuring summer in!*

And I bring word by news of mouth, for women, cattle and corn;
Now has the sun come up from the South, with oak and ash and thorn![5]

Keep singing this last line until you feel that you are done. Using the wand in place of the athame, begin to create your sacred space.

Once you have finished with the invocation of the elements, stand in the center of the circle and invoke:

> *Now is the night when the sweet Maiden shall wed in passionate delight; the Young Stag, eternally in pursuit, meets with the young Goddess in the midst of nature's vibrancy: the corn shall ripen, the blossom shall burst, the birds shall sing in their ecstatic pleasures. I honor their tide of passion, renewing myself in their desire!*

With the phallic wand in hand, begin to dance around the circle once more, slowly, rhythmically, visualizing all your needs and desires. As you tread a spiral dance in your sacred space, begin to wrap the colored ribbons around the wand; each color represents a different desire—the desires become empowered by your dancing to the union of the Goddess and God. Once all the ribbons are wound tightly around the wand, drop to the ground and say, "It is done!"

Bless the food for the sacred meal, honoring the powers of the Maiden and Young Stag that you have invoked this evening. Close the circle, and take the remaining food to be left by a tree or bush as an offering to nature.

Summer Solstice (Midsummer): Late June

Midsummer is the height of passion; the longest day of the year, when, at the height of His power, the God holds the Goddess in the final embrace of death. To represent the passion of summer, decorate the altar with red roses and wildflowers; green garlands should embrace the perimeter of the circle. In the cauldron should be a small fire (if you are outdoors) or an incense made from various aromatic barks such as cedar, sandalwood, and perhaps a bit of frankincense. Create a small God-figure from the stems of wildflowers; it need not be detailed, just a brief suggestion of a human form. Weave the stalks together, and inside stuff it with various aromatic herbs of your own choice. Before casting the sacred space, say:

> *Now is the time of the final passion; our great Horned Lord is at the height of His strength. The Summer Queen can no longer resist His yearnings; She gathers Him in her arms, and they join in the union that sends Him to His death. The strength of summer begins the depths of winter—as the Sun arises to its height in the sky, it must also begin its decline.*

Create sacred space; invoke Goddess and God. Holding the God figure high above your head in invocation, say:

> *Great Light of the Heavens, Might of the Sun;*
> *   powerful God, Mighty Horned One!*
> *We call to thee in thine ancient names—*
> *   Pan, Cernunnos, Balin, Baal, Osiris …*

---

5. This opening chant is extracted from my version of the Gardnerian Book of Shadows.

As you say each name, vibrate it, allowing the sounds to grow into a wordless chant. To the list provided, add any names that hold personal meaning for you. Imagine that the God's energies spiral around you, merging into the small God figure that you hold above your head. Continue with the invocation:

> *Come into this, thy sacred land; touch us all with thy mighty hand. Put to flight the powers of darkness and night; spread about your powerful light!*

Begin a spiral dance around the circle, feeling the energy of the God gathering in the circle. Let the dance grow faster, wilder; gaze upon the image that you hold above your head as you dance. When you feel dizzy, drop to your knees before either the cauldron or small fire. Filled with the power of the Horned One, recite the Charge of the Horned God (Appendix Two). Hold the image above the fire/cauldron, and say:

> *Give us fertile fields, fresh air, pure water, ripening orchards, fields of corn; put to flight the powers of darkness that seek to engulf us; bind the hands and clear the hearts of those who would wish ill to this, our Mother Earth. Horned One, sacrifice yourself now to the Mother, that all may be reborn!*

Throw the image into the fire; watch as it begins to burn in the flames. Smell the scent of the herbs rising on the incense smoke. Take up the plate of bread that you have prepared; before the cauldron, say, "It is done! He has died for the love of the Mother; he has passed into the grain; He is the Spirit of all growing things. I now partake of His essence, that He may continue to live in me." Eat a piece of the bread; consecrate and consume the wine. Close the circle. The ritual is complete.

Lughnasadh: July 31

Prepare for the ritual by decorating the altar with symbols of the harvest: sheaves of grain, wheat, and corn. Bake a loaf of cornbread to symbolize the Horned One. It may be a simple loaf in the shape of a man or elongated to be phallic in shape; this is called the bread of life, and it symbolizes the life-force of the God being released into the Earth. Once everything is prepared, enter your sacred space and say:

> *I come to mourn the passing of Lugh; I come to mourn the waning light. I come to mark the passing of the Lord of Life into the Land of Shadows and Rest. All fades; all passes away; all dies; nothing is eternal in the land of sky and earth. But the Mother, giver and sustainer of life, becomes the Wizened Crone, Reaper of Grain. As the Horned Lord descends into Her dark womb of Earth, She sends him beyond the gates which the living cannot pass; he shall rest; He shall become young again. Light fades; the nights now grow longer; summer is gone—the harvest must be gathered. I come to reap the sacrifice, knowing that as I do, summer melts into autumn.*

Cast the circle, and invoke Goddess and God. Kneel before the altar, facing the bread of Life. Holding your hands high in invocation, recite:

> *O Mighty Mother of us all, bringer of fruitfulness, give us fruit and grain, flocks and herds, and children to the tribe that your hidden children may grow mighty once more upon the breast! Descend, great reaper of grain—bless this bread with the power of thy sacrificed Consort.*

Begin to stroke the loaf lovingly, honoring it as a symbol of life. Build a wordless chant; let the energy from your voice spiral around you, grounding into the loaf. Take it in both hands, gently, and begin to sway and dance deosil around the circle. Slowly, let the wordless chant evolve into, "Summer has passed, summer fades; The God is dead, but His power remains." Speed up the tempo of the dancing and chanting; feel the bread of life throbbing with the power of the sacrificed Consort. Once you are giddy, drop before the altar, holding the bread of life above your head. Say, "I shall eat the bread of life, the life that must die to be born again!" Rip off a piece of the bread and eat it; consecrate the wine, and drink it. Spend a few moments to meditate on the powers of life and death spiraling within you. Close the circle.

Autumn Equinox (Mabon): Late September

Autumn Equinox is the time of the second harvest; the Horned One is seen as passing through the Western Gates into the land of Youth, the underworld, so that in time He may grow young again. This is the grain harvest, the seed-time, and we see His essence carried in the seeds that will be saved to grow new life when the tides are once again ripe. As such, the altar should be decorated with symbols of the harvest, sheaves of wheat and corn; perhaps the perimeter of the circle could be marked out with large grains, such as corn. In the center of the circle should be a plate with a large seed pod still on a stalk, either that of a flower or grain. Cover this with a black veil; you are now ready to begin the ritual.

Begin the ritual with this declamation:

> Now, we celebrate the harvest—the reaping of the grain; this is a time of giving thanks and joy for life. Our lord the sun has set sail toward the Lands of Youth. His journey almost complete, He lies between this world and the next. Day and night face off as equals, yet the day is waning, and the night is waxing. There is naught in the tides of life that remains unchanging … what must rise must also set; whatever grows strong must wane. I come tonight to dance the spiral dance of life and renewal!

Cast the circle; invoke Goddess and God. Begin a slow, widdershins spiral dance beginning at the perimeter of the circle, slowly turning inward until you arrive at the center. As you dance, say, "Behold the spiral dance; the dance of life after life. I will never cease to be." Kneel in the center of the circle. Remove the black veil from the dish of seed. Say, "Behold; in silence and darkness are the seeds of wisdom gained!" Spend a few moments mediating on the dish of grain, sensing the essence of the Horned One within.

Stand and begin a slow, deosil spiral dance; start from the center of the circle, and slowly expand until you arrive at the perimeter. Say:

> Behold the spiral dance; the dance of new beginnings. I was never truly born; I shall never truly die; I go on! I am alive! I move with the tides of life!

Once you reach the outer limits of the circle, celebrate the sacred meal. Close the circle (all grains used in this ritual should be left outdoors on fertile ground as a symbol of the God's future rebirth).

Samhain (Halloween): October 31

Samhain is the final harvest festival and the final sacrifice; to symbolize the season, decorate the altar with sheaves of colored corn and decorated gourds (such as pumpkin and squash). For the sacred meal, provide the usual repast of red wine and bread, but also obtain one pomegranate, one apple, and a knife suitable for cutting. One important aspect of this festival is called the Feast of the Dead; before going to the area in which you will be performing ritual, leave out a plate with some simple food, such as bread, and a glass of red wine. Set the table as you normally would for guests. Light a candle and before it set a picture of your loved one(s); spend some time in remembrance of them. Once all is prepared, retire to your ritual space. Cast the circle; invoke the Goddess and God. Stand before the altar and say:

> *Dread One of the Shadows; God of life and the giver of life, The knowledge of thee is the knowledge of Death! Tonight, open wide the gates through which all must one day pass. Let those who have gone before return this night, this most sacred of nights to make merry with me. And when my time comes, as it will, I will enter thy realm unafraid; For I know that when rested and refreshed among my relations, I will be reborn again by your grace, and by the power of the Great Mother! May it be in the same time, and in the same place, as my loved ones. Bless us with the knowledge, and with the sight, that once again we may know; once again we shall meet, remember, and love again. May your power be with me on this sacred night![6]*

Begin by blessing the wine; drink the glass, and then refill it. Take up the pomegranate from the plate, holding the knife in your power hand. Say, "In my hands I hold the fruit of life; this life leads to death …" Carefully, cut the pomegranate into two halves, allowing the red juices to stain your fingers. Say, "And as I eat the seeds of death, my sight descends to the underworld!" Dance an inward, spiral widdershins dance. Once you are at the center of the circle, kneel. Begin to scry; try to receive some message that your loved ones, or even the Lord of Shadows himself, is with you.

Once you are done, consecrate the wine, drink it, and refill the glass. Take up the apple in your left hand, and the knife in your power hand. Say, "In my hands I hold death's sweet fruit; this death leads to new life …" Cut the apple crossways, revealing the five-pointed star within. Say, "From the Mother darksome and divine; Hers is the scourge; Hers is the kiss. See the mystery sublime—the five-pointed star of love and bliss. Behold the path to rebirth!" Take a bite of the apple; begin a slow, deosil spiral dance from the center of the circle, and end at the altar. Speed up the tempo of the dance; build a wordless chant to give energy to those that have come in spirit to share the celebration. Partake of wine and cakes; close the circle. The remaining bread and fruit should be left outside to "feed the souls of the dead" wandering through the veils to meet with their loved ones.

It is only fitting that our last Sabbat should be both an ending and a beginning; while Samhain is the end of the Witch's year, it is also the beginning of the New Year. Our wheel of life turns on, spanning all times and all places. Through

---

6. This invocation to the Lord of Shadows was extracted from my version of the Gardnerian Book of Shadows.

the power and poetry of the Sabbats, we learn that there is no such thing as a final ending or a new beginning; there is only flow and motion, an eternal pattern that began in the depths of time and space and continues throughout all Cosmos. As Witches, as Pagans, and as Goddess worshippers, it is our birthright to know these natural cycles, to feel the pulsing of Cosmos within ourselves. Once we have come to know the ebbing and flowing of the seasons in sky and earth, once we can look again at the birds, the stars, and the sun and moon hanging high over the horizon and call them our brothers and sisters; only when I can look upon you, my reader, and love you unconditionally as a part of myself, and me as a part of you, can we say that the God/dess has become a part of our lives. I love you; I honor you; may the powers that flow through sky and earth connect us all!

> *The Tree stretched out between the worlds,*
>   *and in the midst its voice was heard:*
> *"Between the Earth and Sky I stand,*
>   *Between the starlight and the land!*
> *From farthest height and deepest depth,*
>   *I form the sphere of life and death!*
> *And in my light, the Wheel of Life is ever turning."*

—From "The Wheel Turns On"
Hillary Jones

THE APPENDICES

Dear Readers,

Magick is an art using natural substances to raise energy: herbs, crystals, minerals, trees, flowers, and perfumes. All these things have life, power, and healing energies; when they are combined in ritual to cast a spell using vibrations of light and sound to weave them into a holisitc whole, true magick is wrought! Within Appendix One's pages, you will find scores of natural substances, colors, names and deities associated with the sephioroth, each preceded by the realm's magickal image. Use these in love; the earth is filled with power, and when certain substances are used in tandem, the forces raised will increase geometrically.

Appendix Two, Words of Power, provides some of the basic liturgical material found in all traditions of the Craft. These have been provided to give you, the reader, a grounding in the God/dess-oriented philosophy of the Craft. They are given as they apear in my Book of Shadows; and although I began my training as a Gardnerian, the myths and declamations presented show influences from various Dianic and self-initiatiory systems. Although some may criticize me for rewriting sacred script, I believe our Craft is a growing entity, an organism that evolves and replicates itself. The Great Mother in all Her forms has been awakened; each who comes to know Her will do so in his or her own way. I encourage you to create, re-create, and renew your spiritual practices as She moves you!

Finally, I would also like to encourage you all to write me about your experiences with my work. Let me know how you work within the Craft and the Qabalah. If this book has helped you take your first fleeting steps to the Great Mother, then I know my work has been successful.

Bright Blessings,
Stuart Myers
Winter Park, Florida

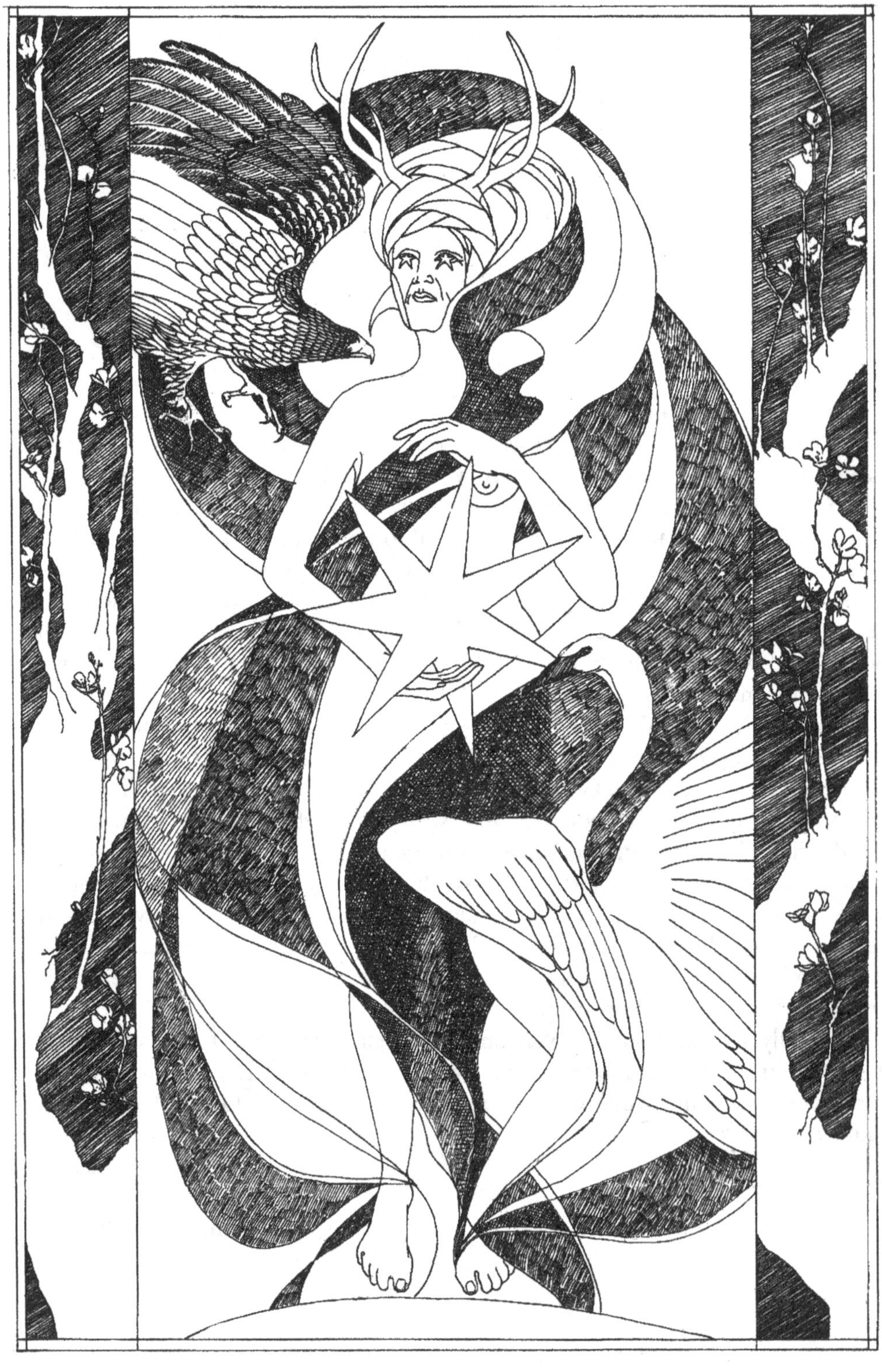

APPENDIX ONE

THE SEPHIROTH

KETHER: THE CROWN (SEPHIRAH 1)

Image: An ancient, Horned Mother in full view.

Deity Name: Eheieh.

Archangel: Metatron. He is responsible for the Tree of Life's reception to mankind. He works in the world of the Cosmic archetypes; his influence among humanity is rare.

Angels: Chioth ha-Qadesh (Holy living ones).

Planetary Attribution: The sphere of the first swirlings; big bang/Neptune.

Element: Root of Air.

Titles: Existence of existences; ancient of days; macroprosopos; lux occulta.

Deity Color/Archangelic Color: Pure white brilliance.

Angelic/Planetary Color: White-flecked gold.

Virtue/Vice: Attainment and completion of the Great Work/No vice.

Symbols: The point, the point within the circle.

Deities: All creator deities—Ptah, Gaea, Achilles. Greek Mother existing before Chaos, giving birth to all; Aditi—self-formed Hindu Mother.

Precious Stone: Diamond.

Plant: Flowering almond.

Tree: Banyan.

Traditional Perfume: Ambergris.

Animals: Swan, hawk.

Tarot Cards: The four aces.

General Energy State: Kether is the primal Light, the Great Mother to all the emanations. She gives the power of comprehension to that which has no beginning or end. She is the Great Mother, the crowning glory of all life.

Magickal Uses: Kether is both the first and the last: it is used for reading the distant path, understanding the present, and knowing the future. It is the sephiroth for working with the higher self, the immortal, divine spark of humans. Knowledge of one's destiny; true will; and communion with the Great Mother.

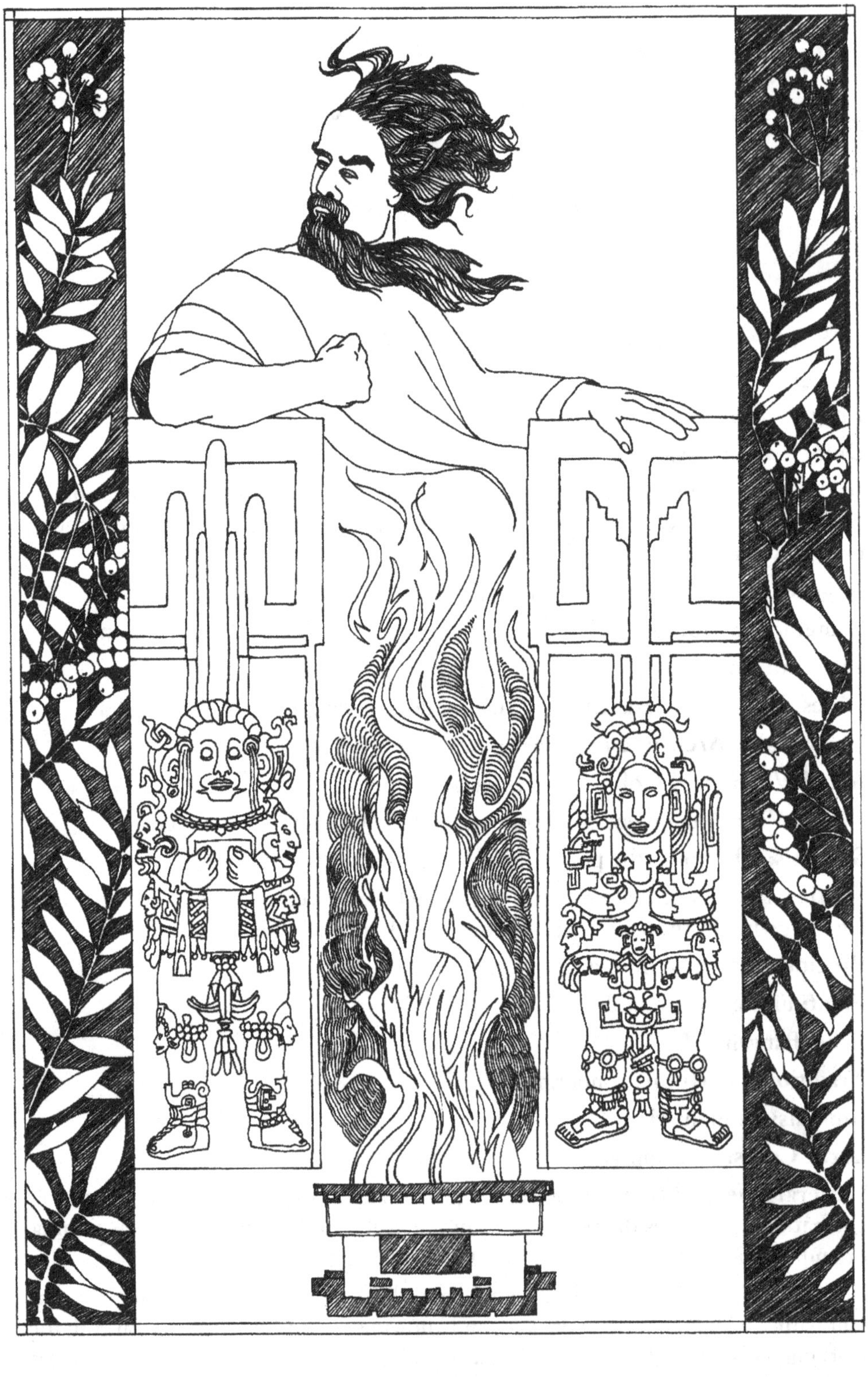

CHOKMAH: WISDOM (SEPHIRAH 2)

Image: A bearded male figure; a penis.

Deity Name: YHVH.

Archangel: Ratzkiel. He guided the creative forces in humanity's early evolution. (The beings of Chokmah and Kether are difficult to formulate in either sphere, for they are beyond all form as we know it.)

Angels: Auphanim (the wheels).

Planetary Attribution: The sphere of the zodiac/Uranus.

Element: Root of Fire.

Titles: Power of Yetzirah, Ab, Abba, the Supernal Father.

Deity Color: Pure soft blue.

Archangelic Color: Gray.

Angelic Color: Pearl gray.

Planetary Color: White flecked with red, blue, and yellow.

Virtue/Vice: Devotion/No vice.

Symbols: The phallus, the tower, the straight line.

Deities: All father Gods; Goddesses of wisdom. Priapic Gods—Great Pan, Osiris, Cernunnos. Acat—Mayan god of life who shaped children in their mother's womb; Anu—Assyro-Babylonian supreme God; Sophia—Hebrew and Greek goddess of wisdom.

Precious Stones: Star ruby, turquoise.

Plant: Amaranth.

Tree: Rowan.

Traditional Perfume: Musk.

Animal: Man.

Tarot Cards: The four twos, knights.

General Energy State: Chokmah is the Father of all Creation; the crowning glory for all the Tree of Life. From the unknown Mother was He born, and unto the Mother shall He strive; this seeking and yearning throughout Cosmos creates and sustains all the forces of all the worlds.

Magickal Uses: Knowledge of the "holy, formless fire" pervading all things; the primal archetype of the Lover and Son, the Witches' God. Useful for destruction of things outgrown and useless; purification. The true model for the male mysteries. Television and radio transmissions, magnetism, unseen radiations (including psychic transmissions).

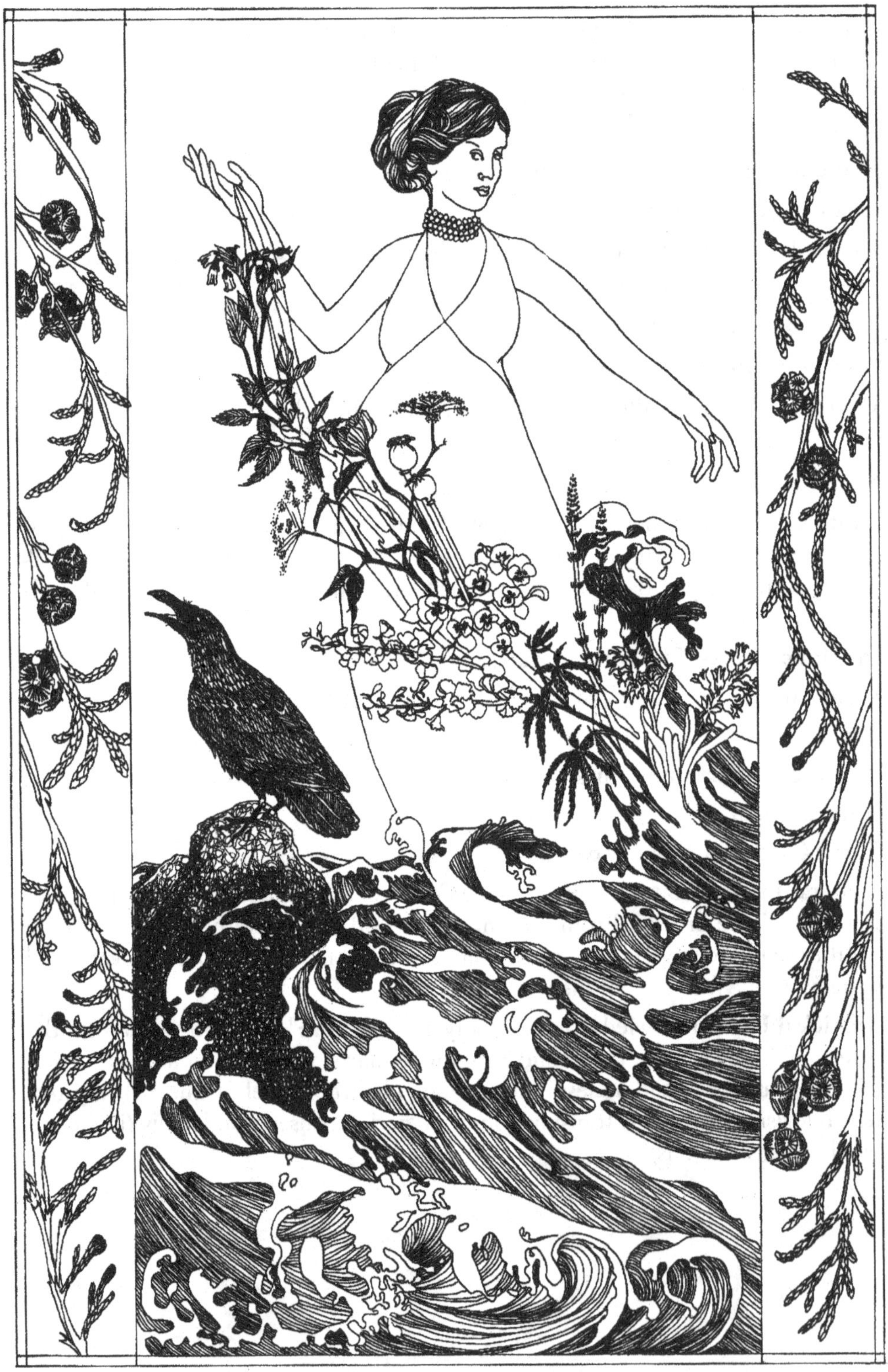

BINAH: UNDERSTANDING (SEPHIRAH 3)

Image: A mature woman; a vagina.

Deity Name: YHVH Elohim.

Archangel: Tzafkiel. He has been behind the formulation of all the mystic cults that have been sent to us from the Inner Planes. He can be envisioned a a great, vast presence shining with a living darkness and a wonderful rose-adorned glow in the center.

Angels: Aralim (the thrones).

Planetary Attribution: The sphere of Saturn.

Element: Root of Water.

Titles: Ama, the dark sterile Mother; Aima, the bright fertile Mother; Mara, the Great Sea.

Deity Color: Crimson.

Archangelic Color: Black.

Angelic Color: Dark brown.

Planetary Color: Gray flecked with pink.

Virtue/Vice: Silence/Avarice.

Symbols: The yoni, cup, or chalice.

Deities: Mother Goddesses, Saturnine Gods. Olwen, Dana, Isis, Demeter, Tiamat, Bran. Adishakti—primeval Hindu goddess of feminine energy; Apsu—Early Babylonian Mother goddess who is the primal abyss of water from which all sprang.

Precious Stones: Star sapphire, pearl, onyx.

Plants: Aconite, asafetida, belladonna, black poppy seeds, comfrey, hellebore, hemlock, hemp, henbane, horsetail, hyacinth, pansy, pepperwort root, Solomon's seal.

Trees: Buckthorn, cypress, yew.

Traditional Perfumes: Civet, ironwood, myrrh.

Animals: Bee, crow, raven.

General Energy State: Binah is the Creatrix of life; from Her all things proceed, and unto Her all must return. She is the gracious Mother of life and death, birthing and destroying all times and all places.

Magickal Uses: Binding, brings destruction and gives death, buildings, comfort in times of sorrow, contact with the Goddess unveiled, death, development of the ability to listen and absorb, help with groups, limitations, knowledge, obstacles, history, time, duties, responsibilities, finding familiars, learning, hatred, discord, works of magick, buildings, meditation, life, doctrines, older people, old plans, debts, repayment of debts, real estate, wills, stability, inertia, conversing with those who died a natural death.

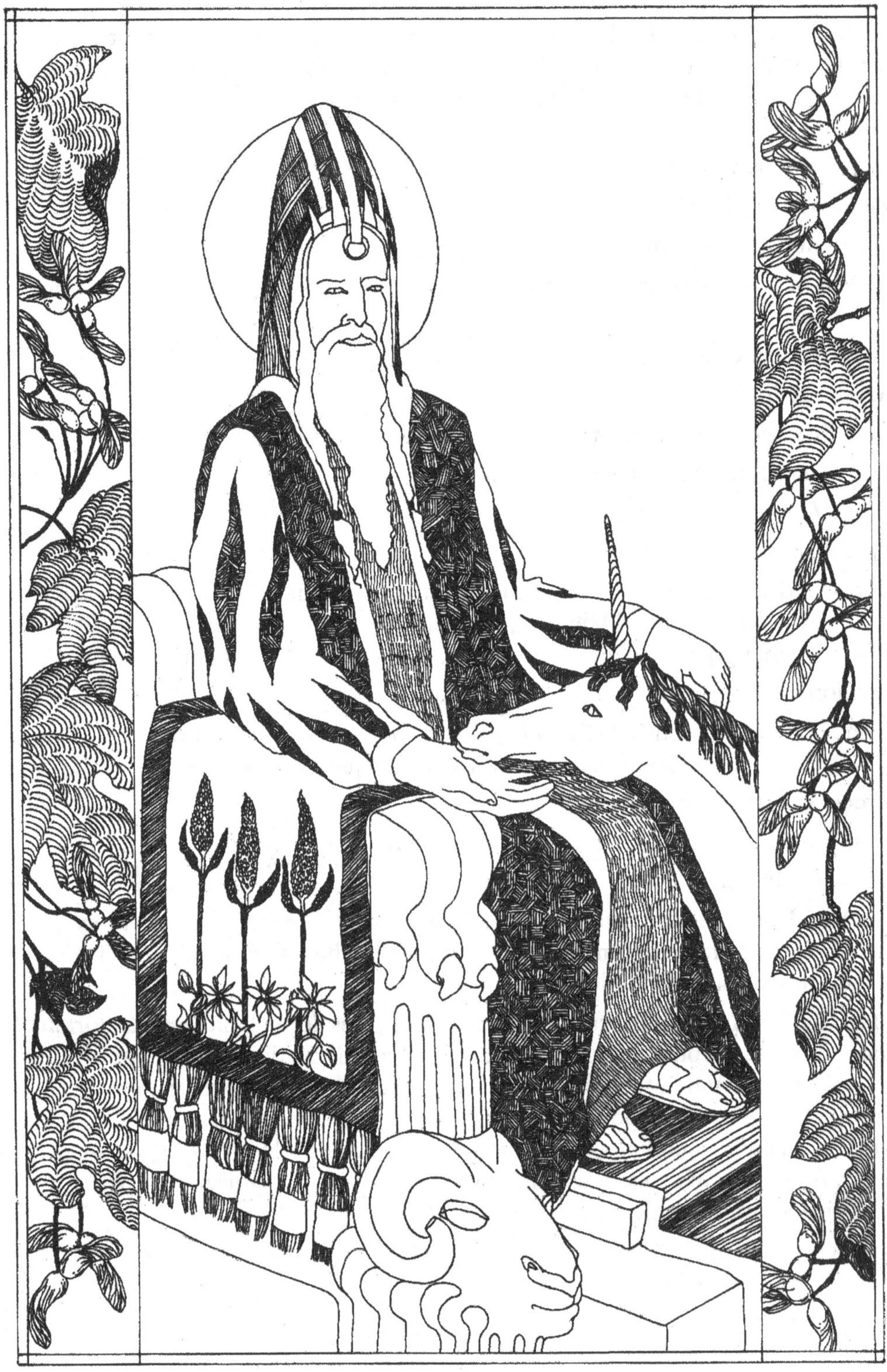

CHESED: MERCY (SEPHIRAH 4)

Image: A mighty crowned and throned King.

Deity Name: El.

Archangel: Tzadkiel. He assures benevolence and the calm of eternal security and certainty, and is of great help to those prone to irritation or unbalance of temper. He may be visualized as a strong, yet slightly feminine, angel standing within an aura of blue light.

Angels: Chasmalism (the brilliant ones).

Planetary Attribution: The sphere of Jupiter.

Element: Water.

Titles: Gedulah; love; majesty; magnificence.

Deity Color: Deep violet.

Archangelic Color: Blue.

Angelic Color: Deep purple.

Planetary Color: Deep azure flecked with yellow.

Virtue/Vice: Obedience/Bigotry, hypocrisy, gluttony.

Symbol: Scepter.

Deities: Benevolent ruler gods, Jupiter, Odin, Zeus. Lola—Indian goddess of fickle fortune; Pax—Roman goddess of peace.

Precious Stones: Amethyst, sapphire, lapis lazuli, chrysolite, turquoise.

Plants: Agrimony, balm, blood root, borage, cinquefoil, hyssop, linden, mint, nutmeg, star anise.

Trees: Ash, maple, olive, cedar.

Traditional Perfumes: Cedar, nutmeg.

Animal: Unicorn.

Tarot Cards: The four fours.

General Energy State: The realm of Chesed holds and controls the holiest of all powers—from this sephirah comes the spiritual virtues of love and mercy. By the power and virtue of the unknowable Mother in Kether, all goodness and purity, bounty and abundance, mirth and reverence of all life is poured upon the Tree of Life.

Magickal Uses: Expansion, growth, help from Ancient Ones, development of punctuality and neatness, correction of stinginess, development of stability, leadership, politics, power, honor, royalty, public acclaim, responsibility, wealth, business, success, obtaining honors, riches, friendships, health, luck, religion, trade, and employment. Treasure, legal matters, abundance, plenty, growth, expansion, generosity, spirituality, visions, dreams.

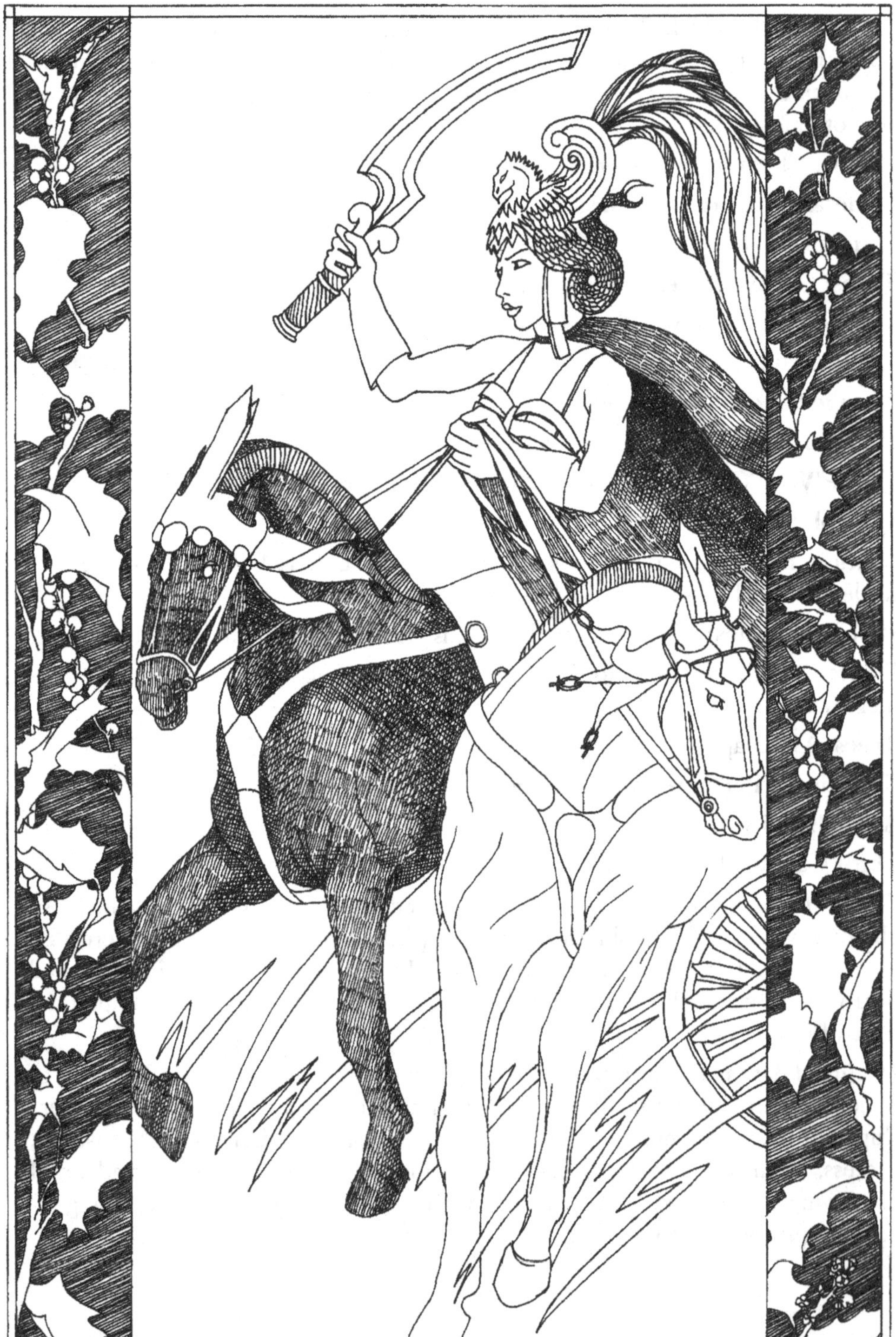

GEBURAH: MIGHT (SEPHIRAH 5)

Image: A mighty warrior in his chariot.

Deity Name: Elohim Gibor.

Archangel: Khamael. He is the protector of the weak and wronged; also the avenging angel who punishes breakers of the law. Visualize him in the archangelic colors for the sphere.

Angels: Seraph (Fiery Serpents).

Planetary Attribution: The sphere of Mars.

Element: Fire.

Titles: Pachad; Fear; Justice.

Deity Color: Orange.

Archangel Color: Red.

Angelic Color: Bright scarlet.

Planetary Color: Red flecked with black.

Virtue/Vice: Energy, courage/Cruelty, wanton destruction.

Symbols: The sword, the scourge, the chain, the cord.

Deities: War, protector, and avenger deities. Smith and forge deities. Mars, Aries, Minerva/Athena, Kali, Morrigan, Lugh. Aerteen—British war goddess; Lewa-Levu—Fijian predatory goddess.

Precious Stones: Ruby, bloodstone, garnet.

Plants: Aloes, basil, betony, caper, carnation, chilies, coriander, dragon's blood, ginger, garlic, lignum, mustard, nettle, oak, onion, pepper, radish, tarragon, thistle, tobacco, woodruff.

Trees: Hawthorne, hickory, holly.

Traditional Perfumes: Tobacco, cypress, pine.

Animal: Basilisk.

Tarot Cards: The four fives.

General Energy State: Geburah is the strength, the courage, the power, and the passion of the Tree of Life; its energies protect and sustain this sacred Tree as it manifests in all the worlds.

Magickal Uses: Energy, courage, defense, getting rid of the unnecessary, vitality, development of will, power and self-discipline, strength, struggle, war, anger, conflict, aggression, courage, surgery, physical strength, oppression, war, defense, endurance, energy, haste, anger, construction or destruction, vitality, magnetism, willpower, overthrow of enemies, wounds.

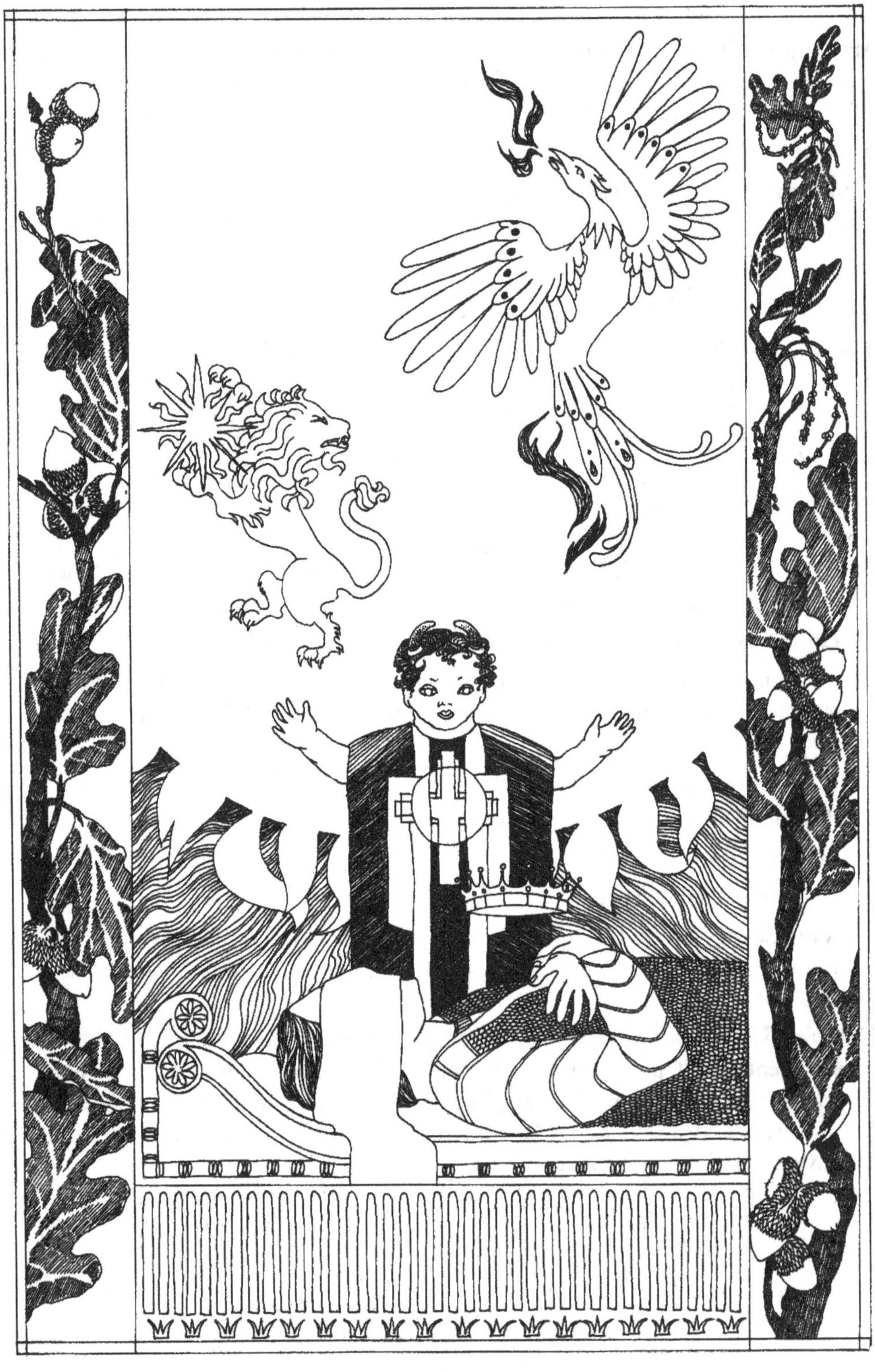

TIFARETH: BEAUTY, HARMONY (SEPHIRAH 6)

Image: A child and a sacrificed god.

Deity Name: IAO.

Archangel: Michael. He holds the healing and sustaining powers of sunlight. Visualize him in the archangelic color of Tifareth.

Angels: Malachim (Kings).

Planet: The sphere of the Sun.

Element: Air.

Titles: The lesser countenance.

Deity Color: Clear rose pink.

Archangelic Color: Yellow.

Angelic Color: Rich salmon pink.

Planetary Color: Golden amber.

Virtue/Vice: Devotion to the Great Work/False pride, extreme ego, bragging.

Symbols: All crosses, the lamen, the cube.

Deities: All sun deities and sacrificial Gods; Apollo, Osiris, Adonis, Bride. Amaterasu—Japanese sun goddess; Li—Chinese, feminine personification of the sun.

Precious Stones: Topaz, yellow diamond.

Plants: Ambergris, angelica, chamomile, citrus fruits, eyebright, frankincense, hazel, heliotrope, honey, juniper, lovage, marigold, mistletoe, myrrh, orange blossom, palinginia, rosemary, saffron, sunflower.

Trees: Oak, acacia, cedar.

Traditional Perfumes: Frankincense, laurel, olibanum.

Animals: Phoenix, lion, child.

Tarot Cards: The four sixes; princes.

General Energy State: Tifareth gathers and mediates the influences of all the higher realms; as they gather, they multiply, and as the powers of the Tree increase, all blessings are poured out to the realms that lie in the lower branches.

Magickal Uses: Honor, power, glory, life, growth, money, healing, illumination, joy, success, advancement, leadership, natural power, friendship, growth, healing, light, superiors, employees, executives, officials, health, healing, confidence, hope, prosperity, vitality, mental power.

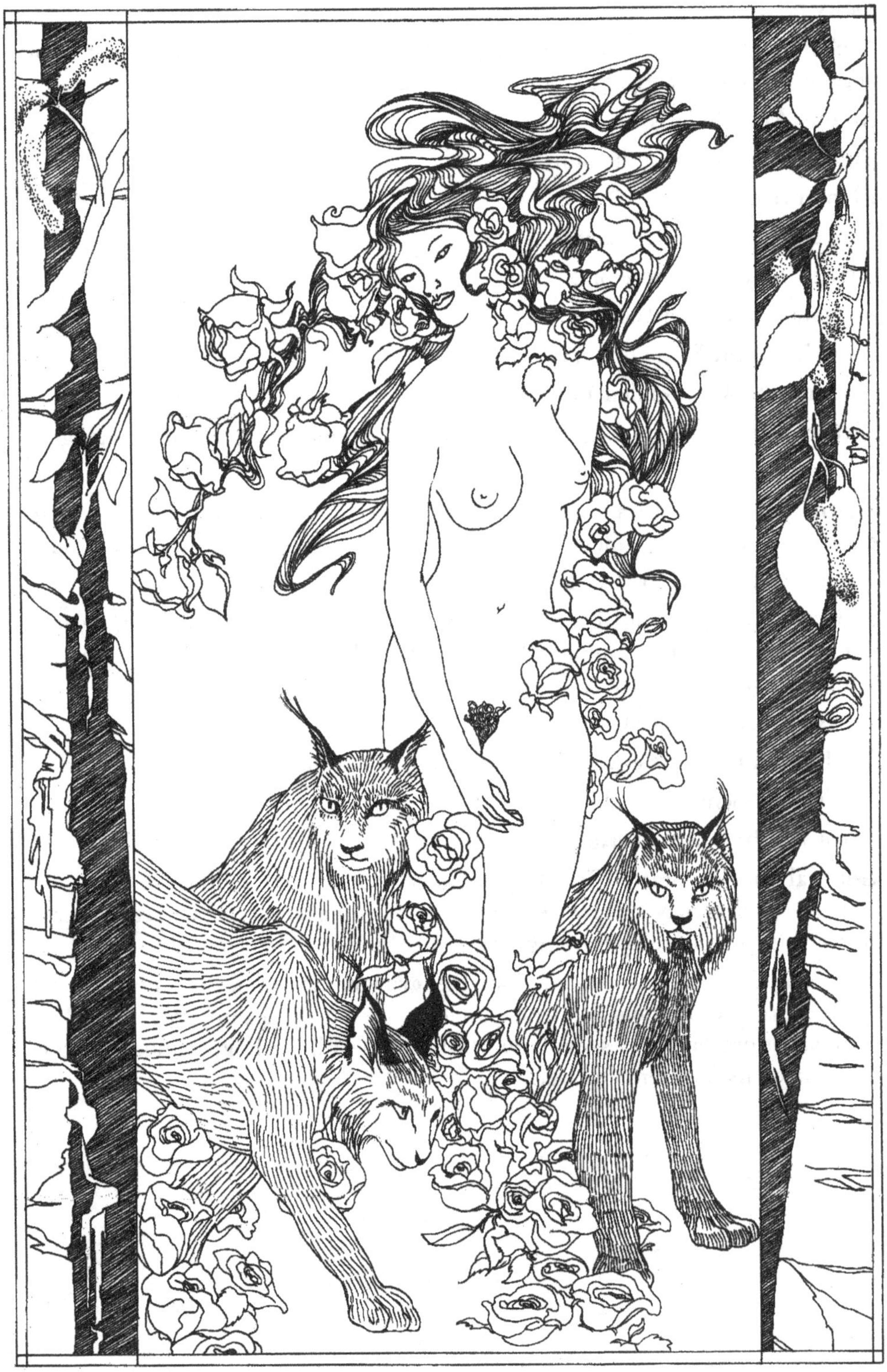

NETZACH: VICTORY (SEPHIRAH 7)

Image: A beautiful naked woman.

Deity Name: YHVH Tzabaoth.

Archangel: Haniel. His sphere is one of harmony and beauty, especially of inner-relationships whether of the spheres, planets, plants, or animal and human life; the great archetype of sympathetic vibration. Visualize Haniel as shining with a green and golden flame with a rose-colored light above his head.

Angels: Elohim.

Planetary Attribution: The sphere of Venus.

Element: Fire.

Titles: Firmness, Valor, Eternity, Triumph.

Deity Color: Amber.

Archangelic Color: Emerald.

Angelic Color: Bright, yellowish green.

Planetary Color: Olive flecked with gold.

Virtue/Vice: Unselfishness/Unchastity, lust for power.

Symbols: Lamp, girdle, rose.

Deities: All love and harvest deities; Haathor, Venus, Ishtar, Aphrodite, Rhiannon, Niamh, Cerridwen. Chasea—Inca goddess who brought forth flowers and attended maidens; Flora—Roman goddess of all growing and flourishing things; Nikkal—Canaanite goddess of the fruits of the Earth; Bachue—Columbian water goddess who protected vegetation and the harvest.

Precious Stones: Emerald, malachite, amber.

Plants: Acacia, acacia flowers, apple, ambergris, daffodil, elder, elderberry, laurel, lignum aloes, musk, olive oil, pennyroyal, plantain, primrose, raspberry, red roses, saffron, strawberry, tansy, thyme, verbena, vervain, vervain, violet.

Trees: Apple, birch, quince.

Traditional Perfumes: Rose, benzoin, red sandalwood, jasmine.

Animal: Lynx.

Tarot Cards: The four aces.

General Energy State: Netzach is the secret moving force behind the material world; through its influence are created all the forms of love, beauty, and harmony that exist in the realm of Malkuth.

Magickal Uses: Love in all forms, pleasure, arts, music, creative energy, inspiration, help in overcoming lack of spontaneity, lack of emotions and lack of subjectivity. Breaking writer's block and similar problems. Love, harmony, attractions, friendship, pleasure, sexuality, all love matters, affections, partnerships, sex, spiritual harmony, compassion, friendships, offspring, arts, music, beauty, extravagance, younger people.

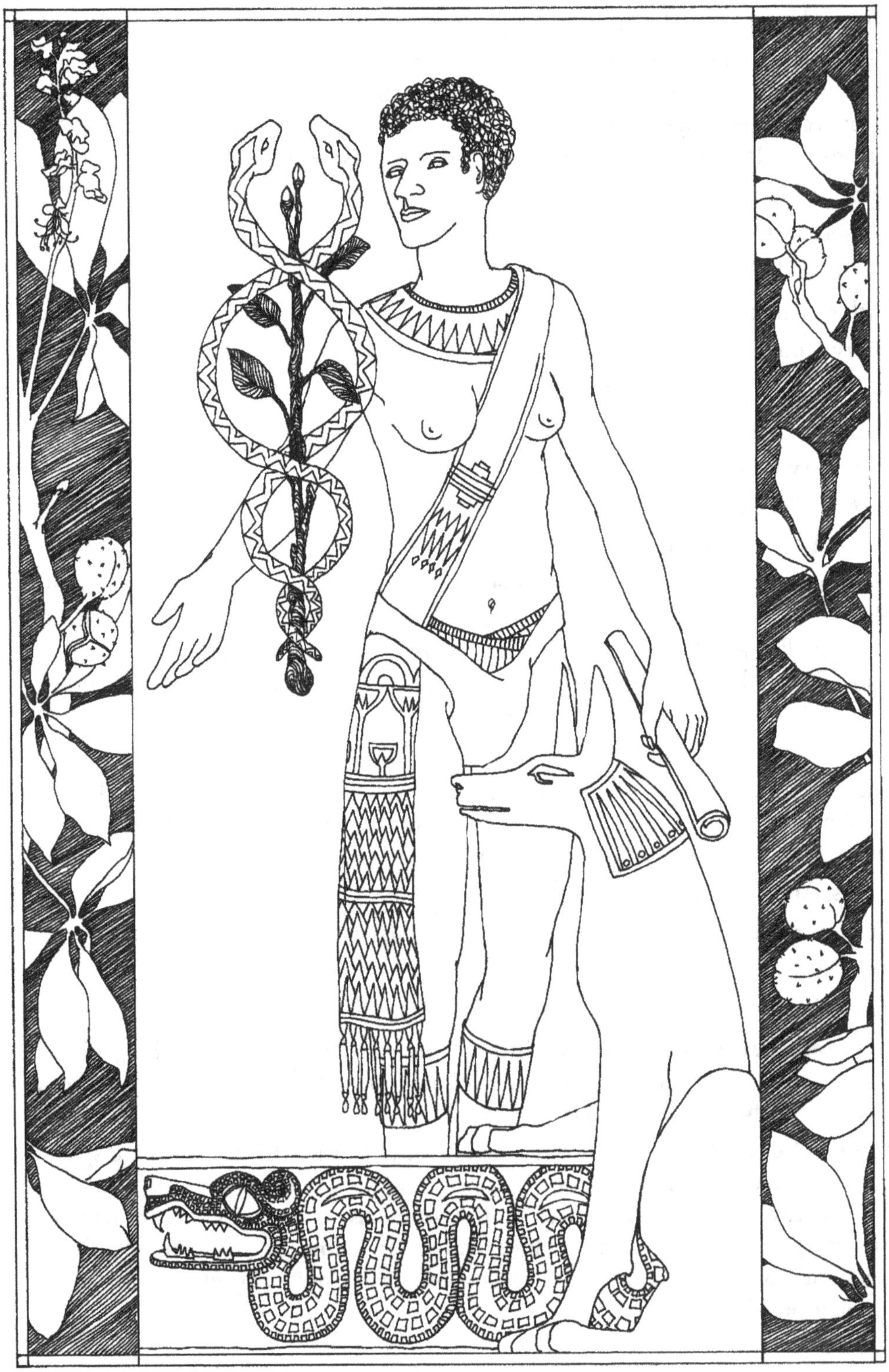

HOD: SPLENDOR, GLORY (SEPHIRAH 8)

Image: A hermaphrodite.

Deity Name: Elohim Tzabaoth.

Archangel: Raphael. He exists in this sphere of magick and holds in control the various evil influences which might escape into the world of men. He both inspires and keeps safe the inexperienced. Visualize him in the archangelic color, with violet light in the wings.

Angels: Beni Elohim (children of God).

Planet: The sphere of Mercury.

Element: Water.

Deity Color: Violet-purple.

Archangelic Color: Orange.

Angelic Color: Russet red.

Planetary Color: Yellowish black flecked with white.

Virtue/Vice: Truthfulness/Falsehood, deceit.

Symbol: Caduceus.

Deities: Messengers and healers; Thoth, Hermes, Mercury. Libon—Irish goddess of healing and pleasure; Aradia—daughter of Diana who came to Earth to teach the ways of Witchcraft; Nike—Greek messenger goddess; Siduri—a minor Sumerian oracular goddess.

Precious Stones: Opal, agate.

Plants: Bayberries, benzoin, carraway, carrots, cascara, cinnamon, cinquefoil, cloves, dill, elecampane, fennel, fenugreek, horehound, lavender, licorice, mace, marjoram, mastic, moly, sweet pea, valerian.

Trees: Hazel, chestnut, walnut.

Traditional Perfumes: Storax, mace, sandalwood.

Animals: Jackal, twin serpents.

Tarot Cards: The four eights.

General Energy State: Hod is the realm of mind and science, for by its influence are laid the rules and logic by which the material realm is created; as such, it is the perfect intelligence for all the Tree of Life.

Magickal Uses: Business, books, legal judgments, travel, information, the intellect, logic, writer's block (not needing inspiration, rather needing the ability to express written thoughts), curb over-emotionalism, organization of thoughts, finding teachers and sources of information, communications, intelligence, cleverness, creativity, science, memory, business transactions, thievery, conjuration, predictions, knowledge, writing, eloquence, speech, speed, improvement of the mind, power, poetry, inspiration, healing of nervous disorders, business matters, writing contracts, judgment. Short travels, books, paper, divination.

YESOD: THE FOUNDATION (SEPHIRAH 9)

Image: A beautiful naked man, very strong.

Deity Name: Shaddai el-Chai.

Archangel: Gabriel. He rules many subtle realms; the Lord of Dreams, bestower of the Sight. He draws the consciousness from the body. His image is a huge silvery ovoid with delicate lilac and violet in his wings. The sound of mighty waters shows his special type of vibration.

Angels: Aishim (the souls of fire).

Planetary Attribution: The sphere of the Moon.

Element: Air.

Titles: Treasure house of Images, the sphere of illusion.

Deity Color: Indigo.

Archangelic Color: Violet.

Angelic Color: Very dark purple.

Planetary Color: Citrine flecked with azure.

Virtue/Vice: Independence/Idleness.

Symbols: The perfumes and the sandals, the mirror.

Deities: All moon deities; Diana, Thoth, Hecate, Sin, Chango, Selene; Laverna—Roman goddess of thieves; Levanah—Chaldean/Hebrew moon goddess.

Precious Stones: Quartz, moonstone.

Plants: Banyan, bay leaf, banana, cabbage, camphor, chickweed, cucumber, damiana, leafy vegetables, mandrake, mushrooms, orchid, sandalwood, white poppy seeds, sea weed, watercress, wild rose, wintergreen.

Trees: Bay, willow, eucalyptus.

Traditional Perfumes: Jasmine, ginseng. All fragrant roots are sacred to Yesod, as this realm forms the sacred root of the Tree of Life, just as sexuality is the root of humanity's existence. Remember also that one must not assume Malkuth to be the root of the system, and thus reality. Malkuth is the fruit of the Tree, an illusion which enables it to perceive itself.

Animals: Elephant, tortoise, toad.

Tarot Cards: The four nines.

General Energy State: Yesod is the final state of force before form; through its actions, all forces and emanations of the Tree are brought to their final state of perfection before manifesting in the material world. It filters, protects, and enlivens all realms, bringing them to final perfection before incarnation.

Magickal Uses: Divination, change, fertility spells, development of intuition, contact with the unconscious, development of memory, women, cycles, generation, inspiration, poetry, emotions, seas and tides, secrets, psychic ability, agriculture, domestic life, medicine, travel, vision, luck, time, publicity, illusions.

MALKUTH: THE KINGDOM (SEPHIRAH 10)

Image: A young, robed woman, standing in a field.

Deity Name: Adonai ha-Aretz

Archangel: Sandalphon. The Archangel of Malkuth is to be invoked by those who have trouble coming to grips with the physical plane. He is in charge of the soul of physical objects. His form may be visualized in the archangelic colors.

Angels: Kerubim (the strong).

Planetary Attribution: The sphere of Earth, the planet, and of the four elements.

Element: Earth.

Titles: The gate; Kallah, the bride; the Gate of Life, The Gate of Death, The Inferior Mother, The Gate of Tears.

Deity Color: Yellow.

Archangelic Color: Ochre, russet, olive, black.

Angelic Color: Ochre, russet, olive, black-flecked with gold.

Planetary Color: Black-rayed yellow.

Virtue/Vice: Discrimination/Inertia.

Symbols: Pentacle, altar of the double cube, the triangle of the art, magick circle, equal-armed cross.

Deities: Earth and grain deities; Pan, Ceres, Demeter, Seb, Cernunnos. Adamah—Hebrew female personification of the Earth; Libitina—Roman goddess of funerals.

Precious Stone: Rock crystal.

Plants: Corn, ivy, lily.

Trees: Elder, elm, pine, pomegranate, poplar.

Traditional Perfume: Dittany of Crete.

Alternate Incense: A mixture often referred to as the "Incense of Abramelin." It is extremely powerful, and is used to control the powers of the four elements as they manifest in the magick circle. Crush equal parts of storax, galbanum, onycha, and olibanum together in a ceramic mortar; seal tightly in a dark glass container for at least one lunar cycle so that the scents can mingle. Use this mixture with caution, for it is extremely powerful! If a physical manifestation of any elemental powers is desired, add one part dittany of crete to the mixture before aging. For the beginner in magick, this recipe is not recommended; it is for advanced students.

Animal: The sphinx.

Tarot Cards: The four tens, princesses.

General Energy State: Malkuth is the result and cause of creation; by its existence, the Tree of Life is allowed to continue, for it draws the powers of Kether into manifestation. It is the fruit and the womb; as such, it is also the seed. By its darkness of matter, it causes the emanations of the Tree to grow brighter; it is exalted above all else, and contains root, the essence, of the Qabalah within.

Magickal Uses: Malkuth is where we first begin all work. Being the realm of physical manifestations, anything done will begin and end in this realm. It is the world of the five elements (fire, water, air, earth, and Spirit), the world of dissolution, and the world of making.

MODERN INCENSE RECIPES

The following incense recipes are among my favorite for the ten sephiroth; they were developed by Ron Jaffe, owner of Magickal Earth, Inc. I am indebted to Ron for allowing me to publish some of his incense recipes. His company provides a full range of oils, incense, and herbal products magickally prepared by hand in accordance with the proper solar and lunar phases; he also guarantees that the proper daily, planetary, and elemental influences are invoked within a magickal circle before the recipes are prepared. His scents are delightful, and he provides them for all practical, magickal needs (not just Qabalistic). His catalog may be ordered by writing to the following address: Magickal Earth, Inc.; P. O. Box 2429; Orlando, Fl. 32802-2429. Please enclose a check or money order for $2.00 to cover postage and handling; allow two weeks for delivery of the catalog.

Notes on the Recipes

If one part equals ½ teaspoon, ten to twelve parts will yield approximately ¼ cup of finished incense.

Saltpeter (Potassium nitrate) may be used in the recipe to help stubborn mixtures burn; use no more than ½ teaspoon per ¼ cup of total mixture. Adding more will cause the mixture to smoke a lot and may cause sparks to burst up and start a fire. It is recommended to first try the mixture without the saltpeter, then add a bit at a time as needed. Use caution!

The incense may be colored in accordance with each sephirah. Combine 6 parts ground bamboo powder with several drops of food coloring; mix until all powder is colored. The more coloring is used, the deeper and richer the resulting incense will be. Let the colored powder dry for approximately thirty minutes before adding to the rest of the incense recipe. Bamboo powder may be created by simply running a belt sander on a piece of bamboo and collecting the powder.

Substitutions may be made to the ingredients as needed, but the best results will be obtained by sticking as close to the recipes as possible. Try not to substitute more than one ingredient; always try to pick an herb with a similar vibration. Substitute a resin for a resin, an herb for an herb, and an oil for an oil if possible.

Most of the incenses will be smoky, even without the saltpeter. This is caused by the burning of the natural dried herbs and their essential oil components.

How to Blend the Incense Recipes

1. Combine the dried herb ingredients and grind using a mortar and pestle, and mix in the resins. (You may use an herb grinder instead, but some of the resins such as frankincense and myrrh may dull or clog the blades as the resins will melt from the heat of the grinder.)

2. Place the ground mixture in a mixing bowl. (Ceramic or plastic bowls are best. Wooden bowls will absorb the oils and powders and are difficult to clean.)

3. After grinding, add any powdered herbs.

4. Add any essential oils.

5. Blend the mixture with a metal or plastic spoon.

6. Store the mixture in a dark, airtight container. Kept out of the heat and direct sunlight this way, the mixture should last for at least two years.

The Recipes

Kether

2 parts rosemary
1 part sage
3 parts chamomile
2 parts yarrow
10 drops cinnamon oil per ¼ cup of final mixture

Chokmah

2 parts vetivert
1 part frankincense
1 part St. John's wort
2 parts peppermint
2 parts fennel or 10 drops fennel essential oil per ¼ cup mixture

Binah

2 parts frankincense
2 parts myrrh
1 part jasmine flowers
3 parts raisins
2 parts hellebore[1] (patchouli is recommended as a substitute)

Chesed

2 parts wood betony
½ part hyssop
2 parts cedar
1 part anise
1 part poppy seeds
1 part cinnamon powder
8 drops nutmeg essential oil per ¼ cup mixture

Geburah

2 parts mustard seed
1 part pennyroyal
2 part tobacco (your favorite or substitute patchouli)
2 parts pine needles (or substitute 2 parts pine bark)
1 part basil
1 part mace or 8 drops nutmeg oil per ¼ cup of mixture

---

1. Hellebore is a poisonous herb. If you must use it, do so outside and do not inhale the fumes. Use patchouli instead; the resulting mixture will smell wonderful, and it will be safe for indoor use.

Tifareth

2 parts frankincense
1 part cinnamon
1 part clove or clove powder
2 parts orange blossoms
2 parts cedar chips or ground wood

Netzach

2 parts rose petals, finely chopped
1 part red sandalwood
1 part vervain
1 part vetivert
2 parts dried ground banana[2]
1 part strawberry leaves

Hod

2 parts lavender
3 parts mace
1 part fennel
3 parts ground or mashed pistachios (shelled)

Yesod

4 parts jasmine flowers, finely chopped
2 parts white sandalwood
2 parts myrrh
1 part fresh ground coconut[3]

Malkuth

2 parts cypress
1 part pine
2 parts cedar
1 part poppy seeds, any color
2 parts magnolia flowers

THE ELEMENTS IN MALKUTH

1. Earth

Hebrew Name: Aretz/Ophir
Divine Name: Adonai ha-Aretz
Cardinal Point: North/Tzaphon
Archangel: Auriel

---

2. Mash the banana and spread it onto a cookie tin. Bake in a 200°F oven until dried (time will vary). You can also use banana chips, which can be purchased at many health food stores and some large grocery stores. Of course, if you have a dehydrator, you can make your own at home.

Angel: Phorlakh
Ruler: Kerub
King: Ghob
Elementals: Gnomes
Time: Midnight
Season: Winter
Colors: Black, brown, green, white
Tool: Pentacle
Name of the Wind: Boreas, Ophion
Sense: Touch
Precious Stones: Rock crystal, salt
Incense: Storax
Plants: Comfrey, grains (corn, rice, wheat, barley, etc.), ivy
Tree: Oak
Animals: All horned animals (deer, bison, earth-dwelling snakes, bull, etc.)

2. Air

Hebrew Name: Ruach
Divine Name: Shaddai el-Chai
Cardinal Point: East/Mizrach
Archangel: Raphael
Angel: Chassan
Ruler: Aral
King: Paralda
Elementals: Sylphs
Time: Sunrise
Season: Spring
Colors: Bright yellow, white, blue-white, all colors of sunrise
Tool: The dagger
Name of the Wind: Eurus
Sense: Smell
Precious Stone: Topaz
Incense: Galbanum
Plants: Myrrh, pansy, primrose, vervain, violet, yarrow
Tree: Aspen
Animals: Birds (especially the eagle and hawk)

3. Water

Hebrew Name: Maim
Divine Name: Elohim Tzabaoth

Cardinal Point: West/Maarab

Archangel: Gabriel

Angel: Taliahad

Ruler: Tharsis

King: Nichsa

Elementals: Undines

Time: Sunset

Season: Fall

Colors: Blue, gray, indigo, black, all colors of sunset

Tool: The cup

Name of the Wind: Zephyrus

Sense: Taste

Precious Stone: Aquamarine

Incense: Onycha

Plants: Lotus, ferns, mosses, seaweeds, water lilies, all other water plants

Tree: Willow

Animals: Sea serpents, dolphins, fish, seals, water-dwelling snakes

4. Fire

Hebrew Name: Asch

Divine Name: YHVH Tzabaoth

Cardinal Point: South/Darom

Archangel: Michael

Angel: Aral

Ruler: Djin

King: Seraph

Elementals: Salamanders

Time: Noon

Season: Summer

Colors: Red, crimson, orange, white, gold

Tool: The wand

Name of the Wind: Notus

Sense: Sight

Precious Stone: Fire opal

Incense: Olibanum

Plants: Hibiscus, garlic, nettle, mustard, onion, red poppies, red peppers

Tree: Flowering almond

Animals: Lions and dragons

Appendix Two

Words of Power

The Charge of the Goddess

High Priest: Listen to the words of the Great Mother, She who of old has been called among men Artemis, Astarte, Athena, Diana Mellusine, Aphrodite, Cerridwen, and by many other names …

High Priestess: Once in the month, and better it be when the moon is full, there shall ye assemble in some secret place and adore the spirit of me, who am Queen of all Witches. There shall ye assemble; ye who are fain to learn all sorcery, yet have not won its deepest secrets, to these will I teach things that are yet unknown. And ye shall be free from all slavery; and as a sign that ye be free ye shall dance, sing, feast, make music and love, all in my praise. For mine is the ecstasy of the spirit, and mine also is joy on earth, for my law is love unto all beings. Keep pure your highest ideal, strive ever towards it, let naught stop you or turn you aside. For mine is the secret door which opens upon the land of youth, and mine is the cup of the wine of life, and the cauldron of Cerridwen, which is the Holy Grail of Immortality. I am the Gracious Goddess who gives the gift of joy unto the heart of man. Upon Earth, I give the knowledge of the spirit eternal; beyond death, I give peace, freedom and reunion with those who have gone before. Nor do I demand aught in sacrifice, for behold, I am the Mother of all living, and my love is poured out upon the Earth.

High Priest: Hear ye the words of the Star Goddess; She in the dust of whose feet are the hosts of heaven, and whose body encircles the Earth …

High Priestess: I who am the beauty of the green Earth, and the white moon among the stars, and the mystery of the waters, and the desire of the heart of man, call unto thy soul. Arise, and come unto me! For I am the soul of Nature who gives life to the Universe. From me all things proceed, and unto me all things return; and before my face, beloved of Gods and men, let thine innermost divine self be enfolded in the rapture of the infinite. Let my worship be within the heart that rejoiceth; for behold! All acts of love and pleasure are my rituals. And therefore let there be beauty and strength, power and compassion, honor and humility, mirth and reverence within you. and thou who thinkest to seek me; know that thy seeking and yearning shall avail thee not unless thou knowest the mystery: that if that which thou seekest thou findest not within thee, then thou wilt never find it without thee. For behold, I have been with thee from the beginning; and I am that which is attained at the end of desire.

THE CHARGE OF THE HORNED GOD

High Priestess: Listen to the words of my Consort, He who of old has been called among men Lugh, Pan, Belin, Cernunnos, and by many other names …

High Priest: Come, and learn the secret that hath not yet been unveiled. For I am the Consort to your Goddess, who, changing form and changing face, ever seeks Her as my other half. I am that secret, eternal flame burning within thy heart, and within the core of every star. I am the keeper of woodlands, fields, orchards, and ripening corn. I am life, and the giver of life; yet is the knowledge of me the knowledge of death. Remember all ye that life is pure joy, that all the sorrows are but as shadows; they pass and are done. But thy immortal soul—that shall remain. So rejoice: beauty and strength, roaring laughter and delightful languor, force and fire, all these things are yours. For I am the Sacred Serpent that giveth knowledge and delight and bright glory to stir the hearts of man. Upon the Earth, I sacrifice myself to Her that all may live; beyond death, I await the souls of those who come for rest and peace and refreshment. So rejoice! There is no dread hereafter, there is only joy and the eternal ecstasy of the Goddess!

High Priestess: Hear now the words of the Horned One, He whose name is mystery of mystery, and whose radiance enlightens the world …

High Priest: I, who am the giver of knowledge and delight and bright glory unto the heart of man, illuminate thy soul! Arise and come unto me! For I am the spear to the cauldron, the lance to the grail. Who but I, who am yearly sacrificed and reborn, can know the secrets of death and rebirth? Let my worship be centered about the true Grail of Immortality, the Goddess, and then shalt thou be strong! Lift up thyself, and thy stature shall surpass the stars! Strive ever towards me, the Son of the Mother, and if thou art joyous the circle of rebirth shall ever be yours. But thou who thinkest to seek for me, know thy seeking and yearning shall avail thee not unless thou knowest the mystery: that I, the Consort of the Starry Queen of Night, am everywhere the center, as She, the circumference, is nowhere found. For behold! From Her womb was I born, and unto Her womb shall I return at the end of time …

THE LEGEND OF THE DESCENT OF THE GODDESS

Through the waxing and waning light of the sun and moon, the flowing of day and night, we see the changing forms and faces of the Great Mother in our world. But in the night sky, as the moon fades from sight for three days and three nights, our Lady also withdraws from the world and descends where the living cannot go.

For when our God disappears within the dark womb of earth, through the Passage of Horns, She follows in secret and arrives at the gates beyond which the living may not pass. The guardian of the portal challenges Her with his sword, "Remove thy jewels, lay down thy garments, for naught may ye bring into this, our land!" She removed her garments and jewels, and was bound as one of the dead who enter Death's realm. Even beyond the bounds of day and night, Her beauty was dazzling as the stars and moon in the sky. The Horned One of Shadows, taken with Her radiance, knelt at Her feet, kissing them as He said, "Blessed be thy feet that have brought thee in these ways. Leave me not; abide with me always, and let me place my cold hand on thy heart!"

But She answered, "I love thee not. Why doest thou cause all things I love and delight in to fade and die?"

"Lady," He said, "'tis age and fate against which I am helpless. Age causes all things to wither; but when they die at the end of time, I give them rest and peace and strength so that they may return; but you, you are my heart's desire. Return not, and abide with me."

"I love thee not," She answered.

"As you receive not my hand on thy heart, you must receive Death's scourge."

"It is fate, better so," and She knelt. Death scourged Her, and She cried, "I know the pangs of love!" The Horned One gave Her the five-fold kiss, saying, "Thus only may you attain to self-knowledge."

For three days and three nights She remained in the land of Death; the moon in the night sky did not shine; all the world was thrown into darkness. And in the powers of night, beyond the eyes of mortals, did they enact the rites of love that sustained the world. Finally, She took up his crown of death, and it became a necklace of acorns that She placed around Her neck, saying, "Behold—the circle of rebirth! Although all passes through you out of life, all passes through me to be reborn. All must die; all must fade; but even thou art not eternal. I am the dark womb of earth; I am the primal mystery of life! Behold, for within me is the cauldron of rebirth. Enter into me; know me, and you will be free of all fear. For as life has become a journey into death, through my grace death shall be a journey into life! In me, the circle shall ever turn!"

Through love, He entered into Her, and was reborn into life; this is the greatest of all magicks. And this magick, this union and passion between the Lord of Death and Goddess of Life, controls all events on earth: birth, love, and death. For to fulfill love you must return again at the same time and the same place as the loved one, and you must remember and love them again. But to be reborn you must die and be ready for a new body, and to die you must be born; and without love you may not be born; and this is the secret of all magick!

THE WITCHES' RUNE

For raising the cone of power.

> *Eko, eko, Azarak,*
> *Eko, eko, Zomelak,*
> *Eko, eko, Cernunnos,*
> *Eko, eko, Aradia*
> (Repeat the above lines slowly three times)

> *Darksome night, and shining moon,*
> *East, then South, then West, then North,*
> *Hearken to the Witches' Rune.*
> *Here we come to call ye forth—*

Earth and water, air and fire,
Wand and pentacle and sword,
Wake ye unto our desire,
Hearken ye unto our word!
Cords and censer, scourge and knife,
Powers of the Witch's blade—
Waken all ye unto life,
Come ye as the charm is made!
Queen of heaven, Queen of hell,
Horned Hunter of the night—
Lend your powers unto our spell,
And work our will by magick rite!
In the earth, and air, and sea,
By the light of Moon or Sun,
As we will, so more it be,
Chant the spell and be it done.
Eko, eko Azarak …

(Repeat until the leader calls to a halt, then fall to the earth to ground the cone.)

GLOSSARY

Aishim: The angels of Yesod; these are under the control of the Archangel Gabriel. Their name translates into the "Souls of Fire."

Alexandrians: Witches following initiatory work of Alex Sanders; although founded by Mr. Sanders, this branch of modern Witchcraft is a direct derivation of the Gardnerian tradition.

Amulet: A charm worn for protection from negative influences (see **Talismans**).

Angel: A spiritual being or entity that carries out the forces and powers of the realm in which it is found; often, angels are seen as mediators and messengers between the God/dess and humanity.

Anima: The inner feminine part of a man's psyche.

Animus: The inner masculine part of a woman's psyche.

Aralim: These are the angels of Binah; they are under the supervision of Tzafkiel. Their name translates into the "Thrones."

Archangel: A high-ranking angel in charge of an order of angels. An archangel is responsible for directing and controlling the realm in which it resides.

Archetypes: Major elements of the Collective Unconscious; not directly approachable, they may be defined only through symbolism.

Assiah: This is the fourth and final World of Creation. Malkuth is the only sephirah contained; it is often called the realm of pure matter.

Astral body: The etheric counterpart of the physical body (see Tselem).

Astral/Magickal temple: A visualization built within the magick circle. Its purpose is to anchor the Witch between the physical world and one of the sephiroth, allowing easy access to the inner planes (see **Sephirah, Astral projection**).

Astral plane: commonly referred to as any plane that is not physical. Qabalistically, the astral plane belong to the world of Yetzirah.

Astral projection: The act of consciously or subconsciously (through the dream state during sleep) transferring one's awareness into the astral body or tselem; one moves about and perceives the astral planes (see also **Tselem, Astral plane,** and **Astral body**).

Athame: A symbol of Witch-hood; each Witch owns his or her own athame. Traditionally, the blade is triple edged with a black handle. The athame is never used to cut physical objects. Some traditional "denominations" of Witchcraft attribute the athame to the element of air; in the Qabalistic traditions, a separate dagger is consecrated to the element of air, while the athame is believed to represent the powers of Geburah (see **Geburah, Dagger**).

Atziluth: This is the first of the Four Worlds of Creation. Including the sephiroth Kether, Chokmah, and Binah, it is often referred to as the realm of pure Archetypes and deity (see **Archetypes**).

Auphanim: These are the angles of Chokmah; they are under the supervision of Ratzkiel. Their name translates into the "Wheels."

Aura: A field of energy surrounding the physical body. Psychics can sense a person's physical, mental, emotional, and spiritual health by sensing the aura's size, shape, and color.

Banishing: Removing any unwanted influences before, during, or after a magickal ceremony.

Bealtaine: This is celebrated by Witches and Pagans on either April 30 (Bealtaine Eve) or May 1 (Bealtaine Day). This festival is one of the greater Sabbats; it is an unashamed recognition of the Earth's fertility (See **Sabbats**).

Beni Elohim: These are the angles of Hod; they are under the guidance of the Archangel Michael. Their name translates into "Children of the God/dess."

Binah: The third emanation of the Tree of Life, also called Understanding.

Book of Shadows: This is a traditional book of rituals, incantations, and spells that is usually passed down from one Witch to the next in a teacher/student relationship. Secret in theory, most traditions have made part or all of their Books public.

Briah: This is the second of the Four Worlds of Creation. The sephiroth Chesed, Geburah, and Tifareth are the three emanations included in this realm; it is also known as the realm of the Archangelic forces and of the mind.

Burning Times: This is a period of persecution which reached its heights during the sixteenth and seventeenth centuries. Historical documents have helped historians to estimate the number of murders at roughly nine million women (their children and husbands go mostly unrecorded)! The Burning Times came about due to the political strength and ignorance of the Christian Church during the Middle Ages. As a special note, I might add that the Witch persecutions are not over; currently (at the time of writing this book) people in South Africa are in fear for their lives. The current date is June 25, 1994; seventy-one people have been murdered for practicing Witchcraft, and an uncounted number of people who have been accused are seeking refuge and safety in police stations. Ignorance and persecution still exist; it is up to those of us currently practicing in the United States to work diligently to correct misinformation.

Cabala, Qabala, Qabalah, Kabbalah: A system of magick and mysticism derived from the early Pagan Hebrew systems. It is based upon the Tree of Life and the system of sephiroth and paths derived from it.

Candlemas: See **Imbolc**.

Chasmalism: These are the angels of Chesed; they are under the supervision of Tzadkiel. Their name translates into "Brilliant Ones."

Chesed: The fourth emanation on the Tree of Life, also called Mercy.

Chiah: The magickal will of the Yechidah. Some also call Chiah the animus; it refers to Chokmah on the Tree of Life.

Chioth ha Qadesh: These are the angels of Kether; they are all under the guidance of Metatron. Their name translates into "Holy Living Creatures."

Chokmah: The second emanation of the Tree of Life, also called Wisdom.

Circle: A magickally created sacred space, believed to lie between the worlds of realities. It is used to channel and contain the psychic energies raised during ritual (see **Ritual**).

Clairaudience, clairvoyance: These are two classifications of psychic abilities. Clairaudience is the psychic sensing of distant events through sound, while clairvoyance is the psychic sensing of events through sight.

Cone of Power: The psychic power raised in a magick circle builds into this structure; the base coincides with the foundation of the circle, while the apex forms above the circle's center.

Coven: An organized group of Witches who regularly work together on both the Esbats and Sabbats. Usually, all the members of one coven are members of the same tradition; they also usually have a set initiation ritual for new members.

Craft: Witch "slang" for the spirituality known as Witchcraft. This term is sometimes used to refer to magick.

Cup, chalice: One of the Witch's four elemental tools. It represents the element of water.

Cauldron: This is used by Witches to represent the element of spirit. Some traditions interchange this tool with the chalice. Qabalistic Witchcraft, however, reserves the use of this tool to represent spirit and the LVX energies that sustain life.

Dagger: This tool is used by Witches to represent the element of air. Some traditions interchange the use of the dagger and athame; however, in the Qabalistic tradition the athame is reserved for Geburah and the dagger is used for the element of air (see **Athame, Geburah**).

Deosil: Describing a movement that is clockwise and rotating with the sun.

Dianic Witchcraft: This tradition is intimately connected with the political/spiritual feminist movement. Covens, as a rule of thumb, do not admit men; the Horned God is given little prominence, if any, in ritual observances. Although spurred by many of the traditional, mainstream sects of Wicca, Dianic Witchcraft is an extremely important political and spiritual path correcting the centuries of Patriarchal control experienced through history. I urge anyone interested in Goddess mythology and Matriarchal philosophy to study the voluminous writings available on this subject: my personal favorites are those by Z. Budapest and Diane Stein.

Divination: An art and science with the goal of obtaining information about future, past, or far-away events. Physical implements like the Tarot, crystals, and runes may be used for this art.

Elemental: A non-human, non-material entity belonging to the elements of earth, air, water, or fire (See also Gnome, Undine, Sylph, Salamander).

Elohim: These are the angels of Netzach; they are all under the guidance of Haniel. Their name translates into "Goddesses/Gods."

Familiar: An animal or spirit helper. Cats, dogs, and horses have a special ability to sense negativity and immanent danger. Witches who own them provide psychic protection in reward for their efforts. Spirit familiars may be either entities, elementals, or deceased relatives and friends (See also **Elemental**).

Festival: Another name for a Sabbat.

Gardnerians: Witches following the work of Gerald Gardner.

Geburah: The fifth emanation on the Tree of Life, also called Might or Pachad, Fear.

Gnome: An elemental belonging to the element of earth.

Great Rite: A ritual involving magickal sex. It may be worked alone (as presented in this book) or by a couple for whom intercourse is a normal part of a relationship. A symbolic Great Rite may be done if the two performing it are not established lovers.

Greater Sabbats: See **Sabbats**.

Guph: Also known as the physical body; it corresponds to Malkuth and the world of Assiah.

Halloween: See **Samhain**.

Hereditary Witches: These claim a continuous family tradition of the Craft beginning before the Gardnerian revival. The beliefs of Hereditary Witchcraft are simple; like most modern traditions, they revere both a Goddess and a God, and they seem to draw off numerous sources for their magickal practices.

Hod: The eighth emanation of the Tree of Life, also called Splendor and Glory.

Imbolc, Imbolg, Oimelc: The greater Sabbat commemorating the first stirrings of spring. It is often known by its Christianized name of Candlemas.

Inner planes: Any level of existence that is not physical.

Invocation: An invitation extended to a higher force; that force is either called to dwell within the self, or within the circle.

Kether: The first emanation of the Tree of Life, also called the Crown.

Lammas: See **Lughnasadh**.

Lesser Sabbats: See **Sabbats**.

Lughnasadh: This is one of the greater Sabbats performed on July 31 (August Eve). This name translates into "Lugh's Festival" (Lugh is the Celtic God of light).

Macrocosm: All of Cosmos, physical and spiritual. In the Qabalah, Macrocosm includes the entire Tree of Life.

Magick: Magick is both a science and an art form; it involves using the powers from Cosmos to create desired changes in one's reality.

Malachim: The angels of Tifareth. The name translates into "Kings"; they are all under the supervision of the Archangel Raphael.

Malkuth: The tenth and final emanation on the Tree of Life. It is also called the Kingdom.

Mercy, Pillar of: Sometimes called the masculine pillar, it includes the sephiroth of Chokmah, Chesed, and Netzach. Within the human energy field, this column is established on the left side of the body (left ear, left shoulder, and left hip).

Microcosm: The Universe, or Tree of Life, in miniature. Humanity is a microcosm of the Macrocosm.

Middle Pillar: On the Tree of Life, this pillar lies between those of Mercy and Severity. It includes the sephiroth that run from directly above the crown of the head, through the spine, and down to the feet: Kether, Daath, Tifareth, Yesod, and Malkuth.

Nephesch: The astral body; it corresponds to the sephirah Yesod. The Nephesch is divided into two parts: tselem and prana. Being the foundation, one's Nephesch is responsible for keeping the physical body's appearance stable throughout the lifetime; as the body loses its connection with the Nephesch, it begins to deteriorate and age.

Neschamah: The magickal understanding of the Yechidah. Some also call Neschamah the anima; it refers to Binah on the Tree of Life.

Netzach: The seventh emanation on the Tree of Life, also called Victory.

Oimelc: See **Imbolc.**

Pentacle: One of the Witch's four elemental tools; it represents the element of earth.

Pentagram: A five-pointed star used to represent and contain the powers of the elements.

Plane: The various levels of being: Atziluth, Briah, Yetzirah, and Assiah. Also, this term may be used to signify one of the ten sephiroth.

Prana: The vital force that forms and feeds the tselem; it permeates all of Malkuth, and everything that lives draws this force to sustain their magickal foundations. This force belongs exclusively to the astral realms; more specifically, Yesod.

Precognition: Awareness of future events.

Psyche: The non-physical structures of a human.

Reincarnation: There are a myriad views of reincarnation. Each supposes: 1) the soul is immortal; 2) the soul must undergo a series of lives on Earth until it is evolved enough to progress beyond the wheel of incarnation. Although there are a multitude of theories on reincarnation, these two premises are prevalent throughout all.

Ritual: This term can mean many things. A ritual may be an established form for a ceremony; it may also be a ceremonial act or action. In the Craft, ritual includes at least one of the paths in the Witch's Wheel.

Ruach: Sometimes called the "empirical ego." It consists of five divisions: will, memory, imagination, reason, and desire. It incorporates the sephiroth of Chesed, Geburah, Tifareth, Hod, and Netzach; also, Ruach forms the link between the lower and higher selves.

Sabbats: These are the eight seasonal festivals of the year, divided into greater and lesser Sabbats. The greater Sabbats are Imbolc, Bealtaine, Lughnasadh, and Samhain. The lesser Sabbats are the Equinoxes and Solstices.

Salamander: An elemental belonging to the element of fire.

Salt: A symbol of purification; it also represents the element of earth.

Samhain: Also called Halloween, it is celebrated on October 31. This festival is the traditional ending and beginning of the Witch's year; it also goes by the name "Feast of the Dead."

Scrying: A form of divination achieved by entering trance with a physical prop (such as crystal balls, mirrors, and pools of ink). The entranced individual receives psychic impressions through symbolism.

Self: The true individual; the perfected psyche achieved through magickal/psychological techniques.

Seraphim: These are the angels of Geburah; they are all under the supervision of the Archangel Khamael. Their names translates into the "Fiery Serpents."

Sephirah (plural Sephiroth): Any one of the ten emanations on the Tree of Life.

Severity, Pillar of: Sometimes called the feminine pillar, it includes the sephiroth Binah, Geburah, and Hod. Within the human energy field, this column is established on the right side (right ear, right shoulder, and right hip).

Sigil: A symbol or sign representative of magickal desires.

Skyclad: Ritual nakedness.

Spell: A symbolic act or rhyming couplet, used to direct energy and redesign reality.

Summerland: A place of rest after death. Here the soul withdraws, preparing for the next incarnation.

Sylph: An elemental belonging to the element of air.

Talisman: A symbolic, magickal object designed for a specific use by an individual.

Temple: A Witch's regular meeting place; temple sites may vary, as the magick circle can be cast anywhere (see **Astral/Magickal temple**).

Tifareth: This is the sixth emanation of the Tree of Life, also called Beauty and Harmony (see **Sephirah**).

Tree of Life: A glyph central to the Qabalah. It contains ten sephiroth and twenty-two paths, denoting the movement of energy from the Negative Veils of Existence to physical existence and matter (Malkuth).

Tselem: One division of the Nephesch; it is also called the astral body or body of light.

Undine: An elemental belonging to the element of water.

Vortex: A mass of energy raised within the circle, flowing in a circular motion that tends to draw more power to its center (see **Cone of Power**).

Wand: One of the elemental tools representing the element of water.

Watchtowers: The guardians of the magick circle, visualized as standing at one of the four cardinal points (see also **Archangels, Angels,** and **Elementals**).

Wiccan Rede: The only dogma of Witchcraft; it may be summed up in the words, "And if it harms none, do as you will."

Widdershins: In a counter-clockwise direction; a banishing movement.

Witch's Wheel: The symbolic representation of the eight paths to power: meditation, trance, invocation, natural substances, dance, the scourge, the cords, and the Great Rite.

Yechidah: The higher, immortal self of an individual. It corresponds to Kether on the Tree of Life.

Yesod: The ninth emanation on the Tree of Life, also called the Foundation.

Yetzirah: Third in the Four Worlds of Creations, it includes Netzach, Hod, and Yesod. Sometimes referred to as the world of angelic forces, it is also the astral plane.

Yule: Also called Winter Solstice, and celebrated around December 20-23rd. It welcomes the newborn child of the Goddess upon the Earth.

BIBLIOGRAPHY

Bonewitz, P. E. I. *Real Magic*. Berkeley: Creative Arts Books, 1979.

Budapest, Z. *The Feminist Book of Lights and Shadows*. Venice: Luna Publications, 1976.

Butler, W. E. *Practical Magick and the Western Mystery Tradition*. Northamptonshire: The Aquarian Press, 1986.

Coppens, Peter. *The Invisible Temple*. St. Paul: Llewellyn, 1987.

Crowley, A. *777*. New York: Samuel Weiser, 1970.

Crowley, A. *Magick in Theory and Practice*. New York: Dover, 1976.

Cunningham, Scott. *Encyclopedia of Crystal, Gem, and Metal Magic*. St. Paul: Llewellyn Publications, 1988.

Cunningham, Scott. *Encyclopedia of Magical Herbs*. St. Paul: Llewellyn Publications, 1990.

Cunningham, Scott. *Magical Herbalism*. St. Paul: Llewellyn Publications, 1988.

Cunningham, Scott. *The Magic of Incense, Oils, and Brews*. St. Paul: Llewellyn Publications, 1986.

Farrar, Janet and Stewart. *The Witches' Goddess*. Custer: Phoenix Publishing, Inc., 1987.

Farrar, Janet and Stewart. *The Witches' God*. Custer: Phoenix Publishing, Inc., 1989.

Fortune, Dion. *The Cosmic Doctrine*. Great Britain: Society of Inner Light, 1976.

Fortune, Dion. *The Mystical Qabalah*. New York: Samuel Weiser, 1984.

Gardner, Gerald. *High Magick's Aid*. New York: Weiser, 1975.

Gardner, Gerald. *Witchcraft Today*. Great Britain: Ryder, 1954.

Gray, W. G. *Ladder of Lights*. Great Britain: Helios Book Service, Ltd., 1968.

Knight, Gareth. *Practical Guide to Qabalistical Symbolism*. Great Britain: Helios Book Service, Ltd., 1965.

Reed, Ellen Cannon. *The Witches' Qabalah*. St. Paul: Llewellyn, 1986.

Regardie, Israel. *Art of True Healing*. Great Britain: Helios, 1974.

Regardie, Israel. *A Garden of Pomegranates*. St. Paul: Llewellyn, 1974.

Regardie, Israel. *The Golden Dawn*. St. Paul: Llewellyn, 1985.

Regardie, Israel. *The Middle Pillar*. St. Paul: Llewellyn, 1970.

Regardie, Israel. *The Tree of Life*. New York: Weiser, 1983.

Sheba, Lady. *The Book of Shadows*. St. Paul: Llewellyn, 1973.

Starhawk. *The Spiral Dance*. San Francisco: Harper and Row, 1979.